ROBIN SCROGGS was
Edward Robinson Professor
of Biblical Theology at Union
Theological Seminary in New
York. His Fortress Press books
include *Paul for a New Day*
(1977), *The New Testament and
Homosexuality* (1983), *Christology
in Paul and John* (Proclamation
Commentaries, 1988), and *The
Text and the Times: New Testament
Essays for Today* (1993).

THE PEOPLE'S JESUS

The People's Jesus

Trajectories in Early Christianity

Robin Scroggs
Edited by Marshall D. Johnson

With a Foreword by Alexandra Brown

Fortress Press
Minneapolis

THE PEOPLE'S JESUS
Trajectories in Early Christianity

Cover design: Alisha Lofgren
Cover image © Keith Reichert/iStockphoto
Book design: The HK Scriptorium, Inc.

Library of Congress Cataloging-in-Publication Data
Scroggs, Robin.
    The people's Jesus : trajectories in early Christianity / Robin Scroggs ; edited by Marshall D. Johnson.
       p. cm.
    Includes bibliographical references and index.
    ISBN 978-0-8006-9791-4 (alk. paper)
    1. Jesus Christ—History of doctrines—Early church, ca. 30-600. 2. Bible. N.T.—Theology. I. Johnson, Marshall D. II. Title.
    BT198.S374   2011
    232—dc22
                        2010045033

Manufactured in the U.S.A.

15 14 13 12 11   1 2 3 4 5 6 7 8 9 10

CONTENTS _____

Foreword _____

Robin Scroggs's passionate commitment to understanding "the everyday lives and social needs and contexts of real human beings" animated his life's work in New Testament interpretation to the very end. From his doctoral dissertation under W. D. Davies (*The Last Adam*, 1966) to his early and provocative applications of psychological theory to Paul (*Paul for a New Day*, 1977) to his essays on "Paul and the Eschatological Woman" and his major and definitive book on homosexuality, *The New Testament and Homosexuality* (1983), Scroggs's writings were profoundly and productively informed by central and enduring existential questions that link ancient texts to contemporary life. It would be a mistake to characterize Scroggs's work as in any sense dictated by the need to address contemporary causes, however. What got his attention was not so much one or another "cause" in our time as the deep human structures of the ancient texts and the ways in which human strivings for and glimpses of liberating transformation are reflected in the biblical witness.[1]

Because his gift was to see the embodied human being in the text, he was among the first New Testament scholars to turn seriously toward the investigation of the social character of the early churches in their primitive environment. Essays and talks he gave in the 1970s, for example "The Earliest Christian Communities as a Sectarian Movement" (1975) and "The Sociological Interpretation of the New Testament" (1977), developed key themes in the social context of early Christianity. His landmark essay "The Sociological Interpretation of the New Testament: The Present State of Research" (1980) not only helped to bring sociological methodology squarely into the mainstream in New Testament studies, but also proved to be an inroad to biblical and ancient Christian studies for sociologists.

Adept though he was at psychology and sociology alike, however, Robin Scroggs was ever and always primarily a biblical theologian. His own mentor, W. D. Davies, kept looking for the New Testament Theology he expected Robin to write. And while his foreshortened life did not allow the full outworking of that comprehensive volume, he was clearly on his way there in the last decade and a half of his life. From the late 1980s, when he moved from Chicago

Theological Seminary to Union Seminary in New York, he devoted his writing energies to the principal matter of Christology that for him was the heart of New Testament theology. His book *Christology in Paul and John* (1988) and his lectures and essays in this period demonstrate his abiding interest in the theological energy and impetus of "realized eschatology" made available through Christ and witnessed in wide variations across the Christian canon. The present volume, completed just before Scroggs's death, is perhaps not in its scope the volume he had hoped to achieve, but in its focus on that essential element of New Testament theology, Christology, it is a remarkably integrated statement of developments in New Testament theology to which he so richly contributed.

In this book, then, Scroggs hopes to bring the reader closer to the earliest non-elite interpreters of the events of the life, death, and resurrection of Jesus of Nazareth. Recognizing that in our earliest texts we are dealing with the literate "elites," he asks, "What did the common folk think?" To what degree are the "thoughts, yearnings, hopes, and fears of those who dared to join with Paul and others to form a group of struggling communities," who are represented only indirectly in the texts that remain, to be allowed to tell their story? Scroggs sets out to find ways of getting "behind the text-authors to a faith shared by people in the early communities, with which the authors themselves were in touch, with which they may mostly have agreed, but with which they were certainly in dialogue, not always positively."

Scroggs's method for getting to the "common folk" rests on the discipline of form-criticism, which he defines as "the study of certain stylized forms through which the early believers expressed their views on the significance of Jesus (based in part on memory)." These forms—christological titles, formulas, and hymns which predate the written texts—could well point us, Scroggs argues, toward popular Hellenistic Christianity. In these formulaic fragments, he contends, we have the bedrock of the earliest Christology as it was known in the Greek-speaking Gentile churches, and because these fragments reflect the faith of the wider church, "they tell us much more than the elitist beliefs of the text-authors." A second step is to move from the evidence of the Hellenistic expressions to explore evidence for the christologies of the Palestinian communities and to ask whether there is consonance there with Hellenistic Christology in substance if not in terminology.

The end product, a creative new reading of the communities behind the documents of the New Testament and their surprising expressions of faith, reflects Scroggs's longstanding interest in and contributions to the sociology of earliest Christianity. But most of all it brings into our hands the culminating work of a biblical theologian who could not and would not forget that the first Christians were real human beings living amidst the everyday strains of stresses of the world and yet knowing, through Christ, a "new day."

Special thanks are due to Marshall D. Johnson for his superb editing of Professor Scroggs's manuscript and to Marissa Wold for her careful work seeing the book through production.

—Alexandra Brown
Jessie Ball duPont Professor of Religion
Washington and Lee University

A Personal Note _____

If Robin could be asked to whom he wished to dedicate this book, I believe he would want it dedicated to the memory of his "Doktor Vater," friend, and mentor, W. D. Davies. Robin followed Professor Davies from Duke to Princeton University to pursue his doctorate with him. Across the years, their friendship continued through correspondence and visits, until Dr. Davies's death.

Although every letter from Davies was complimentary, and he was especially proud when Robin joined the faculty at Union, every letter also included a sentence like this one from March 1987: "I cannot resist—yet once more—expressing the hope for that N.T. Theology."

Two things long prevented Robin from such an undertaking, although it was always in the back of his mind. One was his belief that there is no single New Testament theology, nor even a single Christology, as the present work makes clear. The second postponing factor was Robin's dedication to writing for church people (he loved teaching in churches) and his commitment to showing how Scripture is relevant to, and addresses, the issues of the day. Again and again he heard questions and saw the pain that had been experienced by students, by women, by believers and doubters alike, and he sought to address those issues through his writings. Such concern also led him to address the problem of how it is possible for the first century to speak to the twenty-first.

So this project was put off until after his retirement. Still there were interruptions, such as teaching in several seminaries. Then, about the time it began to take shape, there descended the distraction of living with cancer. It might be said that Robin's determination to finish this book was one of the things that kept him going in those final years. After his last hospitalization, we wrote a belated Christmas letter saying that on January 14, 2005, he came home and immediately resumed work on his New Testament Christology manuscript! Near the end of March, Robin turned off his computer and announced, "It is finished." Less than a month later, on April 25, 2005, he finished this life.

—Marilee Scroggs

The Task of a New Testament Theology

What a grand theological scheme the authors of the New Testament documents hand us! But what did the common folk think? Can we get behind the text-authors to the faith shared by the people in the early communities, with which the text-authors were doubtlessly in touch, with which they may have mostly agreed, but with which they were certainly in dialogue, not always positively? The answer to this question is obviously uncertain. We have only the texts produced by the elites. Are there ways to use these texts to illumine the thoughts, yearnings, hopes, and fears of those who dared to join with Paul and others to form groups of struggling communities, which over time would succeed in ways other religious communities had not? That is the question I have posed in this book.

There are many ways of "doing" biblical theology. All of them offer possibilities and have limitations. The interpreter cannot follow all possible paths but can only map out one path that seems to have integrity and promise for insight. In what follows I identify three issues that involve decisions about which data are appropriate for a New Testament theology—that is, what is or is not included in the term "theology" as it pertains to early Christian expressions. I pose the issues in the form of questions, and my responses will not be technical.

1. *Should the interpreter include the* ideas of Jesus *or should the description begin with* faith in Jesus*?*

This question has divided interpreters since at least the nineteenth century. It might seem obvious to some that what we today call the "historical Jesus" ought to be the basis and fountainhead for any kind of Christianity. But there are at least two separate issues here.

The first has to do with an implicit pejorative in the meaning given to "theology" in the nineteenth century. Theology is speculation, human ideas about the reality of God and the significance of Jesus. In the nineteenth century, many scholars had confidence that they could recover the truth about Jesus, i.e., the "historical Jesus," by sifting out the legends and myths in the Gospels from historical fact.[1] It was this recoverable Jesus who was the presumed fountainhead of Christianity.[2]

But did not Jesus have a theology? That is, did he not teach about God and persons' relationship to God? Going back to at least F. C. Baur in the nineteenth century is the distinction between the "teaching" of Jesus and the "theology" of the church.[3] Jesus did not have a theology; he taught the religion of the fatherhood of God and the brotherhood of man (so Adolf Harnack).[4] And so a distinction was made between Jesus and his true religion, on the one hand, and Paul (honored or vilified, as the case may be) as the founder of theology, on the other.

From this perspective, one could indeed think of a theology independent of Jesus, but it would not be of much worth. Either the theology of the followers of Jesus is a "fall" from the simple religion of Jesus,[5] or the theological reflections of the followers simply express the "value" they attached to the historical Jesus.[6]

While all this may seem obviously the correct path, it is important to see that it can be otherwise. Rudolf Bultmann in his much celebrated *Theology of the New Testament* described the alternative with great clarity:

> The *message of Jesus* is a presupposition for the theology of the New Testament rather than a part of that theology itself. . . . Christian faith did not exist until there was a Christian kerygma, i.e., a kerygma proclaiming Jesus Christ—specifically Jesus Christ the Crucified and Risen One—to be God's eschatological act of salvation. He was first so proclaimed in the kerygma of the earliest Church, not in the message of the historical Jesus.[7]

Bultmann reflects the neo-Reformation emphasis on the importance and legitimacy of theology. His words indicate clearly that the move toward the acceptance of theology (as distinct from the "teaching" of Jesus) affirms the centrality of the faith in Jesus' resurrection as the beginning of the church. Thus theology begins as reflection upon the faith *in* Jesus, and is in no way some "value" derived from the teaching and self-understanding of Jesus. Christianity is rooted in the faith that God has acted through Jesus, not that Jesus claimed divine status. And as long as the neo-Reformation emphasis upon this beginning point lasted, Jesus no longer could be the place one began to reflect on the theology of early Christianity.

A second issue, however, concerns just the *possibility* of knowing enough about the historical Jesus so that one *could* recover, if one wished, his teaching and self-understanding. The search for the historical Jesus goes back to the beginning of the Enlightenment, as Albert Schweitzer pointed out more than a century ago.[8] From the Enlightenment, Christians "learned" that only the historical saves, and thus the race was on to disentangle the true facts of Jesus from the theological (here a pejorative term) legends and myths of the Gospels. Too much, perhaps, has been written about the history of this project, and it need not be repeated here. What strikes me, as I look back on two hundred years and more of the project, is the confidence that scholar after scholar exudes as they tell the "truth" about Jesus over the vanquished bodies of all those who have gone before. Schweitzer himself was not immune from this hubris, nor was Bultmann decades later. What it seems to me we learn from this debacle is that no one can be sanguine about the reconstruction of any historical Jesus. We may—and should—have a more constructive perspective on the "legends and myths" of the Gospels, but these reflect the faith of believers in Jesus and do not necessarily describe the "facts" of Jesus.[9]

There are thus two arguments for beginning the analysis of Christian theology with the faith of the first followers in Jesus rather than from Jesus himself. The first is the theological judgment that faith is *faith in* Jesus, not a repetition of the *faith of* Jesus. The second is the historian's possible judgment that the factual Jesus is inaccessible to any attempts at recovery. The first judgment says the historical Jesus should not be the basis of Christian theology; the second, that the historical Jesus *cannot* be its basis.

I accept the judgment that Christian faith begins with faith *in* Jesus. I argue that throughout the history of church theology, faith in Jesus has always been the starting point (apart from the two hundred years of Enlightenment-influenced thought). I accept that as an appropriate beginning point for today. It is also the case that I am less skeptical than many about the recovery of the historical Jesus.[10] Nevertheless, it is my *theologically* determined judgment that a theology should begin with the earliest recoverable faith in Jesus. In this volume I say nothing about the "historical Jesus."

2. *Should a theology attempt to discover what were the popular beliefs of average Christians, or should it remain content with the authors of the texts, who mostly count as the elites of the Christian culture?*

This question is not as frequently raised as the first but it is equally important. Indeed, it is essential for my program in this book. What is the issue? Until the last decades, investigators were concerned to describe the theology of the authors of the texts—of Paul, for example. Christian theology was seen as the authors' thoughts, and the question about what the "average" believer thought was not considered, or at least was not considered important.

In our more sociologically oriented perspectives today, what the different Christian communities thought has become important. The church is more than the elites. In fact, as is always the case, the elites very often have little influence over popular views, unless an elite also holds political power. And the average participant may have little or no understanding of the subtleties of elite thinking.

If one wants to describe Christian theology in the United States in the last century, where does one go to find the evidence? Does one look to the leaders and write fascinating intellectual histories of the Chicago School, Reinhold Niebuhr, Paul Tillich, and other authorities? Or does one take sociological studies of the views of church members—who may never have had the slightest interest in or knowledge of the intellectual giants of their time? The former would produce rarified reading but provide little information about the average layperson's views. The latter would give a truer reading of just what the person in the pew believed. Surely, insofar as possible, one would ideally like to incorporate both in order to get the most complete picture possible.

But even if one wanted to incorporate popular perspectives into one's account of early Christian theology, would it be possible? After all, all we have are texts.[11] And the texts are, as already suggested, the production of the elites. How would one go about finding data that might provide information about the non-elites?

There are, of course, antagonists mentioned—or attacked—in the texts. Virtually every New Testament text reveals, at some point, that there are opponents out there—enemies who believe in Jesus as much as the authors of the texts. Once one learns not immediately to conclude that these enemies are "heretics" but simply honest people who take viewpoints different from the texts' authors, then a new world manifests itself. Paul opposes leaders who come in from the outside in the Galatian churches. Paul speaks harshly against some believers in Corinth who take some position Paul thinks is opposed to the truth as he sees it. The author of Revelation attacks those in some churches who adhere to points of view he thinks evil (but are held by people who consider themselves believers in Jesus). The Pastorals and 1 John attack other believers who deviate from "their" truth; the author of 1 John even calls them "antichrists."

The problem here is that we cannot be sure whether these enemies represent a kind of popular Christianity or whether they disclose other elitists with other systems of belief and practice. That is, we cannot assume that the texts' authors are opposing a popular Christianity as much as the leaders of a different system. We may have a case of elitists against elitists. Even the people Paul opposes in 1 Corinthians sound like leaders Paul takes to be hubristically motivated.[12] At the least, paying attention to such texts enlarges our views of the extent of early Christianity. Where possible, they should be drawn into the picture.

Another avenue may hold more promise and is the premise upon which this book rests. Nearly one hundred years ago, scholars began to mine the Gospels for materials that were much earlier than the date of the completed Gospels and in which the Jesus materials were incorporated. This discipline came to be called form criticism. It was a study of certain stylized forms through which the early believers expressed their views of the significance of Jesus (based in part on memory). Thus the forms represented an early form of believers' expression. They could well point to "popular" Christianity.[13] They were transmitted orally by "prophets" (who were not part of the elite—if any elite existed at that time!). They were accepted by the hearers and became part of their faith. To the extent that we can put together enough similar judgments about Jesus from this fund, we have as good evidence as it is possible to have of the thinking of the early communities who believed in Jesus.[14] In fact, analysis of these oral traditions could serve as an entry into sociological descriptions of the early communities.[15]

Even more importantly for my purposes, the tools of form criticism were applied to the epistolary material in the remainder of the New Testament. Fragments of liturgical material were discovered in Paul and other writers. This material was cited by the author but not composed by him. Since what was discovered seemed to be hymnic, baptismal, or creedal formulas, these fragments give promise of being examples of what was believed, recited, and sung by believers at large.[16] While there continues to be discussion about whether the original of this or that fragment goes back to the Palestinian communities, in their present form they reflect the faith of the Hellenistic church, now composed largely of Gentiles.

In my judgment, we have in these fragments the bedrock of the earliest Christology as it was known in the Greek-speaking Gentile churches and, because it reflects the faith of the wider church, these fragments tell us much more than the elitist beliefs of the authors. As I argue below, these fragments are consistent in their interpretation of the significance of Jesus. This interpretation is, furthermore, taken for granted by most if not all of the text authors. The evidence extends in time from the earliest Pauline letters (perhaps the early 50s) until the beginning of the second century. Surely here we have a beginning point. It is not necessarily the earliest one, but the earliest one of which we have sufficient information to have confidence of using. Thus I can and will begin this study with what I think is a consensus in popular Christianity of the essence of the faith. Granted, it is a consensus of Hellenistic Christianity, but this is the faith of the church that would become dominant. The question then has to be considered whether it is possible, by inspecting the Gospel material through the lens of form criticism, to see whether the popular Christology of the Palestinian communities is consonant in substance, if not terminology, with that of Hellenistic faith.

3. *In describing early Christian theology, should one remain content with the intellectual system expressed in the words and concepts, or should one also attempt to tease out the experiences that the words reflect and that might live behind the words?*

This question covers an immensely complex set of issues. (a) Is the interpreter's task satisfied when the linguistic theological systems are described and interrelated as best as possible, or does this leave the most significant part of the task ignored? That is, what is most important to a believer who speaks a faith—the words, or the experiences of faith that compel the believer to speak? (b) This assumes that there are such experiences and that one can have access to them. But can one? By what appropriate process or method can one move from words (which is where the interpreter has to begin) to the experiences that produced them? It is one thing to imagine, even to be convinced, that such experiences are in fact there and are crucial to an understanding of the words themselves; it is quite another to have confidence that one can have access to those experiences. (c) Behind these issues lies a basic—shall I say philosophical—question about the relation between words and experiences. Do experiences create words or is it the reverse—that words create experiences? If experiences create words, then one may seek the experiences that create the words. If, on the contrary, words create experiences, then the process has to be reversed, yet the relation between words and experience is equally present.

Surely both positions are, at times, true. In an insightful work, the theologian Ted Jennings argues for the priority of words but acknowledges that there are certain "breakthrough" experiences that also break up the usual words and force one to create new language.[17] This both–and description seems to me appropriate, even necessary, when analyzing the emergence of a new perspective, such as we find in early Christian theology. Paul used the linguistic building blocks of his culture. At the same time he turned them on their heads and created a new structure—at least new for him. Here his experiences influence his linguistic creation. Then he preaches and writes this new structure, intending to recreate in others the same breakthrough experiences he has come to know.

If, indeed, we are to study breakthrough language in early Christian theology, surely it is the breakthrough that is the heart of the matter. To claim that "Christ is Lord" could mean much or nothing, depending upon the commitment of the speaker and the experience that led the speaker first to make that exclamation. Breakthrough language expresses new experiences, and I believe that such experiences are a legitimate subject of theological inquiry. There yet remains, however, a difficult issue: can the interpreter determine *what* experience lies behind the language? Is there an acceptable method that can be used to correlate the two, or is the interpreter allowed to roam freely in his or her imagination about the interrelationship? I do not think there are easy answers to this question, and we should be cautious about making correlations that are too easy.[18]

We can ask about the anthropological implications for theological language. For example, it seems reasonable to think that an expression of God's grace indicates a sense of liberation and acceptance on the part of the speaker. When Paul writes about joy and rejoicing even while he faces a possible death sentence (Philippians), is it not likely that his awareness of God's gift of grace overcomes anxiety about death and enables him to write of joy? Or is he whistling in the dark? No one can live in a changed state without retreating at times back into the older, perhaps safer existence. All of the text writers are human and are subject to the same anxieties as everyone else. Once the new reality is set in vision and in memory, however, the person is able to understand that his or her true life is rooted in that reality, however much anxiety may cause a return to a former self-understanding. Yes, Paul may be whistling in the dark, but his whistle is rooted in the vision of the new life and the memory of his participation in that life. If Paul is whistling in the dark, he is nevertheless saying that if he were able to be at that moment in the new reality, he would be able to rejoice.

In sum, I argue that experiences are a legitimate data source for theological inquiry. We need to know just what the person is and can be in response to God's acts. Given the limitations of our ability to know the past, however, it is easier to say that there are experiences than to know what are their contents. One can say, perhaps, what the experiences *should* be; one needs to have some reserve, however, about saying what they actually were in specific instances. In what follows, I will, where I think it possible, suggest what such experiences might be that lie behind the words. I do not think it possible even to suggest this in every case, because of the limitations described.

I think it helpful to seek out the major linguistic centers around which the early church focused its faith and to trace their trajectories.[19] My attempt is to trace the movement and development of the specific terms and their functions for the meaning given to Jesus that may reflect the basic faith of the church rather than the sophisticated minds of the text authors. As a result of this focus, the detailed theology of the great minds such as Paul or the main author of the Fourth Gospel will not be attended to here. In fact, the chapter on Paul is the briefest in the book, since I am not interested here in his profound, individual articulation of his vision of the truth but only in his use of the trajectory out of which he comes and in which he lived.[20]

The trajectories I explore are given names that highlight specific titles that the early believers used to express their basic faith and commitment. Some might think that I have fallen back into what is now pejoratively called "title research." I hope it will become apparent that by the use of titles I am trying to capture much more than an arid term or two. I aim at using the titles to show not only *what* the titles meant, but *why* early believers found them meaningful and how they helped explain their new situation in the world, both individually and corporately. Alas, it is not always possible, in my judgment, to be sure what this meaning was. But that it meant and symbolized their commitment to a new leader and a new mode of existence seems plain to me. Here speculation, however precarious, seems important, and I engage in such speculation without apology, where facts disappear behind the focus on their new leader, Jesus. Such speculation is not, of course, novel and it has engaged the minds of many scholars. I trust that my attempts are no more off the track of reality than others. In the first century it was not easy or safe to commit oneself to Jesus, and it is only fair to this commitment to take it with utmost seriousness.

I begin with a perhaps unusual point, the Hellenistic church's faith in the resurrected Jesus as Lord of the cosmos. I begin here because the liturgies of this church come through with reasonable clarity and, as suggested above, reflect the basic faith of the church that was to become dominant. For this trajectory I use the term "Cosmocrator trajectory." Obviously there was faith in Jesus before (or alongside of) this trajectory, and I explore this basically in terms of the "trajectory of the Son of Man." Was there a relationship between these two? Did the "Palestinian" trajectory influence and inform the Hellenistic? That is difficult to answer, but I discuss possibilities below. Neither of these two, however, can be complete without introducing the trajectory of the "*Christos*" (the Greek form of "Christ," a translation of the Hebrew "Messiah"). In all ways this is the most uncertain and ambiguous trajectory, despite its early appearance and lingering reality in the Hellenistic church through *Christos* as a name given to Jesus. The original meaning of this title and the faith expressed through it are not clear, and the trajectory tends to peter out in the later church. Finally I look at the Johannine literature to see whether it qualifies as a trajectory—that is, as a reflection of the faith of a continuous community—or whether it stands as an awesome monument to a few great minds. Some of the answer to this depends upon where one locates 1 John in the spectrum, and I have a novel suggestion to make on this troubling issue.

Thus the scope of this book is circumscribed. I do not explore the minds of the text-authors, nor do I wander into crucially related areas such as the new understanding about God or the role of the Spirit. What I have suggested here certainly has implications for many issues I do not find it possible to touch on here. I hope what I *have* done is provocative and illuminative of certain areas in the faith of the persons who were attracted to the proclamation about Jesus and who found it worth the risk to join the ranks, because Christology provided them with new experience and a new life.

Part I

Jesus in the Popular Piety of the Early Churches

I ——

THE COSMOCRATOR TRAJECTORY

"But they declared that the sum of their guilt or error had amounted only to this, that on an appointed day they had been accustomed to meet before daybreak, and to recite a hymn (*carmen*) antiphonally to Christ, as to a god. . . ."[1] These famous words by Pliny the Younger are our earliest specific reference to the practice of saying (probably chanting) a liturgical christological hymn.[2] That such recitation was done antiphonally perhaps reflects the influence of Hebraic poetic parallelism and fits the strophic arrangement of the hymn in Philippians 2, at least in my judgment.

The implication for the importance of the liturgical material embedded in the New Testament and excavated by scholars in the last decades is immense. What we find in these texts are the expressed beliefs and feelings of the Hellenistic churches, the singing and the acclamations of the anonymous members, whether rich or poor, of whatever intellectual status. How Paul and other New Testament authors used these materials is to be accounted to the specific theological reflections of the individuals, the intellectual elite of the early church. But the liturgical materials themselves have a much wider scope and open for us a window into the common faith of the early Hellenistic church, that is, the communities who spoke and sang the Greek of these materials. It needs only to be added that it is *this* church that absorbs other modes of thinking, assimilates them, and presents them, through its own perspectives, to the church of the future.

A primary and absolutely essential conclusion can be quickly reached. Common—indeed central—to most of the discovered liturgical materials in the New Testament is the acclamation of *kyrios Iēsous Christos* (Lord Jesus Christ), the exaltation and enthronement of the resurrected Jesus to the position of Cosmocrator, world ruler.[3] The focus of the liturgical materials on this acclamation is well known and needs no defense here.[4]

The model example is Philippians 2:6-11.

> Therefore God also highly exalted him
> and gave him the name that is above every name
> So that at the name of Jesus every knee should bend
> [in heaven and on earth and under the earth]
>
> And every tongue confess that Jesus Christ is Lord
> [to the glory of God the Father]. (vv. 9-11, NRSV)

The bracketed lines are sometimes held to be Pauline additions.[5] While I am not in complete sympathy with the arguments in either case, discussion is not crucial for the point being made, since the acclamation of Christ as Cosmocrator is clear regardless. The phrase "to the glory of God the Father" does indeed deflect the exclusiveness of the enthronement motif but without calling it into question. If both of these lines are Pauline additions, then the final strophe affirms without any apparent reservation the enthronement of Christ as Cosmocrator:

> So that at the name of Jesus every knee should bend
> and every tongue confess that Jesus Christ is Lord.

Well known about this last strophe is its clear dependence on Isaiah 45:23 (LXX). The startling deflection of the meaning of the Isaianic passage needs to be emphasized. Not only is what is affirmed about God now referred to the resurrected Jesus, but what is for God future has here become potentially present (subjunctive). What is there a future lordship for Yahweh is here a present lordship for Jesus Christ. If verse 11c is a Pauline addition ("to the glory of God the Father"), then at the end of the original hymn, *kyrios Iēsous Christos* (Lord Jesus Christ) stands alone as Cosmocrator.

I begin with the Philippians hymn not because it is necessarily the earliest, although establishing the relative dating of these materials is perhaps impossible, but because it shows most sharply the theme of enthronement to the status of Cosmocrator. Yet all the other materials state the same motif, even if the language differs widely and titles are varied or nonexistent.[6] With regard to dating, what is important for our purposes is to recognize that this theme seems to have been prominent from earliest Hellenistic Christianity throughout the first century. The liturgical materials themselves witness to their early use; the employment by the deutero-Pauline authors attests to their continued importance at the end of the period. A quick survey of the most prominent liturgical materials will attest to the domination of this trajectory in the Hellenistic church.

Romans 1:3f. is widely accepted as a formula independent of Paul:

Who was born of the seed of David
   according to the flesh,
Appointed son of God in power
   according to the spirit of holiness
   by the resurrection from the dead.[7]

Although it may be less possible to isolate layers of traditions than Fuller thinks, the bi-partite Christology must be an original element.[8] Here the second element, "appointed son of God in power," certainly asserts the lordship of the Son, since he is "appointed . . . in power." The aorist participle together with the phrase "in power" points backward in time, doubtlessly to the resurrection, as the final phrase, perhaps a later addition, clarifies. And it is perhaps not accidental that Paul identifies this resurrected authority as "Jesus Christ our Lord" (4b), the same title that comes at the climax of the hymn in Philippians. To be established as Son of God in power means essentially the same thing as enthronement over the cosmos. As we shall see, the combination of *kyrios*, *Christos*, and *Iēsous* (Lord, Christ, Jesus) is the most prominent acclamation of the resurrected Jesus in this thought-world.

Although Colossians 1:15-20 is generally recognized as a liturgical statement, independent of the author of the letter, agreement about the original lines of the hymn is not yet forthcoming. In the first stanza the hymn celebrates Christ as agent of creation in terms of "the all" (*ta panta*). A minimalist reading of the last stanza produces the following:[9]

Who is the head,
   firstborn from the dead,
For in him all the fullness (*plērōma*) dwelled,
And through him to reconcile the cosmos (*ta panta*) to himself.
           (vv. 18b, 19, 20a)

Here lordship is expressed in terms of *plērōma* and reconciliation of *ta panta* to himself rather than enthronement. Yet the resurrection marks the moment of the reconciliation of the cosmos, and it seems hard to deny that the lordship over the reconciled cosmos is implied. Furthermore, it is crucial to note that the savior figure stands on his own, without being overshadowed by God. Jesus Christ is head (*archē*), the *plērōma*, and effects the reconciliation of *ta panta* to *himself* (not to God). Again the hymn ends with the savior figure standing alone on the stage.

That there is a liturgical fragment embedded in Ephesians 1:20-23 seems very likely, although authorial additions probably abound, making difficult any confidence in some original structure. On the argument that Ephesians is dependent on Colossians, it is striking that this material comes in the same place in the letter as does Colossians 1:15-20 and functions in the same way to point to the ultimate lordship of Jesus Christ. Perhaps uneasy with some of the affirmations in the Colossians hymn, the author of Ephesians has replaced that with at least an echo of a more traditional formula, dealing only with the resurrection/ enthronement and reflecting Old Testament terminology. I cite the entire passage, italicizing what seems to be the skeleton and putting in brackets what most likely counts, almost certainly, as additions by the author.

> *Raising him from the dead*
> *And seating* [*him*] *at the right hand in the heavens*
>   above every head and authority and power and lordship
>   and every name named, not only in this age but also
>   in that which is coming.
> *And all things he subjected under his feet*
> *and him he made head over all things*
>   [for the church which is his body]
>   the *plērōma* of the one who fills all in all.

The basic structure is made up of two couplets, the first with participial construction, the second with finite (aorist) tenses in chiastic form. The resurrection is explicitly mentioned (a rare occurrence) and references are made in the first couplet to Psalm 110:1, in the second to Psalm 8:6. The lines after the first couplet clarify the meaning of the seating with phrases that recall Philippians 2:9-10; the lines after the second explain the lordship in terms of the *plērōma* theme, as in the Colossians hymn.

What we may thus have here is a reference to an early, Hellenistic Jewish-Christian formula. In any case, the theme of enthronement is explicit. Jesus Christ is again Cosmocrator, although the presence of God as primary agent in the enthronement is pronounced. Nevertheless, the result is the reign of Christ as Lord of the entire cosmos.

Still another liturgical statement has been detected in 1 Peter 3:18-19, 22. Rudolf Bultmann reconstructed the formula and argued that 1:20 also belonged to it.[10] While the lack of repetitive rhythmic and syntactical relationships do not make it entirely clear that we have before us the formula in its original wording, the movement of the "story" from death to resurrection to enthronement is so close to the other liturgies that it seems safe to claim that at least these verses mirror a liturgical form in use prior to the writing of 1 Peter.

Since I am not concerned primarily with notions of preexistence, it is most helpful to short-circuit Bultmann's proposal about 1:20 (even though I think he is correct in his judgments) and cite the fragment, as Bultmann reconstructed it, in 3:18, 19, 22:

[Christ] once suffered[11] for sins[12]
   to lead us to God
Being put to death in flesh,
   being made alive in spirit;
in which [spirit] he also made proclamation
     to the spirits in prison;
who is at the right hand of God, having entered into heaven,
having subjected to him angels and authorities and powers.

The uncertainty of the meaning of some of the phrases need not detain us, since the point is simply to point to the importance of enthronement in the piece. Most scholars today seem to favor the contrast of flesh/spirit as referring to the two realms of reality in which one participates (cf. Rom 1:3-4; 1 Tim 3:16). In this realm of spirit the resurrected Jesus makes a proclamation to spirits who are bound—most likely a proclamation of victory over the cosmos and its former lords (now bound). In the final line his enthronement (seated at the right hand) and his lordship over the other powers are described.

Again the event results in Christ the Cosmocrator, the ruler over the entire cosmos. Again there is a certain tension between this lordship and God. God does not disappear; the Cosmocrator sits at his right, and the implied agent of the subjection of angels, authorities, and powers is surely God. And yet the final statement shows the complete authority of Christ. The role of God is described simply as the handing over of the world power to Christ.[13]

Conclusions

1. Since these are liturgical fragments, they show more than what the elite, the intellectuals (e.g., Paul) thought, and they come as close as any information we have for this period to revealing what the church as a whole believed. Presumably, community members all sang or recited (or heard sung and recited) these materials. Then as now, liturgy functioned to unify the community into some basic set of affirmations.

2. While it seems to me impossible to date or locate the pre-authorial traditions themselves, the fact that they are repeated in documents that extend from the 50s to the end of the century (or later) indicates the constancy of the basic motif of the resurrected Jesus as Cosmocrator during these early decades.

3. It is equally important to note what is *not* stated in these liturgical materials. No mention is made of an eschatological future. As far as we are led by what is said, the rule of the Cosmocrator is not said to be at the moment deficient, to be perfected only in the future. This is not the same thing as a naive enthusiasm in the present perfection of the rule, any more than Caesar's (or anyone else's)

rule is perfectly exercised. It simply affirms *who* is the cosmic Lord.[14] It may not be too daring to suggest that the enthronement is pictured on a political model of accession to power of a human ruler. One is accustomed to hyperbolic language associated with such events (O King, live forever!). If one approves of the policies of the new ruler, one anticipates a positive reign. One does not expect utopian perfection.[15]

4. No emphasis is laid on individual or corporate guilt and the need for forgiveness of sin or redemption. Other liturgical materials, such as 1 Corinthians 15:3, do imply a saving death, and comments by the authors using the materials may add that (e.g., Col 1:20b). But in the pre-authorial materials inspected, all emphasis lies in the acclamation of the enthronement of the Cosmocrator (even 1 Pet 3:18-22). Granted, a soteriology does lie underneath this claim, but that soteriology is taken from a political metaphor, not a sacerdotal one.

5. The meaning for the acclaimers thus must lie in the enthronement itself, the restoration of the cosmos to its rightful *kyrios*.[16] The world now is a potentially benign reality, in which one can live and breathe freely. The demonic powers and principalities who once enslaved the cosmos are now dethroned, and *kyrios Iēsous Christos* reigns. Since in the cult *this kyrios* is honored, its members can exult in confidence that they are on the right side and that they have some contact with the one who truly rules. Salvation (if one insists on using this term) thus lies in a new meaning-structure given to the cosmos, in which people can now live their lives with new confidence and joy.[17]

6. The meaning includes the dethronement of the powers that have probably been seen as acting to condemn humans to a life of slavery.[18] One is now freed from tyranny. Also crucial is the conviction that this accession is eternal, even if it does not lead to utopian perfection. The Cosmocrator will live forever, although it is not always certain whether the believer is included in that eternality. And, to repeat, the accession is not put into an eschatological structure, but rather into a "political" one.

The nearly unbelievable audacity in this claim has long been noticed. How is it conceivable that a humiliated and executed criminal in such a short space of time has become Cosmocrator? How could a few struggling communities, made up of largely disenfranchised and lower-status folk (at least "not many" were of the establishment—1 Cor 1:26-31), claim that their *kyrios* is Cosmocrator? While any answer is uncertain, the question must surely be asked, how was this audacious confidence possible? This is not a question about the *origins* of the implied mythic story. That question has been long debated and for our purposes can be left aside. What is at issue is not *where* the mythic materials came from, but *why* the Hellenistic church found it important to create the story about Jesus that it did.

This question can be put differently. In the religious faith of Judaism, Yahweh is already honored as Cosmocrator. He is creator, sustainer, redeemer, and judge of the entire world. Why was it not sufficient for the early believers in Jesus, who either were Jews themselves or had had important contact with Jewish mythic structure, to reaffirm that faith? Why could not Jesus remain an earthly agent of Yahweh, a proclaimer of the already and eternal lordship of Yahweh? Surely this would have been easy to do, indeed easier than fitting Jesus into such a grandiose structure of Cosmocrator (and creator). This question has not been sufficiently discussed, largely, I suspect, because interpreters, reading the texts from a later perspective of trinitarian monotheism, have toned down the actual audacity of the material itself. From a structural perspective, the liturgical materials affirm a belief in Jesus Christ as *the* Cosmocrator. And if he is Cosmocrator, he has in effect become God. Simply stated, the structure implies a replacement theme. Yahweh as God has been replaced by *kyrios Iēsous Christos*.

That Christ replaces Yahweh says at least that for the creators of this new structure, the old one was believed or felt to be deficient. I say "felt" because it is not necessarily the case that we are dealing here with self-conscious theologians who have come to certain rational conclusions. Rather we may have at the basis of this dramatic change an expression of an alteration of existence at a level not entirely available to rational reflection.

This may even suggest that the use of "deficiency" is leaning too much to a negative perspective. It may perhaps be the case that the cause of the change is an awareness of something positive that has happened that cannot be easily related to the old mythic structure. If one does not pour new wine into old wineskins, one equally cannot rest content ascribing what is perceived as a new reality to an old mythic structure.

This is not to say that the framers of the materials would ever admit that Yahweh no longer is God. Yahweh always remains in the background. Given the close relation of Christianity to Judaism, even for Gentiles, it would be no more possible to deny the reality of Yahweh than to deny the fact that Jesus was crucified. There is no question of a theme of usurpation; no competition could be permitted to exist between them. The story always unfolds within the framework of Jewish belief in the one God. Yahweh somehow retains at least an honorific position.

Thus the function of the texts is replacement rather than usurpation.[19] Nevertheless, the audacity of the material is actually intensified. Not only is Christ Cosmocrator, he has de facto replaced Yahweh. The question now becomes why this replacement was important to the communities that created the story? How did the motif of replacement function? I am ultimately interested in what that motif may say about the perceived alteration of reality within Christian groups.

From the perspective of sociology of knowledge, the question becomes: What is the relation between the motif as objectified in the mythic story and the human situations, individual and societal, of the creators of the story? These situations, of course, include religious thinking and cultic activity as a central focus.

There is, obviously, no direct way of answering that question. We have too little information about such creators and their social scene to enable us to establish a sure correlation. There is an indirect approach, however, which perhaps will enable us to make educated guesses about the correlation. The indirect way lies in an investigation of instances of the divine replacement motif found in other religious expressions. If a pattern can be established in which correlations between the social situation and the mythic theme can be reasonably suggested, then it may be possible to insert the early Christian replacement theme into that pattern. It is to such possible instances in other expressions that I now turn.

Replacement Motifs in Other Religions

Historical connections are not the issue here. Whether one of these expressions has influenced another is a subordinate and ultimately non-crucial matter, although it may well be that in one or more cases some historical connection can be suspected. What is crucial are possible functional similarities. To speak of a functional similarity, two criteria must be satisfied. (1) There should be structural similarity in the myth. (2) There should be some likelihood that a change in the social situation of the mythmakers is involved. The first criterion can be answered with more confidence than the second. I operate, however, out of a conviction that a change in the mythic structure always implies some sort of important social alternation, whether it can be discovered or not.

The Enthronement of the Son of Man in Daniel 7

The structure of the mythic picture in Daniel 7:9-10, 13-14 is clear, even if the meaning is disputed. God, as the ancient of days, holds a heavenly court in which "one like a son of man" is presented to him and enthroned as cosmic lord:

> To him was given dominion and glory and kingship,
>   that all peoples, nations, and languages
>   should serve him;
> his dominion is an everlasting dominion,
>   which shall not pass away,
> and his kingdom one
>   that shall never be destroyed. (v. 14, RSV)

God appoints the new ruler, but structurally it is a replacement of the old god by the new. "The old god, the 'Ancient of Days,' abdicates in favor of a young god, who takes his place."[20] Colpe writes: "The transfer of dominion from the Ancient of Days to the Son of Man would seem to go back to the wresting of power from an old god by a young one. . . ."[21] From now on the new god reigns.

While the story line of Daniel itself closely relates the one like a son of man to the people of Israel, it is very likely that the mythic structure itself assumes that this figure is divine. Many see the structure dependent on the myth of two Canaanite gods, El and Baal, the latter of which assumes power over the former.[22] To that background I will return. Others, in a complementary but not contradictory argument, think that since "saints" in verse 18 likely refers to angels, the one like a son of man is perhaps also an angel; Michael seems to be the angel of choice.[23] Since Israel is the special people of Michael, the people participate in the kingdom ruled by the angel (cf. v. 27).

Assuming that the mythic structure of the material about the one like a son of man is pre-Danielic, it is impossible to speak about the social situation that may have lain behind the function of that structure in its original setting.[24] We can only speak with assurance of the *use* of that structure by the author of Daniel, and about his situation we know quite a lot.

The usual judgment is that the author of Daniel wrote in 164 B.C.E., after the initial successes of the Maccabees but before the rededication of the Temple. If that is the case, the phrase "now but not yet" would be appropriate for the sense of faith's confidence in the ultimate victory of God's people over its oppressors. This confidence is expressed in the exultant language of the enthronement of the one like a son of man. In words that perhaps echo the Israelite enthronement ceremony,[25] this figure is (proleptically) given the power of the eternal kingdom.

Why the replacement theme? Why did the author not remain content to exult in *Yahweh's* impending victory? Only speculation is possible, yet it may be productive. Israel had long lain under the domination of foreign rulers. Since about 174 B.C.E., the continual and increasing threat to the Jewish religion, at least as it had been traditionally practiced, may have been undermining confidence in the old theology of Yahweh as Lord of history. With the startling successes of the Maccabees, a new expectation arose that could not be comfortably expressed within the confines of the old theology.

Yahweh could never be denied. The vitality of the new hope, however, needed some new form in which the old theology could be amplified and a place found for new expectations. This amplification was found in the heavenly enthronement myth of the one like a son of man (Michael?) who was strong enough to carry out Yahweh's program, a program that long centuries of subjection may have made it difficult simply to ascribe to Yahweh any longer. Hence there is continuity between old and new; yet the implicit replacement theme allows for the present hopeful expectations of that time.

There is no space here for exploration of the later uses of Daniel 7 in Jewish and early Christian myth. Such exploration has been made difficult by the raging controversy over the function of the term *Son of Man*, even to the extent of denying its titular form and function.[26] On the other side, writing of the uses in the Jewish materials, Emerton concludes: "It may fairly be claimed that all four Son of Man passages fit well into the background of the enthronement festival and of the Canaanite and Israelite ideas associated with it."[27] Despite vociferous judgments to the contrary, this still seems to me a judicious conclusion.

The same titular meaning is present, in my opinion, in those New Testament uses in which the resurrected Jesus is, or will be, the enthroned and powerful Son of Man. This motif is taken up in the exalted conclusion to Matthew, where the resurrected Jesus claims divine power in allusion to Daniel 7: "All authority in heaven and on earth has been given to me" (Matt 28:18). Since it may well be that such notions of Jesus as enthroned Son of Man lie behind the Hellenistic liturgical materials with which I began, it will be instructive to pursue such directions in the following chapter.

El and Baal in the Ugaritic Texts

The ultimate origin of the mythic structure of Daniel 7 lies, in the judgment of many scholars, in the Ugaritic myths of El, the old god, and Baal, the young power.[28] Although the texts are obscure, scholars seem confident that Baal has, at least in some of the mythic structures, gained authority and power in place of El. Here is either a replacement or a usurpation motif—the end result of which is the same.[29] Unfortunately it seems impossible to detect the social situation behind the mythic change.

The Enthronement of Yahweh

Even Yahweh may not always have been the supreme god in Israel. According to some scholars, early Israelites lived in the shadow of the supremacy of the Ugaritic deities, El and Baal. In the move toward political and military supremacy, David also moved to make Yahweh not merely equal to the other deities (by absorbing traits that belonged to them); Yahweh now came to control all nations and was thus supreme over other deities. J. J. M. Roberts finds texts such as Psalms 82 and 47 expressive of this emerging supremacy of Yahweh.[30] The social setting of this "theogonic revolution"[31] is clear: David's march to political and military supremacy over the territory of Israel. Roberts concludes with regard to Psalm 47: The setting of the psalm is "a cultic celebration of Yahweh's imperial accession, based on the relatively recent victories of David's age, which raised Israel from provincial obscurity to an empire of the first rank."[32] What is not clear is whether this enthronement is purely a political move on the king's part, or whether it reflects as well the increasing pride of the populace as a whole. Regardless of how one assesses this question, it is clear that the enthronement of Yahweh to supremacy over other gods is due to a specific social setting. It is not armchair theologizing.

Ancient Near Eastern "Enthronements"

While adequate description is not possible here, mention can at least be made of Marduk and Inanna. The accession of Marduk to supremacy over the council of gods is well known from the *Enuma eliš*. Of the connection between this structure and the political changes of the Near East, Mann writes: "*Enuma eliš* provides perhaps the most salient example of the typology of exaltation, especially in the correlation between theogonic and political events."[33] W. Hallo and J. van Dijk have studied a poem in which Inanna is exalted to supremacy among the gods. In their judgment, this is related to Sargon I's effort "to lay the theological foundation for a united empire of Sumer and Akkad."[34] We have here the "first example of its kind attested in the literature."[35] Again this supports the judgment that enthronement motifs are closely related to social settings. In the words of Hallo and van Dijk, the Near Eastern examples can be used "to emphasize the close dependence of major 'theogonic' revolutions on historical events."[36]

Conclusions

These examples show that at least in the ancient Near East the replacement of one god by another was a not uncommon theme. They show further that in the instances about which we have information, the replacement theme is closely related to a social setting in which change is occurring or has occurred. The change in the divine world reflects a change in the human society that produced the myth. These changes are largely political and involve significant alterations in entire segments of society. Only in the Germanic tension between Wotan and Tiwaz (see note 36) does it seem likely that the changes reflect an inner-societal situation.

At the same time, the myths are expressive of a hope that the experienced change in the social situation will become complete and permanent. At the time of the writing of Daniel, the Maccabees have not yet vanquished the armies of Antiochus Epiphanes. The success of the Davidic-Solomonic empire was impressive, but given the volatility of Near Eastern politics no complete assurance could have been experienced (as later events amply demonstrated). The same can be said for the political situation that lay behind the enthronement of Marduk. Thus the enthronement-replacement theme celebrates the in-breaking of something new that is both a present reality and a hoped-for future.[37]

The Social Dynamic of the Enthronement of Jesus Christ

I have argued that the Hellenistic liturgical materials reflect a replacement theme, whereby Jesus Christ becomes *kyrios* and de facto functions in the place of Yahweh. I have also produced examples of the replacement theme in other religious settings. These examples express both a present change and a hope for complete and permanent change. Can these examples help us better understand the audacious claim of the Hellenistic church that Jesus Christ *kyrios* now functions as Cosmocrator?

One difference between the affirmations of the church and the examples given may seem too great to allow comparison. Whatever the change experienced in the church, it could not have been based on any observable political alteration as seems to be the case in most of the examples adduced. For believers in Jesus, life in the provincial cities and under the emperor went on as usual. There is no evidence that they even hoped for a change in the political structure.

Yet social changes are not only political. When people attached themselves to a new community, especially one that made exclusive claims, they were in effect making a significant social change for themselves and participating in a new social setting. The change is thus individual relocation and social transformation, since the believers are now incorporated into a community with a new cosmic vision. They were switching worlds, entering a social realm in which the only adequate mythic expression seems to have been to affirm Christ as Cosmocrator. The new demanded something more than just an affirmation, or reaffirmation, of Yahwistic faith, however much the new mythic structure needed to fit somehow within the old. The audaciousness of the claim implies an equally significant transformation in the experience of believers. The term "transformation" is appropriate, because to enter a new structure of meaning is to become a new self.

The liturgical forms themselves offer no explicit content to the new world over which Jesus Christ is *kyrios*, and the temptation to let Paul or some other New Testament author speak for the church must be resisted. Can the mythic structure itself tell us anything? I can suggest the following implications from the structure.

1. Affirmation of a new cosmic Lord implies a new meaning structure, where the believer has a new and positive place in that world order. It is even possible that the new meaning structure replaces not an old meaning but what was essentially a meaninglessness, a wandering among the pluralities of other possible centers of meaning. The reduction of centers from many to a single one (that is, for Gentile believers) is in itself potentially a powerful impetus for the world-switching.

2. Furthermore, this new *kyrios* is the "legitimate" Lord. That is, he represents a return of ownership to the creator. This is expressed in the Colossians hymn by the explicit identification of creator and reconciler. Elsewhere it may be implied by the fact that Yahweh as creator hovers in the background. For those still able to affirm the goodness of creation, this return would be a powerful dimension of self-understanding in the new world. Here then would be one place where the refusal of the church simply to affirm a new Lord without the backdrop of Yahweh speaks in an important way.

3. This linkage between the new *kyrios* and Yahweh may function in still another way, although this is nowhere stated in the liturgical material. For Gentiles who would ask, "And who is Yahweh, the creator?" the rejoinder could only be: "Read the story in Scripture." The basic content of understanding the reality of the *kyrios* and the reality of persons under that *kyrios* would be found in the story of Israel. What is affirmed by the replacement theme is not a content different from that found in Scripture, but the powerful declaration, based on a transforming experience, that this reality is now available in the church.

4. In the available materials, however, Christ is more than cultic Lord; he is primarily cosmic ruler. What is experienced in the cult becomes hope for the world. Here the audaciousness is revealed in its extreme. Through the hymns and formulas the little church, few in numbers and of no political significance, claimed that its experience was and would become normative for all people everywhere. Nothing less than a vision for the cosmos is captured in its confessions.

This is the vision expressed by the liturgical materials in early Hellenistic Christianity. In an important way this is the trajectory of the church that was to become dominant. The Cosmocrator trajectory thus lies at the heart of the faith of the church. This is not, of course, the whole story. What was to become of this trajectory has yet to be explored. And what lay behind it and to its side is the subject of the chapters that follow. Is it possible to discover the trajectory and experience of early Palestinian believers, those emerging from a Jewish culture, for whom other building blocks were more germane to their religious culture? I turn next to the trajectory of the Son of Man.

2 _____

THE SON OF MAN TRAJECTORY

Early Stages

In chapter 1, I outlined the heart of Hellenistic faith in the resurrected Jesus. Obviously, this is only the beginning point of any full description of Hellenistic theology. And it is not even a beginning point, since Hellenistic Christology is itself, in some important, indeed, crucial ways, a development from points of contact with the earliest followers of Jesus centered in the culturally Aramaic communities in Jewish Palestine.[1]

Having described the direction and terminology of Hellenistic Christology, however, the question immediately emerges what the points of contact with Aramaic faith might be. On the surface, Hellenistic Christology, with its lack of interest in Jesus traditions and its implicit political thrust, seems almost like a different religion, with no contact with the founder, Jesus. Indeed, such a difference gives one pause before one dismisses out of hand the proposals of Arthur Drews a century ago and of Burton Mack in the late twentieth century.[2]

My tasks in this chapter are thus difficult. First, I will search for the beginnings of Aramaic Christology among the first followers of Jesus. What texts are the bases for this search? The answer: pre-authorial traditions in the Synoptic Gospels. For reasons that will become clear below, I exclude the Gospel of John from this section.

The Gospels exhibit a number of different levels of material. The most obvious distinction lies in the level(s) of pre-authorial tradition, compared with the ideas of the authors at the stage of the final composition of the texts. In this chapter I attempt as consistently as possible to bracket out what seem to count as authorial additions and creations. I am interested in delineating the earliest stage of the Son of Man trajectory. In my judgment there is no literary evidence prior to the authorial passion predictions in Mark of an identification of the Son of Man with Jesus. My questions in this first section are twofold: What is the function of the Son of Man figure in these earliest strata, and How is Jesus understood in relation to the Son of Man?

At some point a crucial step was taken: Jesus was identified with the Son of Man. Is it possible to pinpoint this step, or must it remain shrouded in mystery (which is a euphemism for our ignorance)? Although these questions might ultimately prove unsolvable, at least I will present the evidence and draw whatever conclusion is possible from that evidence.

As could be imagined, and as I try to demonstrate, the Son of Man trajectory is rooted in a quite different ideational context from that of Cosmocrator. Yet the question is crucial: Are there points of correlation, if not terminology, that might link the two trajectories in internally cohesive ways—ways that would support the contention that we are dealing with *one* religious faith in God's act in Jesus? To relate the Son of Man trajectory with that of the Cosmocrator is so difficult, on the surface, as to appear an impossible task. Indeed, as I try to show, the trajectories run their different courses without showing any significant amount of influence of one upon the other. As far as our evidence exists for the "great church," that is, Hellenistic Christianity as it became dominant in the West, it is more a matter of the survival of the one over the other. Certainly at the stage described in this chapter I do not think a relationship can be established. Yes, the function of the Son of Man with its eschatological structure bears some similarity to the rule of the Cosmocrator. But one thing is clear: the person of Jesus does not yet dominate the Son of Man trajectory as he does that of the Cosmocrator.

Terminology obviously changes and must change. The history of Christian thought is an object lesson in such changes. Is the theology of New Testament times in a somehow "true" relation to Nicean formulations, which were influenced by Greek philosophy? Do the influences of Neoplatonism and later Aristotelian perspectives alter the basic theology of the church? Or are they *acceptable* translations into terminologies and structures compatible with different cultures? That the church has accepted such changes alerts us to be open to consider them as normal "experiments" to be expected as a new faith community struggles to find the ways to mirror its religious experience.

But what is an acceptable translation? I take it that "acceptable" means assurance that the different translations are at heart affirming the same basic faith about what God has done in Christ. My task is thus not only to describe the terminology and conceptual world of the Son of Man trajectory. It is also to ask whether the two trajectories are compatible with each other—indeed, whether they affirm the same basic faith in God's act in Jesus. We should not, however, expect compatible systems to emerge magically at the same time, as if we did not need to struggle and ponder what their claims mean and what the implications might be.

Why Choose "Son of Man" as the Title for the Aramaic Trajectory?

As mentioned above, the choice of the terms "Cosmocrator" and "Son of Man" is an effort to find labels that point to a total framework into which faith in God's act in Jesus is incorporated. As such, they are, I hope, useful as long as the terms are not themselves reified. The phrase "Son of Man," however, obviously needs explanation.

On the surface, the omnipresence of the term "Son of Man" in the Gospels seems to make this an obvious choice. The phrase occurs more frequently than any other title used in the Synoptics (it is found frequently also in the Gospel of John).[3] That it occurs only on the lips of Jesus in the Synoptics is frequently cited as an indication of confidence that the term goes back to Jesus himself. If one argues, as I do, that Christian theology centers on faith *in* Jesus and is not an attempt to replicate the faith *of* Jesus, then the authenticity of such sayings, or of some of the sayings, says nothing about the earliest faith *in* Jesus. To the contrary, if one should argue that *none* of the sayings is likely "authentic" as sayings of Jesus, that would be a strong argument for the importance of the term in understanding the faith of the earliest church. How the phrase functions in the Jesus traditions does indeed give us key knowledge about what the followers thought about Jesus, regardless of the origin of the tradition, and regardless of whether or not Jesus is identified as the Son of Man. I think, however, that once the identification of Jesus with the Son of Man was made, all of the earlier traditions came to be understood from the perspective of the asserted identification. Thus all of the Son of Man traditions become statements about the meaning that followers ascribed to Jesus as Son of Man.

Even if my judgment, however, about the significance of the title "Son of Man" is correct, there are other titles to consider. Of the alternatives, the complex Christ-Messiah-Son of God (I argue that they frequently mean the same thing) surely is the most important. For many people in the church, it would seem that the key term, in fact, is "Jesus Messiah." To be sure, the Greek translation of *mashiach, Christos*, became so popular in Hellenistic Christianity that it quickly assumed the status of a proper name of Jesus. Jesus is "Jesus Christ." All of this is true, but the evidence actually works against the presumed importance of the title.

In the first place, although one or another of the terms occurs in key passages in the Gospels (for example, the "confession of Peter"), the frequency of the term in the Gospels is less than that of Son of Man.[4] And the fact that *Christos* becomes a proper name in the Hellenistic church is an indication not of its titular importance but of its lack thereof. Hellenistic believers did not "hear" *Christos* as a title; therefore it became a proper name. Even Paul, although he most probably knew the significance of *Christos* as a title,[5] uses the word simply as a proper name of Jesus.

The fact of the matter is that, while Jesus as Messiah did function as a minor trajectory, the evidence for that is surprisingly obscure. Its presence in the Gospel tradition is not overwhelming, and it quickly lost any significance it had in the Hellenistic churches. Obviously, its rapid spread to the Hellenistic churches suggests that it had *at that early time* titular significance. Unfortunately, we have little evidence for that early time. By the time Paul's letters were written, such importance had dimmed. In later chapters I will pursue the ambiguities of that trajectory. For now, however, I conclude that any *Christos* trajectory does not have the significance of that of Son of Man, as far as our evidence enables us to judge. And yet there is perhaps a link between the *Christos* trajectory and that of the Cosmocrator that may show that the Cosmocrator trajectory developed out of an aspect of the *Christos* trajectory. For that, the reader must await a following chapter.

The Son of Man in Early Judaism

Virtually every assertion that has been—or can be—made about the phrase "Son of Man" has been challenged.[6] Is it or is it not a "title"? Does it stand for a semi-divine figure, or is it just a phrase for a human reality, individual or collective? Again, it is not my purpose here to argue about matters erudite researchers have pondered for decades. I simply wish to lay out the judgments upon which my exegesis of the New Testament passages rests.[7]

"Son of Man" is basically a phrase that indicates that one belongs to the human race. Just as "son of a prophet" means that one is a member of the prophetic guild, so "son of man" indicates a human person. Ezekiel amply demonstrates such a common usage. In Daniel, however, the term appears in an unusual way. Here the Son of Man is a figure in the heavens who "comes" to be enthroned by one who is "ancient of days"—usually thought to be God. Ultimate power is given this figure to reign as God would. "To him was given dominion and glory and kingdom, that all peoples, nations, and languages should serve him; his dominion is an everlasting dominion, which shall not pass away, and his kingdom one that shall not be destroyed" (Dan 7:13-14). While it is true that the human form of the new ruler is contrasted with the previous beast arising out of the sea, and also true that the *author* of the book takes the ruling figure to represent Israel, the passage leaves the strong impression that the Son of Man in these verses comes from a prior tradition of a divine figure enthroned by God.[8]

The parable section in Ethiopic Enoch (chaps. 37–71) certainly understands the term in this way—and indeed expands this concept. Here the Son of Man is a divine figure who "lives" in heaven. His task is to wait until the eschatological denouement, when he becomes the judge of the world and the leader of the elect.[9] Somewhat similar traditions are to be found in 4 Ezra 13. Thus, while the evidence is not plentiful, it seems safe to conclude that in some circles, however esoteric they may have been, the term "Son of Man" did denote a more than human figure who was expected to rule and judge at the eschatological denouement and to be the leader of the elect flock. That the New Testament passages are often entirely consonant with the Jewish texts cited above lends confidence that such a belief did exist in early Judaism.

The Son of Man in the New Testament

The expression "Son of Man" is prominent in the Gospels. It occurs eighty times in the four documents, and with the exception of John 12:34 (twice) the term is always spoken by Jesus. The occurrences, however, are varied, and whether all uses are titular is disputed.[10] In some late, compositional insertions, the term seems simply to refer to Jesus and to be interchangeable with other titles.[11] Rudolf Bultmann, following some nineteenth-century scholars, arranged the Son of Man sayings into three main categories: the Son of Man "as coming; as suffering death and rising again; and as now at work."[12] In his judgment, only the future category contained old tradition. The death and resurrection material was clearly *ex eventu*, and the "present" sayings were non-titular. All three categories, however, eventually *become* instances in which the believers see Jesus as the titular Son of Man. Even the "present" category belongs to the faith of the followers. This use probably reflects a late christological development in which the primary future orientation is being amplified by acclamation of Jesus as Son of Man, in whichever form he exists.

The Future Son of Man

With the future Son of Man sayings we have the closest parallels with the Jewish traditions, and it seems clear that these represent the earliest category of the Son of Man traditions in the New Testament. What is remarkable about these sayings is that Jesus and the future Son of Man are never *explicitly* identified in the pre-authorial traditions. For the following analysis, I urge the reader to set aside any tendency to assume an implicit identification or to allow the awareness that later traditions do make such an identification to inform a judgment on the matter.

Thus we must make a very careful and sharp distinction in evaluating the Son of Man sayings. The earliest traditions about the Son of Man depict Jesus teaching about the eschatological figure who would come to exercise judgment, but who is in no way identified with himself. I argue below that it is Mark who makes the first literary identification of Jesus with the Son of Man. Once this identification has been made, then readers and hearers of the future Son of Man sayings would have made the identification there as well. Thus *all* the Son of Man sayings would have come to be interpreted christologically. If we are engaged in attempting to trace the history of the emergence of the Son of Man into the faith of the followers of Jesus, however, it is essential to keep the distinction clearly in mind.

The material called "Q" is significant in the analysis of the Son of Man sayings. Q is a hypothetical document, construed in the nineteenth century as part of the explanation of the relationships among the Synoptic Gospels. It is by definition a collection of sayings common to Matthew and Luke but absent from Mark. Much scholarly controversy rages over issues related to Q; these issues cannot be discussed here. I simply record my judgment that Mark is probably the earliest Gospel, making the Q hypothesis attractive, and if we leave Q unreified as probable but hypothetical, it is useful to include in this discussion.[13]

Q is a document of some coherence, in which, at least in its final form, Son of Man is a prominent title in contrast to *Christos* (which does not occur), and in which there is no explicit mention of Jesus' death or resurrection. This document (or firm set of oral tradition) shows us a community that honored Jesus but did not ascribe significance to his death or resurrection—if it acknowledged his resurrection at all. What it did was to portray Jesus as the prophet of the Son of Man, who is sketched in traditional Jewish colors, and who is soon to come. God's eschatological agent is the heavenly Son of Man who is soon to appear. Jesus' role is to proclaim this agent and his imminent coming.

In the Cosmocrator trajectory the resurrection of Jesus is, as I have shown, the focal point of the faith. We are so accustomed to generalizing this centrality of the resurrection that any other possibility seems strange indeed—so strange that most investigators, I suspect, think that Q assumes it. But if Q assumes it, why is there no mention of it? Surely this would be an important argument in promoting the significance of Jesus. Equally mysterious is the failure to refer to the death of Jesus. But if his death had no theological significance, it might have been considered an embarrassment and therefore not necessary to deal with. Jesus' death did not affect the significance of Jesus as the prophet of the Son of Man. The focus of Q would be on the warning that Jesus gave to Israel—to prepare for the coming Son of Man.[14]

The future sayings are preponderantly about the coming Son of Man in judgment, even if many of them speak of his coming without explicit reference to judgment. If there is a gap implied between coming and judgment, that is evidence that the saying is already applied to the resurrected Jesus. I will first discuss the Q material, but I do not by this wish to imply that Q is necessarily earlier than other instances in which a future Son of Man, not identified with the resurrected Jesus, occur. These others are scattered throughout the Synoptics and suggest that the non-identification was a common strand in the Aramaic Jesus movements.

The Q Material

Luke 11:30 (par. Matt 12:40). "Just as Jonah became a sign to the people of Nineveh, so the Son of Man will be to this generation."[15] Here the Son of Man is compared to the preaching of Jonah, who became a "sign" to the Ninevites.[16]

Luke 12:40 (par. Matt 24:44). "You also must be ready, for the Son of Man is coming at an unexpected hour."

Luke 17:24 (par. Matt 24:27). "As the lightning flashes and lights up the sky from one side to the other, so will the Son of Man be in his day." The analogy here is to the coming of the Son of Man in a cosmic lightning flash. The emphasis is not only on the suddenness but also the universal manifestation of his coming to judgment.

Luke 17:26, 30 (par. Matt 24:39). "Just as it was in the days of Noah, so too it will be in the days of the Son of Man. . . . it will be like that on the day that the Son of Man is revealed." The suddenness is compared to the suddenness of the flood during the days of Noah.

Luke 12:8 (par. Matt 10:32-33). A separate kind of logion relates the judgment of the Son of Man to obedience to Jesus' teaching. "Everyone who acknowledges me before others, the Son of Man will also acknowledge before the angels of God; but whoever denies me before others will be denied before the angels of God." In the Q saying (as also in Mark 8:38), a relationship is established between the teaching of Jesus and the criterion of judgment by the Son of Man—but no identification. As the prophet of the Son of Man, what Jesus says becomes the criterion of the Son of Man's judgment.

Luke 12:10. A logion that seemingly conflicts with Luke 12:8 occurs in Luke 12:10: "Everyone who speaks a word against the Son of Man will be forgiven; but whoever blasphemes against the Holy Spirit will not be forgiven." This is difficult to understand in any case, but especially if the Son of Man has been identified with Jesus. Thus the saying probably assumes a stage earlier than that of Luke 12:8.

Luke 6:22-23 (compare Matt 5:11-12). Here is a particularly difficult saying, and whether the Q original spoke of the Son of Man is for me the key issue.

> Blessed are you when people hate you and when they exclude you, revile you, and defame you on account of the Son of Man. Rejoice in that day and leap for joy, for surely your reward is great in heaven; for that is what their ancestors did to the prophets. (Luke 6:22-23)
>
> Blessed are you when people revile you and persecute you and utter all kinds of evil against you falsely on my account. Rejoice and be glad . . . for in the same way they persecuted the prophets who were before you. (Matt 5:11-12).

What is surprising is how similar the two Gospels sound, although there is scarcely a common word between them. The structure, however, is similar. A blessing on the persecuted is followed by the assurance (?) that similar treatment happened to the prophets. The structure alone gives some confidence that the material is basically from Q. But if it is Q, how can we explain the discrepancy in wording? If it is Q, and if we follow the Lukan version as generally more likely to be original, how can we explain Luke's wordiness and, specifically, the use of the phrase "Son of Man"?

Whether "Son of Man" occurred here in Q is a judgment call. Some opt for the Matthean "I," on the basis that Matthew secondarily adds "Son of Man" in 16:13 and would not, therefore, have omitted it had it been original.[17] This argument does not hold. There are also instances where Matthew omits the title and replaces it by a personal pronoun (Matt 16:21; 10:32-33). The judgment about Matthew seems to be that "Jesus" and all that the name stands for is more important than any single title. Thus Matthew feels free to use or not use any specific title. The likelihood is that "Son of Man" is original to Q, but that still does not help us get at the meaning.

What can we say about the beatitude in general? It clearly reflects a situation of persecution in the life of the early communities that, in some way, "believe" in Jesus. A traditional Jewish way of thinking is assured by the reference in both versions to the prophets and their mistreatment—a not uncommon theme in Q. These communities are being mistreated in some way by the larger Jewish communities because of the communities' commitment to the Son of Man. We cannot jump to the conclusion that there is an assumed identity between Jesus and the Son of Man. But, if not, what would cause the persecution? Is it conceivable that the intense proclamation of a coming Son of Man in and of itself could evoke such hostility?

At this point it is instructive to consider the judgments of George Nickelsburg in the introduction of his commentary on *1 Enoch*.[18] Looking at the various sections of the writing synoptically, Nickelsburg sees a theme of conflict and persecution running through what he accepts are "communities" that are the recipients of the writings. "The dualism that is constitutive of *1 Enoch*'s worldview expresses a recurring perception on the part of these authors that they, their communities, and their nation were parties to conflict and victims of violence, oppression, and persecution."[19] He cites the "Parables," the section in which the profession of a judging and coming Son of Man is prominent. "According to 46:8, the kings and the mighty 'persecute the houses of his congregation, the faithful who depend on the name of the Lord of spirits.'"[20] If this judgment is sound—the judgment of a scholar who has reflected on the Enoch materials for a long time—then it is not impossible to think that the Q community, by proclaiming passionately a coming Son of Man who is to right the wrongs of God's world, could also incur the ridicule or wrath of larger, perhaps more comfortable sections within Judaism. The community has sent out prophets (cf. Matt 10:23—a saying I strongly suspect was in Q); they have largely, it seems, been rejected, but none of this need assume that Jesus has been identified with the Son of Man. Jesus is portrayed as the catalyst of the intense expectation, but we do not need to assume what Q otherwise is silent about, that Jesus is thought by the community to be the Son of Man.

I judge Luke's "Son of Man" to be authentic Q over against Matthew's personal pronoun. By using the pronoun, Matthew makes an identification of Jesus and the Son of Man, an identification that is not stated in the earlier Q passage.

At least in the Q communities some outsiders are badmouthing the Son of Man. In Luke 6:23 the title refers to something in the present, but that is neither Jesus in his earthly activity nor the proclamation about Jesus, but the community's proclamation of a coming Son of Man who will right the wrongs of the world.

Matthean Material

Matthew 25:31. At the beginning of the parable of the sheep and the goats, Matthew introduces the judgment scene with the following: "When the Son of Man comes in his glory and all the angels with him, then he will sit on his glorious throne." Here is a typical scene of eschatological judgment by the Son of Man. And it is completely "Jewish." The Son of Man judges the nations, the criterion being how they have treated Israel, who are here the "brethren." Matthew, of course, identifies the Son of Man with Jesus and the "brethren" with the Jesus community (or individuals within it). But in the stage prior to Matthew's redaction, the parable in the Jesus community must have functioned as a parable told by Jesus about the coming Son of Man, at which stage there was no identification of that august figure with Jesus.

Matthew 13:41-42. "The Son of Man will send his angels, and they will gather out of his kingdom all those who oppose faith and all evildoers and they will cast them in the fiery furnace." Here the act of judgment is given a violent metaphor. The judgment takes the form of angelic (!) seizure of evil people and forcible thrusting into punishment. The criteria for the judgment are not stated clearly.[21]

Matthew 16:27. "The Son of Man is to come with his angels in the glory of his Father, and then he will recompense every one for what he has done." Here is a by now familiar statement pointing to a judgment of works in Matthew. The criterion *might be* obedience to Torah. The theme of the law court occurs, instead of the more violent metaphor of the logion previously cited.

Matthew 10:23. "You will not have gone through all the towns of Israel before the Son of Man comes." This is a startling statement of the imminence of the eschatological judgment, implied by the coming of the Son of Man. Again, there is no identification of the Son of Man with Jesus.

Lukan Material

Luke does not use as many future Son of Man logia as does Matthew, but he at least shows that he was aware of a tradition of such thought. In Luke 21:36, at the end of a "watch and be ready" statement, the final sentence reads, "But watch at all times, praying that you may have strength to escape all these things that will take place, and to stand before the Son of Man." Clearly, to stand before the Son of Man means to receive judgment from the Son of Man. The "standing" thus must mean the ability with a clean conscience to approach the Son of Man in a future judgment (cf. also Luke 12:40). The tradition gives no hint of identification with Jesus.

Markan Material

Even though Mark does identify Jesus with the Son of Man, he uses early traditions in which no such identification is implied.

Mark 13:24-27. Here is the most elaborate Son of Man description in any of the Gospels. Here is vividly described the assumption of power of the eschatological Son of Man. The powers fall before him, "and then they will see the Son of Man coming in clouds with great power and glory" (verse 26). This is *not* a coming to earth. The world ruler takes power in heaven. Indeed, in the next verse he sends his angels to earth to gather the elect. Neither the passage nor the context makes any identification of Jesus with the Son of Man (contrary to Mark 14:62b).

Mark 8:38. "Whoever is ashamed of me and of my words in this adulterous and sinful generation, of him will the Son of Man also be ashamed, when he comes in the glory of the Father with the holy angels." This is a typical statement about judgment, relating God's glory and the coming of the Son of Man with the accompaniment of the angels. That this is a judgment saying is confirmed by the use of shaming. In certain Jewish contexts, to "be ashamed of" means to reject. The Son of Man will reject certain people—clearly, a judgment saying. What is distinctive here is that the rejection by the Son of Man has as its criterion a person's rejection of Jesus and Jesus' *teaching*. This is, in part, similar to the Q saying in Luke 8:12, the difference being Mark's insistence on the teaching as a criterion, but different from Matthew 13:41 and 16:27, where no mention is made of Jesus at all. In both Mark and Q the distinction between Jesus and the eschatological Son of Man is clear, yet a relationship has been established. The judgment of the Son of Man will vindicate the person and mission of Jesus when he was on earth. Is this perhaps a hint of an increased value placed on Jesus by the followers? Jesus is not the Son of Man, but his mission will be vindicated by God through the eschatological judgment of the Son of Man. It is interesting and perhaps of importance that in this saying the acts (including teaching) of Jesus are seen as crucial in the eschatological denouement.

The Leader of the Elect

Also echoed in these early Gospel traditions is the notion, found in *1 Enoch*, that in heaven the Son of Man will be the leader of the elect flock. In *1 Enoch* 62:11-15 the elect are destined for the joy of eternity. "The righteous and elect ones will be saved on that day, and from henceforth they shall never see the faces of the sinners and the oppressors. . . . The Lord of the Spirits will abide over them; they shall eat and rest and rise with that Son of Man forever and ever."[22] We have already seen in Mark 13:27 the angels gathering together from the earth the elect (*eklektous*). The text does not say explicitly for what purpose the gathering is done, or even where the elect are taken once gathered. Much is assumed, doubtlessly because it is common tradition regarding the hope expressed in the passage from *1 Enoch* cited above. It is a word of comfort and hope for those who consider themselves the elect. When the final day arrives, they will live in the presence of the Son of Man.

The word *eklektos* does not appear frequently in the New Testament (22 times). It occurs three times in Mark, all in chapter 13. Apart from the parallels with Mark 13 in Matthew, in that Gospel the word occurs only one other time (Matt 22:14). In Luke the word appears only twice, and it is absent in the Gospel of John. One of the two Lukan occurrences is in 18:7-8: "And will not God vindicate his elect, who cry to him day and night? Will he delay long over them?[23] I tell you, he will vindicate them quickly. Yet when the Son of Man comes, will he find trust on earth?" (cf. also Luke 21:36). These verses appear at the end of a parable about an uncaring judge and a nagging widow. The appended verses draw the moral from the parable. God will act more earnestly and caringly than did the human judge. It is in verse 7 that the notion of the elect appears. What might be a second addition is the line in 8b about the coming of the Son of Man. Thus in the presumed pre-Lukan tradition, the Son of Man might not have had anything originally to do with the elect. Nevertheless one should be cautious. Since Luke only once elsewhere uses the term "elect," verses 7-8a are likely pre-Lukan tradition, although they fit his "moral" nicely. And verse 8b is also surely pre-Lukan.[24] Since "Son of Man" and "elect" are complementaries in tradition, the likelihood is that the two logia were already joined when Luke used them. If that is correct, then either there was one logion that included both elect and Son of Man or, under the attraction of the two, an early transmitter joined them. In any case, it is not Jesus who is over the elect, but the Son of Man.

While the word "elect" does not appear in Matthew 19:28, the content may be similar. In biblical language, that a ruler judges can indicate a continual role, not just a one-time event. In fact, judicial and royal language has to be eschatologized before it can primarily point to a one-time event. It is interesting to speculate that the saying in Matthew 19:28, although certainly an eschatological saying, may suggest that even here "judging" means a continual rule. "Truly I say to you, in the new world, when the Son of Man shall sit on his glorious throne, you who have followed me will also sit on twelve thrones, judging the twelve tribes of Israel."[25] This is a remarkable statement. That the population in heaven can be identified as the tribes of Israel surely indicates a very early tradition, prior to the acceptance of Gentiles into the communities (cf. also Matt 18:17). For my purposes, the hard task is to decide whether Jesus and the Son of Man are identified. Nothing in the passage hints at that. It reads as if the Son of Man is a separate figure from Jesus. Yet Jesus seems to have the authority to appoint the twelve. And does he not have a throne? What would it be if not the throne of the Son of Man, in which case the identification has already been made? Regardless of this issue, the fact that the twelve tribes of Israel live under the Son of Man is clear. The twelve tribes are the elect, an idea that is surely not foreign to the ideas in *1 Enoch*. It should be noted that in the other two passages about the elect discussed above, there is no hint of an identification. Thus there may not be one in the Matthean passage.

Summary and Implications

The Portrayal of Jesus

The view of Jesus that emerges from this evidence is so unusual as to invite skepticism—which might seem a mild word to those who accept the traditional interpretation. At least I can put together the evidence and see how it appears.

Jesus does *not* set himself forth as the Son of Man. He proclaims the coming to judgment and rule of that angelic figure. All his energy seems to be devoted to preparing his followers for that eschatological event—which for the elect will be a time of eternal rejoicing. Hence his teaching becomes the criterion for judgment by the Son of Man. Thus he not only teaches about the Son of Man but also about how the people are to live in conformity with God's will. His followers are convinced that Jesus teaches the truth and that it is incumbent on people who wish to survive the apocalypse of the Son of Man to follow his teaching. This may, in fact, be one reason Jesus' teaching is a prominent heritage in the early Aramaic communities.

Jesus has no title. He is not even expressly called a prophet, although he functions as one. John the Baptist was a prophet—indeed, perhaps more than a prophet.[26] The anomaly is thus that, while the people follow Jesus and his teaching, Jesus extols the figure of the Baptist. But now the Baptist is dead, and Jesus takes his place, meekly, it would seem, not even claiming to succeed John.[27] It is true that the fate of the prophets is to be killed, and it may be that this is the way his followers understood Jesus' death, although nothing explicit is said about it. It goes without saying that there is no resurrection in this perspective. What lies ahead is the coming of the Son of Man, just as Jesus proclaimed before his death.

At some point the Son of Man entered the thinking of the earliest followers of Jesus with respect to their belief in him. Whether this was due to Jesus as an originating figure or whether behind Jesus and his earliest disciples lies the Baptist tradition cannot be stated with any assurance.[28] But it became a dominant title to use to describe the power and authority of the figure. It must have competed with the *Christos* title for pride of place. While the fate of the *Christos* title is unclear, the evidence indicates that in circles associated with the Jesus traditions the Son of Man title was the preferred one, even though Jesus was not yet identified as the Son of Man. Can we imagine why it won out in spite of the non-identification? At the least we can describe the differences in conception and see what the alternatives were.

The *Christos* title seems in some quarters a primarily political-military one.[29] The Messiah is basically a king who will lead the Jewish people to freedom. As God's son, he does this with the essential support of God. But armies may be required, and the political-military structure is needed rather than superseded. The War Scroll of the Qumran community and the claim by the military hero Bar Cochba to be Messiah indicate the intimate relationship of the military-political structure with the concept.[30] For those, like peasants, who have been oppressed by the political structure (including Herod and the priesthood), messianic hope may not have been an exciting expectation. It may rather have seemed more of the same.

The Function of the Son of Man

The Son of Man figure is basically a religious one. He has no contact with the earthly political, military, and priestly structures. The Son of Man is a heavenly persona who comes to judge the nations (in this sense he does perhaps imply a political role, but he acts as the direct agent of God) and to gather the elect flock. The criterion of judgment is not certain—but nothing is said that would imply obedience to the Torah as essential (unless that is implied in Matt 16:27). That is, the Son of Man bypasses the political-religious establishment of Judaism. It does not seem surprising that the followers of Jesus, who seem to be from the peasant, oppressed class in Palestine, would gladly accept the figure of the Son of Man over that of a Messiah. With this possibility in mind, I review the New Testament evidence adduced above.

Central to the assertions about the Son of Man is that he is or will be enthroned (the "coming" motif), and that he will judge the world. The standards by which he will judge the world are mostly tantalizingly unclear. That they have to do with the response to Jesus' earthly life and teachings is, however, explicit in some sayings (Mark 8:38; Luke 12:8; 6:22) and may be implied in others. Assurance is given that the followers of the Son of Man will have a special place in the end time (Mark 13:27; Luke 18:7-8; 6:22-23; Matt 19:28).

While nothing can be said with complete confidence about the experience that lies behind such beliefs, the relation between the original audience of Jesus, as oppressed peasants, and the religious figure of the Son of Man as judge and leader of the elect needs to be seriously considered. This community needs a figure who is not related to the military-political-priestly establishment; they require a figure who sides with their needs. They need a figure who will judge the world by real standards of righteousness—which for the community means, at least in part, their allegiance to Jesus. They need to have confidence that they are on the right side—or, more accurately, that God is on their side in the activity of the Son of Man. By claiming the authority of the Son of Man, they anticipate the coming judge of the world and leader of the elect. They claim that their faith is based in God's reality and is not mediated through religious and political structures. And who is Jesus? He is both prophet and friend, and they believe that his proclamation is true. That he died like other prophets only proves the correctness of his teaching.

A second major issue concerns one of the other key differences between the Son of Man and the Cosmocrator trajectories. Essential to the Son of Man trajectory was the importance of the Jesus traditions, while the Cosmocrator trajectory apparently ignored them. One simple reason may well have been that the Jesus traditions were close to the earliest followers of Jesus. They had known Jesus, or knew those who had known him, seen him, and heard him. They would have expected that traditions would have been passed down.

But was there also a theological reason why the traditions were important? The answer lies in Mark 8:38 and Luke 12:8-9 (Q). The criterion of judgment by the enthroned Son of Man was based on acceptance of the person and teaching of the earthly Jesus. Thus it was imperative that the followers pass on this earthly Jesus to others who knew him only through the traditions. It may also not be accidental that the traditions are full of acceptance of excluded peasantry and rejection of authorities who oppressed them.[31] The Jesus traditions told of a Jesus who was on their side—thus of a Son of Man who would also be on their side when the day arrived.

The Identification of Jesus with the Son of Man

I have so far described the earliest stage of the Son of Man trajectory. Before long Jesus became identified with the Son of Man. In a later chapter I will explore the meaning that that identification had for the Aramaic communities of believers. Here I simply ask *when* this identification may have been made. Alas, many questions are legitimate, but not all have answers; I nonetheless hope to be able to clarify the obscurity that surrounds this fateful step.

The earliest *literary* evidence for the identification of Jesus with the Son of Man occurs in the famous (or infamous) Markan "passion predictions."

> 8:31. And he began to teach them that the Son of Man must suffer many things, and be rejected by the elders and the chief priests and the scribes, and be killed, and after three days rise.

9:31. He was teaching his disciples, saying to them, "The Son of Man will be delivered into the hands of people, and they will kill him, and when he is killed, after three days he will rise."

10:33-34. Behold, we are going up to Jerusalem, and the Son of Man will be delivered to the chief priests and the scribes, and they will condemn him to death, and deliver him to the Gentiles, and they will mock him, and spit on him, and scourge him, and kill him; and after three days he will rise.

Although Jesus does not explicitly say, "I am the Son of Man," the identification of the fate of the Son of Man with the fate of Jesus leaves no room for doubt. But note that these "predictions" are also the first Synoptic evidence for the belief in Jesus' resurrection. The key question is whether, as in earlier scholarship, these predictions are pre-authorial or whether they were composed by the author of the Gospel, as current scholarly opinion has it. There are several arguments in favor of the view that they are pre-Markan. (1) The three are closely similar in form. The third has obviously been expanded to include details from the passion narrative, but that does not distort the basic similarity. Not only are the three similar, but they also have distinctive wording that sets them off from other confessions about the death and resurrection of Jesus. Thus (2) the Son of Man is the clear title for Jesus. (3) Jesus will be "killed" (*apokteinō*) rather than "crucified." (4) The phrase "after three days" (*meta treis hēmeras*) is unique to Mark. (5) Jesus "rises" (*anastēsetai*) rather than the slightly more frequently used passive of *egeirō* (be "raised").

The view that these predictions are pre-authorial is not widely accepted in current scholarship, perhaps for the following reasons. When compared with the Cosmocrator formulas, they are unusual, but one must allow for an author like Mark, who is not influenced by such formulas, to create his own. That Jesus would be killed rather than crucified surely goes back to the idea of basic responsibility for the death: Jews or Romans. Since crucifixion was a specifically Roman punishment, if one wished to implicate the Jews it would be more natural to use the word *apokteinō*. Thus in Acts 3:15, when Peter wishes to lay the blame on the Jews for Jesus' death, he claims they killed him. Just so in the Gospel of John, when the issue is the fight between Jesus and the Jews, the Jews wish to kill him (*apokteinō*), not crucify him (e.g., 5:18; 8:37). In the first two predictions, the Romans are not mentioned, so that *apokteinō* is perhaps more natural. In the third, the "Gentiles" are specifically mentioned, and "crucify" could have been used.

The use of *anistēmi* rather than the passive of *egeirō* may also easily be a natural non-theological choice. Although we are accustomed to attribute heavy theological significance to Paul's use of *egeirō*, even Paul can use *anistēmi* (1 Thess 4:14), as can Acts (10:41). And the distinction between "after the third day" and "on the third day" may reflect more a move from a Jewish idiom to a Greek than anything else. At any rate, the evidence is so small as to be inconclusive. In all the Pauline corpus the phrase "on the third day" occurs but once (1 Cor 15:4), and nowhere else in the New Testament apart from Acts 10:41 and the places in Matthew and Luke that are parallel to the Markan passion predictions. As far as I know, however, only Mark uses "after three days."

Particularly interesting is to see how Matthew and Luke treat the Markan passages. Matthew copies Mark's *apokteinō* in the first two predictions (Matt 16:21; 17:22) but changes it, logically enough, in the third, where the Gentiles enter in and the influence of the passion narrative is strong. Luke keeps Mark's verb in two instances (9:22; 18:32-33). In the third, he uses only the verb "to deliver" (9:44). Matthew, on the other hand, in all three instances changes the verb of resurrection to the passive of *egeirō*, while Luke vacillates, once keeping Mark's preference for *anistēmi* (18:33) and once altering it to the passive of *egeirō* (9:22). Matthew and Luke are, however, entirely consistent in changing "after three days" to "on the third day" (Luke does not mention the resurrection at all in 9:44).[32]

The evidence here is confusedly ambiguous. We cannot tell from the Markan predictions, in relation to comparable passages, whether or not Mark's predictions are pre-authorial formulas. To a certain extent they reflect wordings that are different from the Cosmocrator formulas, but then Mark does not stem from that tradition. Why could not the Son of Man trajectory have different formulas? The only sure judgment is that only Mark uses "after three days," a Jewish expression that might reflect a stage before the resurrection of Jesus had been fixed as being *on* the third day. The formulas certainly fit with Mark's Christology and he uses them as significant parts of his structure. But before I turn to Mark himself, I ask whether there are other hints of the identification of Jesus with the Son of Man prior to the writing of the Gospel of Mark around 70 C.E.

Possible Evidence for Pre-70 Identification of Jesus with the Son of Man: Acts 7:54-56

> But he [Stephen], full of the Holy Spirit, gazed into heaven and saw the glory of God and Jesus standing at the right hand of God; and he said, "Behold, I see the heavens opened, and the Son of Man standing at the right hand of God."

This narration is remarkable, because it reports a vision of the resurrected Jesus *in heaven* as Son of Man. Nowhere else in the New Testament is there such a combination. So unusual is it that I have often characterized it to my students as "the earliest post-resurrection appearance story in the New Testament." The question, however, is whether the story is earlier than authorial Mark.

I believe that it is likely that in the earliest times post-resurrection stories did not yet exist. Our earliest evidence for "appearances" is 1 Corinthians 15:3-8—and this evidence is a list, not a set of stories. The announcement (or claim) that the resurrected Jesus had appeared was sufficient for the proclamation. This would explain why there are no extant stories for most (or all) of the recipients of an encounter with the resurrected Jesus in that list.[33] I would add that 1 Corinthians 15 in general suggests that the earliest encounters were not with the resurrected Jesus on earth but with the exalted Jesus in heaven. So 1 Corinthians provides a list of individuals or groups who claim to have seen the resurrected Jesus as he appeared to them from heaven.

In Mark there are also no post-resurrection appearance stories.[34] The reason, I think, is that by the time of authorial Mark, stories as we know them from Luke and John had not yet been created. Even in Matthew there are no pre-authorial stories. In Matthew 28:9-10, the resurrected Jesus encounters the women who have just left the tomb—but what Jesus tells them is a reprise of the angel's words—surely a Matthean expansion. And in the famous concluding story in 28:16-20, Matthean themes are so prominent that it has to be seen as authorial creation. Only with Luke and John do we have real stories, and even these may not reflect pre-authorial traditions. They are unique in being stories taking place on earth (granted, Matthew's creations are on earth as well) and having as themes issues that had begun to concern the late first-century church—like docetism. They are thus to be dated toward the end of the first century. Mark 8:27-29 would then be too early to be taken as a post-resurrection story.

Given this scheme, where does the appearance to Stephen fit? It differs from the stories in Luke and John by taking place in heaven, and it is the only story that uses the title "Son of Man."[35] But is it the earliest post-resurrection appearance story, or is it a Lukan creation (as commonly thought)? Some think that the reference to the Son of Man derives from Luke 22:69 ("From now on the Son of Man will be seated at the right hand of the power of God").[36] But the words differ significantly. In Acts the Son of Man is standing, not sitting, as in Luke 22:69. Stephen sees the glory (*doxa*), while the Gospel account refers to the power (*dynamis*). In Acts the story emphasizes the opening of the heavens, about which the Gospel is silent. It is to be granted that certain features of the Acts story may reflect Gospel tradition about Jesus (the loud cry; the motif of forgiveness), but similarity might be based in tradition. I conclude that the Son of Man

material in Acts 7 is so distinctive in the vocabulary of Acts that it is unlikely
that Stephen's words are based on those of Jesus in Luke.

In addition, the title Son of Man is highly surprising in the context of Acts.
Already in Luke 24 the author is preparing for the title that is definitive for
him, *Christos*. In 24:6-7 the two "men" speak the last reference in the Gospel to
"Son of Man," in words reminiscent of Markan terminology. But in verse 26 the
incognito Jesus reminds the disciples that the *Christos* should suffer and enter
into his glory. Likewise in verse 46 the resurrected Jesus says that "the *Christos*
should suffer and on the third day rise from the dead." The reader is thus prepared for the avalanche of *Christos* affirmations that are to come in Acts. Eight
times before the Stephanic vision, the title *Christos* appears, beginning with the
confession in 2:36 ("God has made him for Lord and *Christos*") to the summary
in 5:42 ("And every day in the temple and at home they did not cease teaching
and preaching Jesus as the Christ").[37] The *Christos* title continues consistently
after the vision. It seems highly unlikely that the author would change his presentation of Jesus as the *Christos* unless "Son of Man" was already there in the
tradition.

If it is tradition, whence comes it, and is the tradition earlier than authorial Mark? Long ago I argued that the speech of Stephen in Acts is indebted to
Samaritan Pentateuchal readings.[38] I concluded that the speech of Stephen was
not a creation of the author of Acts but reflected the movement of the Stephanic
group into Samaria. Is it possible that the vision of Stephen was also associated
with the Stephanic group's Samaritan mission? Assuming that the story of the
vision *is* tradition, this would be a likely judgment. Against it, however, is the
absence in Samaritan Judaism of a Son of Man figure (its Bible presumably did
not include Daniel). The author of Acts seems to want to associate the *Christos*
title with the Stephanic mission. Philip proclaims the *Christos* to the Samaritans
(8:5). Acts also mentions the arrival in Antioch of members of the Stephanic
group and immediately adds that believers were first called "Christians" there
(probably not nearly as soon as Acts implies, however). If the early center of the
Christos trajectory was Jerusalem, as I think likely, the Stephanic acceptance of
the *Christos* title would not be surprising. To claim the Stephanic vision as a
tradition of the Stephanic group would thus have no real support, as far as the
Son of Man title is concerned. Nevertheless, John 4 indicates that some believers
could combine Samaritan expectations with the figure of the wonder-working
Messiah. This is but another point where our lack of knowledge forces us to
silence.

The main question, however, is whether the story is earlier than authorial
Mark. If the story is a Lukan creation, that obviously settles the matter. And the
pursuit of a location of an earlier traditional unit has been unsuccessful, however much I suspect that there was such a tradition.[39] We are back to the only

criterion we have: there are no certain pre-Markan post-resurrection appearance stories. Thus the possibility that there was a tradition behind Acts 7:55-56 does not help us assess the Markan passion predictions.

Pre-authorial Son of Man in the Gospel of John?

The most significant collection of Son of Man materials outside of the Synoptic Gospels is in the Gospel of John. In chapter 11, I discuss in detail the history of this title in John. Here I briefly summarize what I think to be the development.

All of the Son of Man materials in John assume an identification between this figure and Jesus. Jesus *is* the Son of Man. Thus there are no Q-like sayings in which no identification is stated or implied. In my judgment Jesus as Son of Man was not the earliest Christology of the Johannine community. The earliest seems to have been Jesus as a wonder-working *Christos*. In fact, I argue that the split with the synagogue, so clearly stated in the texts (especially 9:22), occurred at a fairly early date over the issue of whether Jesus was or was not the *Christos*.

After the split, a second stage of thinking about Jesus intruded onto the community, namely, that Jesus is more than *Christos*; he is the Son of Man. I believe at this second stage Jesus is thought to evidence this title by his resurrection. He ascends to heaven as Son of Man. No text says that he *becomes* Son of Man at the resurrection. This is because, in my analysis, still a third stage occurs, in which Jesus has become the preexistent Logos. Thus Jesus descends to earth. What this intrusion does is to force the Son of Man to become a descending as well as ascending figure (as, for example, in 3:13). This means that Jesus on earth is Son of Man, not in lowliness as a mere human. He is Son of Man in all his authority and power (9:35-38).

Thus the earliest Son of Man traditions in the Gospel of John assume the identity of Jesus with the eschatological figure. Are they therefore post-authorial Mark, or are they evidence of a tradition independent of and perhaps earlier than Mark? This is an extremely difficult issue and is inextricably tied with the question of possible dependence of John on Mark or one of the other Synoptics. Into these briar patches I cannot go. In this discussion, I accept the judgment of many scholars that the Gospel of John is independent of direct influence by any of the Synoptics.[40] This means that the identification of Jesus with the Son of Man was an intrusion into the Johannine community not caused by Mark, Matthew, or Luke. Does that judgment imply that the identification occurred independently of, and perhaps prior to, authorial Mark?

Influencing that judgment is the question of the dating of the intrusion into the Johannine community of the Son of Man Christology. Alas, that question cannot be answered with any assurance. The usual dating of the final (at least, the "first edition") Gospel is somewhere toward the end of the first century, although most who opt for such a date know that it is in large part speculation. I too accept a date toward the end of the first century, basing that on my reading of 16:2, "Indeed, an hour is coming when those who kill you will think that by doing so they are offering worship to God." I assume that the "killing" of the believers refers to the threat of Roman persecution, not likely earlier than the end of the century. This is, of course, not strong evidence. I do not think the expulsion from the synagogue that so threatened the Jesus community (John 9:22) need be related to the curse on the Nazoreans, presumably inserted into the Jewish liturgy during the time of Gamaliel II (presumably at some point after 80 C.E.). In fact, I expect that the expulsion was a local act of a synagogue or synagogues at an earlier stage when the fight was about Jesus as *Christos,* before the Son of Man Christology influenced the community's faith. And since the Son of Man Christology was in turn influenced by the Logos Christology, all we can say is that the Son of Man's entrance into the Johannine community occurred after the break with the synagogue over Jesus as *Christos* and before the emergence of the Logos Christology. That is not much to go on. As far as I can tell, there is nothing in the texts that would deny either a pre-authorial or a post-authorial Markan dating.

One question remains. Is there any linguistic connection between the Johannine Son of Man material and the Markan passion predictions? The clear answer has to be no. (1) The most distinctive phrase in the predictions is "after the third day." In John there is no reference to a third day in whatever linguistic form. (2) "The Son of Man will be killed." Yes, John refers to Jews wishing to kill Jesus, but these are all prior to the actual death of Jesus, which, in the passion narrative of John, is referred to only as crucifixion. (3) Jesus will rise (*anistēmi*). John uses an extraordinarily rich vocabulary to indicate the resurrection of Jesus: *egeirō* (in the passive, 2:22); *anistēmi* (20:9); *anabainō* (6:62; 20:17); *doxazō* (7:39; 12:16, 23); *hypsoō* (usually in a double entendre alluding also to crucifixion, 3:14; 7:28; 12:34). In this list *anistēmi* is a rare use, although it is used to refer to the act of Jesus or God raising the dead (5:40, 44; 11:23, 24). (4) Mark uses *paschō* (to suffer) once in the predictions (and only once elsewhere, also in relation to the Son of Man, 9:12). Given John's triumphalist Christology, it is not surprising that the word does not occur at all in his narrative.

Thus neither in authorial Mark nor in the passion predictions (if there is a distinction to be made) are there indications of verbal connections with the Gospel of John. Most convincing, however, is the fact that the basic structure of the predictions is nowhere replicated in John. The conclusion is clear: there is no indication of Johannine connection with any known Synoptic view or words, except the basic claim that Jesus is the Son of Man.

Conclusion

I find myself confronting a frustratingly insoluble conundrum. There is no sure evidence that other occurrences of the Son of Man Christology, as identified with Jesus, pre-date authorial Mark, or that they are in any relationship with authorial Mark.[41] The hint is that the Son of Man Christology (by which from now on I mean an identification with Jesus) had origins more than in authorial Mark, but these origins are unavailable to us. These origins are unlikely to be later than authorial Mark, and the hint is that they are earlier, but to this point we have no access.

There is at least one final question we can ask about possible origins. Is there any view of the Gospel of Mark that might help us answer the question whether the Son of Man Christology is authorial Mark's creation or whether he is indebted to pre-Markan traditions? In other words, does the Gospel of Mark itself give us hints that the Christology is pre-authorial Mark?

The issue here concerns the predictions. As indicated, they read formulaically, and it is not surprising that earlier judgments tended to conclude that they were pre-Markan. The problem is to find an argument that would lead to a convincing decision. The Christology expressed in the predictions seems consonant with what Mark says elsewhere about the Son of Man. The only way I know to get at the issue is to ask how authorial Mark uses the predictions. Is this use consonant with the predictions themselves, or is there some friction that might indicate that Mark uses the predictions in a way that is not identical with the thrust of the predictions themselves, thus indicating that authorial Mark may have found the predictions at hand?

According to broad consensus, the predictions are a focal point of the central, crucial section of the Gospel, 8:22—10:52. First, Mark cites the prediction. Next occurs an explicit or implicit rejection of the anti-triumphalist thrust of the prediction and its implied Christology. Finally, Jesus retorts that not only is the way of suffering his way; it is also the way of those who would be true disciples.[42]

Prediction	Rejection	Discipleship
8:31	8:32	8:33-38
9:31	9:33-34	9:35-37
10:33-34	10:35-40	10:42-45

In between these three sections Mark has incorporated other materials. But the structure of the entire section is clear and is buttressed at beginning and end by stories of the healing of a blind man.[43] Mark certainly concurs with the Christology of the predictions. But the section as a whole shows that Mark uses the predictions for slightly different purposes than the christologically thrusted predictions themselves. How should one assess this difference? Is it an argument for the pre-Markan origins of the predictions, that is, that Mark found the form of the predictions in tradition, used them because he agreed with them (or was persuaded by them), but his own hand is shown by the use he makes of the predictions? Or is this too subtle a distinction to make, so that the use authorial Mark makes of the predictions is not an argument against the likelihood that he created the predictions?

Like everything else posed so far, the answer is a judgment call, without convincing justification for either position. If I had to judge, I would incline to the view that the predictions are pre-Markan. That simply throws the entire issue of the origin of the Son of Man Christology into obscurity. But that, in my judgment, is where it has to remain. We simply do not know how or why the Son of Man Christology emerged from an earlier point of view, in which Jesus proclaims a Son of Man who is not himself. We can see a perhaps intermediate stage in which the criterion for the eschatological judgment of the Son of Man is response to Jesus. We can also imagine that the Christology was a way of incorporating the resurrection into the Son of Man trajectory, a resurrection honored by the Cosmocrator trajectory but for which the early Son of Man trajectory had neither need nor rationale. But this remains within the realm of speculation.

Excursus: Mark 8:27-29 as a Resurrection Story

Rudolf Bultmann believed that the confession of Peter in Mark 8:27-29 was originally a post-resurrection appearance to Peter, of which the original ending, cut off by Mark, is to be found in Matthew 16:17-19.[44] The view, which had many earlier adherents,[45] seems to be rejected by most subsequent scholars.[46] What can be said about the argument?

1. It is usually implied that Mark 8:27-29 is the primary passage, while a comparable statement in Mark 6:14-16 is a secondary formulation. I am convinced that it is the other way around. Similar in both stories is the expressed opinion that some take Jesus to be Elijah or one of the prophets. Similar also is the identification with John the Baptist. But it is only in Mark 6 that this identification is explained. There Herod Antipas, to explain the miraculous activity of Jesus (fearfully?), supports the judgment that John has been raised (*ēgerthē*) in Jesus.[47] This seems like a primitive, popular explanation of Jesus' ability that would hardly have been created by Mark. Thus I think it highly likely that 8:27-29 is the later formation. That it is later is supported by Bultmann's form-critical judgment that early pronouncement stories do not begin with Jesus raising an issue.[48] Thus I think it is likely that 8:27-29 is a Markan composition based

on 6:14-16. Bultmann's argument that it is pre-Markan and based on the resurrection faith has no support in the text itself. I think it is most likely that Mark uses the *Christos* title in order to reject it for his preferred title, Son of Man. Thus the passage *in its context* is polemical, not confessional.

2. In Mark Jesus is resurrected as Son of Man, not *Christos*. That Jesus is resurrected as *Christos* seems to have its origin in the Jerusalem church (cf. 1 Cor 15). Mark has little or nothing to do with the Jerusalem traditions and, indeed, seems to avoid them (e.g., the young man's advice to the disciples to go to Galilee and not stay in Jerusalem, 16:7). The purpose of the Markan formation in 8:27-29 would be, in fact, to reject the Jerusalem tradition according to which the appropriate title for Jesus is *Christos*—not to affirm it. While it is conceivable that Mark retrojects a Jerusalem tradition of a post-resurrection appearance to Peter in order to reject both the prominence of Peter and the status of *Christos*, that 8:27-29 reflects dependence on 6:14-16 makes this unlikely.

3. Much depends on the assessment of the Matthean "ending" (16:17-19), since it has been argued that there are resurrection motifs in the passage: the notion of revelation, the building of the church, the binding and loosing. Yet, none of these is specific, and we are again reduced to a judgment call. Recent scholarship seems in agreement at least that Bultmann was wrong,[49] whether the passage is taken as Matthean redaction (e.g., U. Luz) or as a pre-Matthean tradition (Davies and Allison).[50]

The passage offers many puzzlements, such as the disputed presence of Semitisms, the prominence of Peter, and the naming incident. None of these can be explored here. Suffice it to say that it seems unlikely that the Matthean "ending" was an ending anywhere but in Matthew's scheme, and that the passage cannot be taken as supporting a Markan post-resurrection appearance story in Mark 8:27-29. The most curious aspect of Matthew's section is the exaltation of Peter (including the naming in Greek), which is so "un-Markan" and which does not seem to have a clear rationale in the Gospel. To this issue I shall return in a later chapter.

3 ——

The Christos Trajectory

Despite (or because of?) the heavy and omnipresent appearance of *Christos* as a title and/or name of Jesus throughout the New Testament, its possibly various meanings and functions and, even more importantly, its history are not at all clear. To put together all the evidence into some coherent whole requires imagination and conjecture. This is the case because, despite the frequent occurrence of the term in the New Testament, there are major gaps in our knowledge of the history. The term obviously begins as a title applied to Jesus by the early followers. One supposes this occurred in the Palestinian churches. To judge from Paul, by the time of the 50s, the term has exploded in use in the Hellenistic churches to the extent that *Christos* frequently seems to be a proper name of Jesus, as in "Jesus Christ."[1] Since the term occurs with some reservation in the Gospel tradition, one has to imagine how and why the title became more popular in earliest Hellenistic Christianity than in Palestinian, and why it began to lose there its titular significance.

The statistics are impressive. *Christos* appears in the Gospels 53 times; in the remainder of the New Testament, 478 times. In the UBS Greek text, the Gospels take up 415 pages; the remainder of the New Testament makes up 480 pages. Thus for the Gospels there are 53 instances in 415 pages, while in the remainder of the New Testament there are 478 appearances in the 480 pages. This means that in the Gospels the term occurs about once in every eight pages, while in the remainder of the New Testament it appears about once on each page.

Since the title began to be used of Jesus in the Palestinian communities, it is necessary to begin with Gospel materials, in which such traditions are recorded. It is true that, as *writings*, the Pauline corpus is earlier than the final composition of the Gospels. Nevertheless the Palestinian beginnings need to be discussed before the continuation in "Hellenistic" churches.

My aim here is to construct, as far as possible, a trajectory of the emergence and function of the title *Christos*. This means that it is important to distinguish between tradition and composition by the final authors. Such distinctions are not always easy to make, nor does it seem to me possible to distinguish between early and later traditions. What I will do in the following pages is to describe each appearance of the title, plus the related terms, "Son of God," "son of David," and "king," and, eventually at least, to order these appearances in terms of tradition or composition. The organization is thus not neat and simple. I ask the reader's patience.

Mark

The earliest Gospel uses *Christos* seven times (compared with fourteen uses of Son of Man). Of these appearances, only one is connected with another title. This exception is the presumed heading for the Gospel: "Beginning of the gospel of Jesus Christ, Son of God."[2] Clearly, this is compositional and does not help us in our search for tradition. One can argue whether *Christos* is a proper name, as in Hellenistic custom. Much depends upon whether one reads "Son of God" as part of the original text. If Son of God is read, *Christos* is probably titular. If "Son of God" is not read, the use is ambiguous.

The other uses are almost certainly titular, if varied. Apart from the title, the first appearance of the term does not appear until 8:29 when, under prodding from Jesus, Peter responds simply: "You are the *Christos*." Here we have a clear titular use that belongs to pre-Markan tradition. In Mark's composition, Jesus tends to play down the title in preference to Son of Man—indicating where the Gospel writer stands on the issue. The traditional narrative itself gives no clue as to the meaning of the title, except that it is contrasted with the possibilities that Jesus is John *redivivus*, Elijah, or one of the prophets. It is assumed that the meaning of the title is obvious.[3]

At the night trial, often considered to have been composed by Mark from traditional elements,[4] the high priest asks Jesus, "Are you the *Christos*, the son of the Blessed?" (14:61). Jesus responds, "I am," but then speaks of the coming Son of Man. Just as in the context of Peter's confession,[5] Mark accepts the Messiah title but subordinates it to the title Son of Man. While the entire story is compositional, the *Christos* title certainly comes from tradition and is used here in controversy, as it often is in the tradition.

In the crucifixion narrative, the only appearance of the title occurs in a taunt by the high priests and scribes: "Let the *Christos*, the king of Israel, come down now from the cross" (15:32). On the assumptions that this narrative is largely composed of traditional elements (however it may have been put together by the final author) and that Mark shows no particular interest in the title, we can assign this occurrence to the pre-Markan passion tradition. The ridicule comes from a political perspective. The enemies of Jesus claim that he has made political assertions, the falseness of which they think is amply demonstrated by the mortal predicament Jesus is in. One should note that Pilate has already engaged in such ridicule. From the enemies' point of view, Jesus is definitely *not* the king of the Jews or Israel. What, however, does the narrator think of this ridicule? It is amazing that the narration remains completely silent about the messiahship of Jesus. It is almost as if the narrator agrees with the ridicule, at least to the point of conceding that the title of Messiah is not an appropriate one for Jesus.

Controversy about the title in relation to the Davidic line occurs in 12:35-37. Here is the only place in Mark where any hint comes as to the meaning(s) of the title. Unfortunately, the meaning of the saying is shrouded in scholarly controversy.[6] Is the title itself rejected? Or just the linkage with the Davidic line? On the surface it would seem that the *Christos* term is accepted as a valid one (although in this case not applied directly to Jesus), but that the point of the saying is to claim that "Messiah" and "David" are not to be joined. This will relate it to traditions in other Gospels (to be inspected shortly) in which the relation to the Davidic line is an issue. We can consider the passage a saying that stems from tradition, in which, implicitly, the messiahship of Jesus is affirmed as valid regardless of lack of association with the Davidic line.[7]

A strange saying occurs in 13:21-22, embedded in the so-called little apocalypse, usually thought to be (more or less) a unit Mark has received from tradition. "And then if anyone says to you, 'Behold, here is the *Christos*, he is there,' do not believe. For false christs and false prophets will arise and give signs and wonders to deceive, if possible, the elect." Jesus does not identify himself with either *Christos* or prophet. He simply says that such will arise, claiming that status or claiming that others have such status, and that they will perform miraculous feats. Who such wonder-workers could be is not more exactly defined. Notice that the true followers of Jesus are said to be the "elect"—a term that elsewhere seems to adhere to a Son of Man Christology. Is the Jesus who speaks here the Son of Man who warns against false messiahs and prophets in the last days? At any rate, if the tradition had wished to identify Jesus as *Christos*, it could have been clearer about it. Even Matthew makes no move in that direction (Matt 24:23-24).[8] It is perhaps not irrelevant that in the Markan context, which Matthew does not alter, the Son of Man seems to be the dominant title.[9]

Another unusual appearance occurs in 9:41. In the context of the mission of the early disciples (so the usual location asserted of the materials), Jesus says, "For whoever gives you [plural] a cup of water to drink because you are a follower of *Christos* will by no means lose his reward." This is interesting, because it seems to reflect a mission in which the followers are proclaiming Jesus to be the Messiah. Rarely in the Gospels is *Christos* linked with the discipleship of community.[10]

If one asks which of the traditional uses reflects a confessional context, in which a follower asserts Jesus to be the Messiah, only 8:27 and 9:41 seem to fit. The others fall into a context of what I will call "controversy." That is, the title is used either to bolster the followers' claim that Jesus *is* the Messiah (12:35-37) or to imply that others dispute such a claim (13:21; 15:32). Mark 1:1 clearly belongs in the confessional category, in this case compositional rather than traditional.

Since "Son of God" is a royal term in Psalm 2:7, a psalm used frequently by early Christian exegetes, it is necessary to look at this phrase as it appears in the Gospel. In 14:61, the high priest asks, "Are you the *Christos*, the Son of the Blessed?" Here it is obvious that "Son" is a synonym for "Messiah."

The divine word at Jesus' baptism is more complicated. "You are my beloved Son; with you I am well pleased" (1:11). Many scholars consider this an echo of Psalm 2:7 and, with the mention of the descent of the spirit upon Jesus, leads them to say that here the baptism is the beginning of the messiahship of Jesus. Scholars debate whether Mark took this perspective from his tradition, or whether it is a specifically Markan idea.[11]

Interpretation of the command of the divine voice in the transfiguration story is even more uncertain. Here the words of 1:11 are partially repeated: "This is my beloved son, listen to him." The last phrase may reflect the passage about the prophet who will arise after Moses in Deuteronomy 18:15: "The Lord your God will raise up for you a prophet like me from among you, from your breth- ren—him you shall heed."[12] If so, then the divine voice probably acknowledges Jesus to be both the Messiah and the "new Moses." Much depends upon judg- ment about the function of the story, and certainty eludes us. The likelihood is that it affirms that Jesus, rather than Moses or Elijah, is the ultimate authority. Also uncertain is whether the divine voice comes from the tradition or is a Mar- kan composition.[13]

Another ambiguous occurrence of Son of God is the statement of the cen- turion, who, seeing the portents surrounding Jesus' death exclaims: "Truly this man was a son of God" (15:39). One can argue whether or not the anarthrous "son" has significance. Of course the "original" meaning and that heard by the hearers of the Gospel could well be different. In the context, the centurion is probably expressing amazement about the close relation Jesus must have had with a higher power, due to the portents—hence *a* son of God. The believers may well have glossed the saying to think the centurion was acknowledging *the* Son of God. That the opening title of the Gospel also uses "Son" anarthrously supports this reading by the later church.

This leaves two instances in which the demonic world acknowledges Jesus to be the Son of God (3:11; 5:7). While these are almost certainly traditional elements (although 3:11 may count as a Markan summary), it is most likely that the term arises out of a context in which the powerful magician is related to divine powers and is thus a son of God, rather than out of a context of messianic acclamation.[14] How the believing communities understood the demonic confession, however, may not be the same as the original context. If miracles and messiahship are related, as I suggest below, the believing communities may well have interpreted the demonic acknowledgment as messianic.

A special separate category may pertain to the several uses of *basileus* in the crucifixion account. All of these (15:2, 9, 12, 18, 26, 32) are ironic in character—both for Christian as well as for Jewish sensitivities. Pilate, for example, calls Jesus the King of the Jews before Jewish leaders. Not surprisingly the Jewish leaders respond in a completely negative way. A kind of double irony occurs, however, in the last instance (verse 32), because the chief priests join in the taunting with the title King of Israel (is there significance in the change from "King of the Jews" in the mouths of the Romans?). In general, the function of the title King of the Jews seems to represent a Gentile perspective. While the Christians and the Jews fight over whether Jesus is *Christos* or not, the Gentiles look back from their superior station and see it all as a meaningless fight over a King of the Jews—something the Gentiles know is an unreality.

If we add the references of Jesus as Son of God to those in which *Christos* is used, we get the following results. We have seven "confessions"—counting those of the demons (as they would probably have been understood by the followers)—all stemming from pre-Markan tradition and 1:1, which is certainly compositional. Four belong to controversy, that is, denials that Jesus is what the followers claim—counting 14:61 which is probably compositional in its present form. To this number we can probably add the five occurrences of the ironic *basileus* in chapter 15.

That the occurrences fall into these two categories is significant. For one thing, the two categories are certainly related: one category affirms what the other denies. This suggests as a working hypothesis the following: the *Christos* title (and "Son of God" when it is equivalent to *Christos*) appears in debate with the Jewish communities about whether Jesus is or is not the Messiah. The instances tell us nothing about the meaning of the term and nothing, really, about what the application to Jesus does to explain, define, or delimit his status. That means that the debate occurs about what is for the participants a known item. The term *basileus*, in addition, may reflect awareness of how the Gentile world makes fun of the entire debate.

In sum, at some point in time tradition appears in which Jesus is named Messiah and Son of God. Whether Son of God was originally a synonym for Messiah or whether it came out of a sense of awe in Jesus' reputation as a miracle worker (or both) is difficult to say. By the time the tradition becomes visible to us, the claim that Jesus was *Christos* occurs in an implicit or explicit debate between Jews who believe in Jesus and those who do not. The author of the Gospel accepts *Christos* as a title but prefers that of Son of Man. Whether the author is still engaged in the debate about Messiah is not, in my judgment, certain. What is instructive in our search for trajectories is that the author, writing c. 70 C.E., prefers Son of Man as a title over *Christos*. If he is still engaged in the debate about the Messiah, his preference for Son of Man might be one way of defusing the argument: yes, Jesus can be called *Christos*, but his real significance lies in his being the Son of Man.

Matthew

Matthew seems to handle titles rather freely. For him, "Jesus" is *the* category, and he can play with the traditional titles. For instance, although he eliminates Mark's Son of Man from the first passion prediction (16:21) and replaces it with a personal pronoun, yet he keeps the title in the other two passion predictions. On the other hand, his change in Jesus' response to the high priest about messiahship leaves the Messiah acknowledgment more ambiguous than in the Markan account: "You say so" (Matt 26:64). Thus his alterations do not seem to suggest a preference for one title over another.

In Matthew the title *Christos* appears some sixteen times.[15] First we must search for the traditional elements in the Gospel. In four instances he records Markan material using the term *Christos*: 16:14; 22:42; 24:23-25; and 26:63. These need no further discussion. Not surprisingly, five instances occur in the opening messianic genealogy and birth narrative (1:1, 16, 17, 18; 2:4). Since the purpose of these narratives is to demonstrate that Jesus is the Messiah (why else does he have to be born in Bethlehem?), it would be surprising if such instances did not occur. In 1:1 *Christos* is equated with being son of David. Since the intent of the genealogy is to argue for this sonship, the equation does not surprise. The title is repeated at the end of the genealogy, this time in the phrase, "Jesus who is named *Christos*." Interesting is the use in verse 17 of *Christos* without "Jesus." All of the uses so far seem clearly titular; obviously verse 17 has to be. Verse 18 announces the birth story with the title "Jesus *Christos*." And, finally, in 2:4, Herod asks of the Jewish leaders where the *Christos* is to be born. In the tradition that we call Matthew's birth narrative, *Christos* is undoubtedly a title, even when it occurs in conjunction with "Jesus." Implicitly this narrative is an argument that Jesus is *Christos*, son of David and was born, as the prophet Micah (5:2) foretold. Obviously, the counter argument is that Jesus was born in Nazareth and therefore could not be *Christos* son of David. These uses of *Christos* are thus part of a controversy with other Jews.

Whether the next use is composition or tradition is uncertain. In a chapter carefully crafted by Matthew (chap. 11), the opening scene is the question (a Q tradition: Matt 11:2-6, par. Luke 7:18-19) that the imprisoned John asks Jesus (11:2-6; Luke 7:18-19). In Q John queries whether Jesus is "the coming one" (*ho erchomenos*).[16] Since Q has no explicit use of *Christos*, one wonders whether the coming one is the *Christos*, the Son of Man, or some other figure. In the Matthean text John's query is, however, explained by his having heard about "the works of the *Christos*." Clearly Matthew takes "the coming one" to refer to *Christos*. The phrase, *erga tou Christou*, sounds formulaic (cf. John 11:27), but it does not occur in the Lukan parallel. If the general judgment that Luke usually is truer to Q than Matthew holds here, then Matthew's phrase, wherever it comes from, is compositional. On the other hand, Matthew does not use the title *Christos* in the remainder of the section. Does this mean that the phrase was in Q and that Luke omitted it? Were it not for the fact that Q apparently uses the title Son of Man but avoids *Christos*, I would incline to think that the phrase "works of the *Christos*" is traditional. In any case, the "works" of the Messiah must refer to miracles performed by Jesus. That the Messiah does miracles is not attested, to my knowledge, in Jewish tradition, but in the Gospel tradition he clearly does, an argument to be presented below. For the moment, it may be safest to assign the phrase in question to Matthean composition, although I have reservations. If it is compositional, it shows that at the date of Matthew's writing (90s?) the idea that the *Christos* is a miracle worker is still alive.

Equally problematic is the admonition of Jesus to his disciples in 23:10. "Nor call yourselves teachers, because your one teacher is *Christos*." The apparently parallel saying in verse 8 gives as its rationale the equality of church members, not the sacred leadership. In what sense the Messiah was seen as a teacher is also not clear. Thus the ambiguity of the injunction as it now stands is sufficient to make a judgment between tradition/composition by Matthew difficult. If, in the earliest church, there was an egalitarianism among church members (cf., e.g., Matt 18:15-20), then verse 8 might count as traditional.[17] Is verse 10 Matthew's version of the saying? Did he change the egalitarian flavor of verse 8 and create a saying in which Jesus as *Christos* assumes (as resurrected?) the status of the one who tells the church what to believe? It should be noted, however, that the saying does not nullify the notion of equality among members. If the saying *is* Matthean, why did he choose the *Christos* title, when it did not have, as far as we know, the connotation of teacher? The answer here surely would lie in the basic Christology of the Gospel, in which Jesus is the true interpreter (teacher) of the meaning of *torah*. At whatever stage the saying emerged, it witnesses to a believing community in which its exalted leader, called *Christos*, guides the church into what is true.[18]

Five instances seem clearly compositional. In 16:20 he adapts Mark's warning by Jesus not to speak about him (after Peter's confession); but Matthew makes explicit that Jesus accepts the *Christos* title handed him by Peter: "Not to tell anyone that he is the *Christ*." To Jesus' warning in Mark that one should watch out for eschatological deceivers, Matthew makes it clear that these are deceivers who claim the name *Christos* (24:5). In the traditional taunt scene after the trial, Matthew inserts a vocative *Christ* into the taunt of some members of the Sanhedrin (26:68). Twice Matthew changes the Markan questions by Pilate. Mark has Pilate ask about the "King of the Jews." Matthew writes "Jesus called *Christ*" (27:17, 22). All these are obviously compositional changes, but they do not add new content to the *Christos* trajectory.

The phrase "Son of God" (or the absolute "Son") appears in Matthew fourteen times. Which are traditional? Almost all of them. Of the fourteen, seven are taken from Mark.[19] Two come from the Q tradition of the temptation story. The possible deeds imagined here for the Son of God are to command stones to become bread and to jump from the pinnacle of the temple. It seems divine-man notions are at work here, although in the larger context the story exhibits a strong Jewish piety. Clearly there is controversy here. But is the issue whether Jesus is able to perform the miracles or, assuming he can, whether he will use his divine power for personal advantage (or is this a modern moralistic importation into the story)?

Three of the fourteen occurrences display the absolute use of "Son," that is, they do not contain the phrase "Son of God" explicitly, but in these, it should be emphasized, "Father" and not "God" is the correlative. One is from Mark (24:36), one from Q (11:27), and one from a baptismal formula (28:19). There is something exalted about these three sayings that almost makes one affirm that they are claiming more than messiahship for Jesus. What this "more than" might be, however, is not clear. We should certainly resist later creedal trinitarian linkage. There is, furthermore, no hint in Matthew of Jesus' preexistence. That the sayings are traditional and not compositional makes one see how quickly a "high" Christology began to develop in the Palestinian communities. Thus eleven of the fourteen occurrences are from pre-Matthean tradition.

The three apparently compositional instances are additions to a Markan context: 14:33; 16:16; 27:43. Two of these probably do not add to the Markan intent, since "Son" is a synonym for the *Christos* of the Markan text. Mark records Peter's confession of Jesus as the *Christos*. Matthew adds to that: "Son of the living God." In 27:43 he adds the Son title to the taunt about being the King of Israel. Here those who taunt claim that *Jesus* claimed to be Son of God. These additions seem to indicate that "Son of God" is tantamount to *Christos*. More startling is his addition to the Markan account of Jesus walking on the water. To this miracle the disciples respond: "And those in the boat worshiped him saying, 'Truly you are the [or "a"] Son of God'" (14:33). The anarthrous "Son" would fit well with a response of awe to one who could do such a great miracle, to a person perceived as a "divine man," rather than as an acclamation of messiahship. Would Matthew himself, however, have had such an intent in mind? Had this statement then been added to the tradition prior to Matthew? The wording is easiest to explain if that were the case. If the addition to Mark is pre-Matthean, I am inclined to read this use as one that is not messianic. How Matthew himself intended the title is another matter. As we shall see, miracles may be one indication in Matthew that Jesus *is* Messiah.[20]

Finally, Matthew has seven occurrences of the phrase "son of David."[21] Two of these seem to be taken from the story in Mark of the healing of Bartimaeus (9:27 and 15:22)—apparently parallel accounts with slight variants. Matthew seems to find such a setting non-problematic, because he adds this title to the Canaanite woman's address to Jesus in a healing story (15:22). He also has the crowd express the possibility that Jesus might be the son of David because of his healings (12:23). This is apparently a Q saying, but Luke does not have "son of David" (Luke 11:14-15).[22] Matthew's version almost reads like a confession of a unique authority—that is, it might be the case that here "son of David" has explicit messianic content. The same is surely true about the two instances in which the crowds (and later the children in the Temple) cry out, "Hosanna to the son of David" (21:9, 15).[23]

These occurrences of the term "son of David" are mostly related to Jesus as miracle worker, and they mostly appear to be compositional. Matthew himself likes the term and finds no hesitation in relating it to Jesus as miracle worker. The acclamations in 12:23 and 21:9, 15 seem to be messianic in character.

In sum, as far as pre-Matthean tradition using *Christos* is concerned, we have little evidence to go on. Once we eliminate instances taken from Mark and those clearly due to Matthew's own hand, only a few remain. The five uses of *Christos* in the birth narrative belong to the tradition that insists Jesus was born in Bethlehem and thus is the Messiah. The only issue here is *why* such a narrative arose. Since the birth narratives in Matthew and Luke are so disparate, the purpose can hardly be to pass on historical information. Both narratives have as their primary purpose to have Jesus born in Bethlehem, so that at least one argument for Jesus' messiahship is in the church's favor.[24] While the narratives are basically seemingly irenic, they must belong to the controversy about the messiahship of Jesus.[25] Otherwise evidence for traditional uses may occur only in the phrase "the works of the Christ" (11:2), and the notion of *Christos* as teacher (23:10). Hesitantly, I think it likely that both are compositional. If they are traditional, they witness to ideas applied to Jesus of the Messiah as miracle worker and teacher.

Nor is the fund of information from the title "Son of God" larger. In the Q temptation story, the phrase occurs twice in connection with miracle. The response of the disciples in 14:33 to Jesus' miracle of walking on water also sounds like a response to a divine man. Finally, Matthew uses the Q statement of the intimate relation of Son to Father (11:27) and the baptismal formula (28:19). These traditions point in quite different directions. In the tradition behind Matthew there was, seemingly, both a divine-man understanding of the power of Jesus as miracle worker and a "high" Christology of a close relation between God and Jesus. Matthew's use of "son of David," while in one instance related to Markan tradition, is almost entirely compositional.

And where does the Gospel writer stand in the trajectory? I find it difficult to put him in any obvious place. The author does insert the title at least five, and perhaps seven, times into his narrative. These insertions, however, seem to be mostly explanatory (at least from his perspective) and do not add to the argument or further a description of what it means for Jesus to be *Christos*. The two instances in which the text seems really to communicate something about the Messiah are those two that are of uncertain provenance (11:2 and 23:10). In general, the author seems to stand at a point where Jesus, rather than any particular title, has become the issue. This is perhaps surprising because if Matthew, as is generally thought, represents a believing community close to and yet in significant conflict with the synagogue, one would expect more explicit controversy about Jesus' messiahship—such as we find in the Gospel of John. Yet the differences between Matthew and John make this divergence understandable. For Matthew, the conflict with the synagogue is about torah, while in the Gospel of John, it is about Christology. In Matthew, Jesus is the true teacher of torah; in the Gospel of John, he is for the insiders the divine Logos, and for outsiders he is claimed to be Messiah. For Matthew, Jesus can be named *any* of the honorific titles, as long as his function as true teacher of torah is included as central. It is perhaps for this reason that Matthew seems not to regard to any specific title as definitive. Clearly his redactional uses of *Christos* indicate that he honors Jesus as Messiah. Jesus is also son of God, perhaps in more than one sense, as well as son of David.

Luke

Comparison of Luke with Acts is interesting. In the Gospel, there are twelve occurrences of *Christos*, while in Acts (roughly the same length), there are thirty-one. True to the traditions, Luke's use of *Christos* in the Gospel is muted, while in the story of the church, where *Christos* is an established title and name, the usage more than doubles.

Of the twelve appearances in the Gospel, four are taken from Mark.[26] Two occurrences are in the birth and infancy section. This is not in itself surprising. In fact, that there are *only* two is perhaps what is surprising (Matthew has five in a shorter text). What is interesting is the acclamatory character of the two. In

2:11 the angels announce to the shepherds the birth of "a savior who is *Christos kyrios*." Apart from the use of *sōtēr*, this is much like the acclamations in early Hellenistic liturgies. *Sōtēr* is not a Lukan word, and that fact militates against his composition of the acclamation.[27] In 2:26 the narrator remarks that it had been promised to Simeon that he would not die until he should see "the Christ of [the] Lord." "Lord" obviously here refers to God. The syntax is unusual, and it probably belongs to the tradition Luke found.

The other six occurrences of *Christos* appear to be compositional. One startling use appears in a Markan context, connected with the encounter with demons. In this case Mark's summary of healings says, "And he would not permit the demons to speak because they knew him" (1:34). Luke supplies an acclamation for the demons: "You are the Son of God," and then explains the reason for his command to silence by Jesus: "Because they knew he was the *Christos*" (4:41). Here a divine man acclamation is supplied, yet with a gloss that Son of God is an equivalent for Messiah.[28]

The remaining five occurrences are disparate in character. In 3:15 the people (*laos*) are so impressed with John that they wonder if he is the *Christos*. John, of course, denies the possibility, using the words of Mark.[29] The trial scene before Pilate produces a second example. Only Luke supplies the charges by the Jewish leaders to Pilate against Jesus. One of these is that he claims to be *Christos*, a king.[30] Clearly the intention of the Jewish leaders, according to the narrative, is to convince Pilate that Jesus is an insurrectionist. The unrepentant thief also taunts Jesus with the *Christos* title (23:39).

The last two occurrences connect the *Christos* title with Jesus' suffering. (1) "Was it not necessary that the *Christos* should suffer these things and enter into his glory?" (24:26). These are the words of Jesus to the two disciples on the road to Emmaus. "These things" refers to the brief recapitulation of the crucifixion narrative told by the disciples and "necessary" clearly points to the prophetic prophecy mentioned in the previous verse. (2) To the disciples Jesus says, "Thus it is written, that the Christ should suffer and on the third day rise from the dead" (24:46).

"Suffer" (*paschō*) does not often occur in Luke. The author follows the wording in the Markan passion predictions. When Mark writes (8:31) that the Son of Man is to suffer, Luke repeats it (9:20, using the Son of Man title). Luke virtually inserts the phrase in 17:25, clearly referring to the Son of Man, who is mentioned in the previous verse. Perhaps reflecting this use, Luke apparently inserts a reference to Jesus' suffering into the account of the last supper (22:15).[31] Otherwise, the verb appears as a reference to Jesus only in the two passages cited above. Luke has taken up the notion of the necessity of Jesus' suffering from Mark (and perhaps last supper tradition), expressed this twice with the Son of Man title (9:28; 17:25) and twice in the resurrection narratives, but with a changed title—*Christos*.

Why does Luke focus on suffering rather than dying? In none of the passages is the suffering said to have salvatory significance—a notion essentially absent from the entire Gospel. The scriptural necessity—which Luke emphasizes in the two resurrection occurrences—probably functions as an apology for the humiliating death of Jesus. And while Luke has followed Mark earlier in associating the suffering with the Son of Man, in these last two instances Luke changes the title. But why? Since he seems to have no problem with the Son of Man title, it is not due to preference for *Christos* over Son of Man. Could it be due to the fact that the association of scriptural necessity with suffering was traditionally associated in Hellenistic Christianity with the *Christos*, as is sometimes asserted?[32] The evidence for this joining is, in my opinion, thin (a possible support would come from one textual tradition in 1 Pet 3:18). Or perhaps these verses in chapter 24 mark a transition to the next volume (Acts) in which the title Son of Man virtually disappears (appearing only in 7:56) while the *Christos* title becomes more customary (31 instances). Whatever the cause, Luke seems to emphasize at the end of the story of Jesus the scriptural necessity of Jesus' suffering and ties this in with the *Christos* title. In general, apart from the two post-resurrection sayings, one can say that Luke's uses of *Christos* follow the tradition. He does not seemingly have much interest in pushing the title back into the life of Jesus.[33]

The same dependence on tradition can be seen in his uses of "Son of God" and "son of David." The title "Son of God" appears ten times. Four of these are from Mark (the baptism, 3:22; the Gerasene demoniac, 8:28; the transfiguration, 9:38; the night trial, 22:70). Two are from the birth traditions (1:32, 35). Two are from the Q account of the temptation (4:3, 9). One is from the Q saying about revelation between Father and Son (10:22, here used absolutely). The only addition due to Luke's hand is his insertion of the title into the Markan summary about the healing of demons (4:41, discussed above).

The appearance of son of David is even sparser in the Lukan narrative. The title occurs once in the birth traditions, in a passage that seems patently political (1:32). Here the angel announces that Jesus will be Son of God, son of David (lit., of "his father David"), and that "he will reign over the house of Jacob forever."[34] Then the angel couples "son of David" with "Son of God" (verse 35). Luke also repeats the Markan story about Blind Bartimaeus, with its double use of "son of David" (18:38-39), and the controversy about *Christos* being a son of David (20:41-44). There are no compositional uses of the title.

In sum, the search for pre-Lukan tradition about *Christos* produces little of substance. Apart from the two occurrences in the birth narrative, there is no other sure pre-Lukan use. One would expect in a narrative that goes to great length to square Bethlehem and Nazareth that the *Christos* title should appear. Yet the announcement by the angel to the shepherds sounds strikingly Hellenistic. Does this mean that already in the Palestinian communities such an acclamation was in use? Or is this an example of an importation from Hellenistic culture (by whom?) into a basically Palestinian set of stories? And is the meaning that messiahship and lordship begin at the birth rather than the resurrection? Finally, what does Jesus save from? These are questions for which I see no easy answer. The evidence suggests that the acclamation is not a Lukan addition; rather it must have existed in the narrative used by Luke. At the same time, if there is anywhere a political messiahship attributed to Jesus it is in the Lukan birth narratives—something one would hardly expect from a Hellenistic environment. What the birth narratives express about Jesus as *Christos* is both startlingly diverse and atypical for the New Testament in its political program. Sadly, we cannot yet locate this narrative in a reasonable way. The political implications and the kind of acclamations do not fit the main christological trajectory as it is unfolding in our study.

Similarly, the appearances of Son of God help us little in getting a sense of this trajectory. The title appears twice in the angel's announcement to Mary, and there it is definitely tied to messiahship (*Christos* does not appear) when the angel adds that God "will give to him the throne of his father David" (1:32). Again, this identification is only to be expected in such a narrative.[35] At any rate, Son of God is clearly equated with Messiah. I have already evaluated the two instances in the Q temptation story. Luke's narration is similar to Matthew's.

I conclude that Luke's fund of tradition does not suggest that the *Christos* and Son of God titles were frequently used among early believers. The same lack of interest seems to accrue to the author as well. While Luke is not averse to using *Christos* for Jesus' earthly life (cf. 4:41), in general he seems to assume this is primarily a title for the resurrected Jesus. Once Jesus has been resurrected, *then* it is appropriate for Jesus to speak of himself as the *Christos* who had to suffer. The same can be said of the Son of God title. Only once does the author add it to his narration (also 4:41).

It does seem possible to put several of the non-Markan instances into the controversy and acclamation categories. *Controversy:* Here belong the appearances in the birth and infancy narratives, those in the Q story of temptation, the question about John as Messiah, and the charge before Pilate. *Acclamation:* The appearances in the birth narrative are also acclamatory. One must acclaim what is controverted. One could add to these the compositional insertions of *Christos* and Son of God into Mark's summary in 1:34 (Luke 4:41).

John

John surprises. There are more occurrences (19) of the word *Christos* here than in any of the other Gospels. The surprise is due to the usual—and basically correct—judgment that John's Christology is "high"—that it concerns the transcendent divine Logos come to earth to reveal God and to grant eternal life to those who "see" in Jesus that divine reality. Why then would the author and his community be seriously interested in a title that carries earthly meanings? And yet the conclusion to the original Gospel (20:31) focuses on Jesus as Messiah. "These are written that you may believe that Jesus is the Christ, the Son of God, and that believing you may have life in his name." Some layering is clearly going on, and this needs to be sorted out as far as possible. It is also difficult to separate between what might be early tradition and the position of the community at the time the author wrote.[36]

First it is necessary to detail the appearances. The pattern we have discovered in the other Gospels becomes in these instances even clearer: controversy and acclamation. *Controversy*: The Baptist emphatically denies that he is *Christos* (1:20, 25; 3:28). The Samaritan woman questions whether Jesus might be the *Christos*, presumably because of his power to know more than a normal human could know (4:25, 29).[37] In a major controversy section, the argument about whether Jesus could be the *Christos* reaches a fever pitch. Six uses of *Christos* occur in 7:26-42. The criterion of messiahship in verses 26-27 is that no one knows the origin of the *Christos*. In verse 31 it is the doing of miracles (signs); in verses 41-42, that the *Christos* should come from Bethlehem. While the first and the third criteria seem contradictory, the situation is clear: the *Christos* title emerges when there is debate with the Jews as to Jesus' messiahship. In 12:34 a further criterion is suggested: that the *Christos,* once arrived, is to abide forever.[38] The result of a positive judgment is highlighted in 9:22 when the confession of Jesus as *Christos* causes the removal of a member from the synagogue. In 10:24 the crowd at Jerusalem demands that Jesus tell whether he is or is not the *Christos*. In all, these make up fourteen of the nineteen occurrences. Clearly, controversy between the Johannine community and the Jews focuses around the *Christos* title.

The remaining five occurrences can be put into the category of *acclamation*, i.e., the Johannine answer to the controversy. The first appears at the end of the prologue: "For the law was given through Moses; grace and truth came through Jesus *Christos*." Andrew tells Simon that "we have found the Messiah, which means *Christos*" (1:41). In 11:27 Mary confesses, "I believe that you are the *Christos*, the Son of God, he who is coming into the world." Jesus even speaks about himself in 17:3: "And this is eternal life, that they know you the only true God, and Jesus *Christos* whom you have sent." And finally comes the confession at the end of the Gospel in 20:31, quoted above. Perhaps one should add Peter's confession in 6:69 that Jesus is "the holy one of God."[39]

The two categories are so closely related that they might even be joined into one: argument between the Jews and the believers about Jesus' messiahship.

The Christology of the Gospel seems to operate on two levels. Within the community Jesus is the divine Logos; but in the controversy with the Jews, the still dominant issue is whether Jesus is or is not the *Christos*. What is surprising is that the controversy with the Jews *always* focuses on the *Christos* title, never around the "higher" Christology affirmed on the inside. Do we have here a demarcation between what the believers said to themselves and how they argued with the Jews about the significance of Jesus? Since the controversy with the Jews seems still an issue at the writing of the Gospel when the high Christology is essential, this distinction seems likely.

The Gospel of John also uses the phrase "Son of God" nine times. The uses are varied and not always easily categorized. Twice the phrase is explicitly related to "Messiah." Nathanael acclaims Jesus the Son of God, the King of Israel (1:49). And Mary confesses Jesus to be the Christ, the Son of God (11:27). Two times the title appears in a conflict situation between Jesus and the Jews: 10:36; 19:7. Here it seems to be equivalent to "Messiah." Caution, however, is advised, since in 5:18, in response to the parable (or simile) of "son" as apprentice to the father, the Jews see this as "making himself equal with God."

The last citation suggests that for the Johannine community, "Son of God" points to a more exalted status than the Messiah—although we must remember once more the final statement in the original Gospel that its purpose is to have people believe that Jesus is the *Christos* the Son of God (20:31). Certainly 3:18 puts sonship very close to divinity itself: the condemned person has not believed in the only Son of God.[40] The Son of God is the Lord of the eschaton in 5:25. Strangely, in the next verse the Son is used in the absolute, and in the verse after that the title is Son of Man. The supple mind of the author becomes almost slippery here. At any rate, it seems clear Son of God means more here than the traditional Messiah. A similarly exalted sense occurs in 17:1, relating to the mutual glorification of Father and Son (again absolute). The Son of God will be glorified as well in the raising of Lazarus (11:4). Finally, the Baptist confesses that Jesus is Son of God, but here hints at interpretation are lacking.

In sum,[41] *controversy* and *acclamation* are suitable categories for understanding the titles in the Gospel of John. Yet the Christology of this Gospel is understandably complex, as our brief march through the titles indicates. "Son of God" is a particularly ambiguous title, since it can mean more than one thing. Probably the Johannine community also took it to mean more than one thing, at times indicating a divine status for Jesus, at times (and perhaps when in controversy situations) accepting equation with Messiah. If we made a ladder of the four most prominent terms—Logos, Son of Man, Son of God, Messiah—we might see these in some descending order, yet with overlap. "Logos" is surely the apex of the terms, although it appears only in the prologue. "Son of Man" appears when the author wants to emphasize the acts of God in Jesus. "Son of

God," when not a synonym for Messiah, appears to point to an intimate relation with God as Father. "Messiah," as we have seen, is primarily a term used in controversy with Jewish opponents, although obviously the term is still honored.

A Sketch of a Possible Trajectory

This is a daunting task. One does well to approach it modestly, with awareness of the tentative nature of all such enterprises. Let me begin with my original assessment of the situation. *Christos* is not a dominant title in the Gospel literature. It has become so common, however, in the Hellenistic church that the title has become in many instances a proper name—the second name of Jesus. It hardly makes sense to suppose that *Christos* applied to Jesus was a creation of the Hellenistic church. Thus an adequate trajectory would explain how the term arose in the Palestinian communities, why it did not become dominant, how it moved to Hellenistic communities and became such a dominant title—even in a culture in which the title is not at home, culturally or linguistically. In this chapter I will struggle only with those issues that pertain to the earliest Palestinian communities. Alas, for none of the questions is there a certain answer.

Why was the term applied to Jesus? The discrepancy between the image of the Messiah in Jewish literature and the portrait of Jesus in the Gospels is staggering. In Jewish tradition the Messiah is a royal figure, reigning either by military power or by the power of God (or both). In the Gospels, Jesus is an irenic figure who speaks to the poor and dispossessed, who is crucified and rises. Only in the Lukan birth narratives is Jesus in any way described as a royal, reigning Messiah.

I agree with the many scholars who do not think Jesus himself claimed to be the Messiah. Given what we know from Jewish culture, it would have been absurd for him to do so. It has often been said that Jesus (or the communities) reinterpreted "Messiah" to mean something different. But, as Rudolf Bultmann has rejoined, there is no evidence in the Gospels of any such reinterpretation. As we have already seen, the *Christos* title is used without any explanation; it seems assumed that one knows what it means.

One possibility often suggested is that messiahship was not ascribed to Jesus until the resurrection faith emerged. Peter's confession is then taken to have been originally a post-resurrection appearance story in which Peter acclaims the resurrected Jesus as Messiah. The Messiah titles then are gradually worked back into the life of Jesus. This is not implausible, but it has its difficulties. In this reconstruction, it is presumably the resurrected and *coming* Jesus who will function as Messiah. *Then* he will exercise rulership over the world. One could then appeal to a passage such as Acts 3:18-21, which speaks of a *Christos* appointed who is now in heaven, but who will come in the future to fulfill all the divine prophecies.[42] In this view, even the resurrected Jesus is not yet Messiah—that enthronement awaits the eschaton. This may be parallel to the idea that the resurrected Jesus is the future Son of Man.

Two questions need to be put to this suggestion. (1) It is hard to imagine that the term *Christos* suddenly, out of nowhere, emerged in the Aramaic communities when the resurrection faith arose. There could have been other explanations of the resurrection. For the title Messiah to be applied because Jesus has been raised surely presupposes some sort of notion about messiahship prior to the resurrection faith, but what could it have been, since Jesus never fits—nor is there any evidence he tried to fit—the traditional image of the Messiah? (2) Why is it that in none of the Gospels does the title *Christos* appear in post-resurrection narratives, with the exception of the two Lukan compositional sayings, by Jesus about himself, that as Christ he had to suffer?[43] Some have argued that Peter's confession was just such a post-resurrection appearance story. Then the question presses why Mark put the story into the life of Jesus and why this dislocation was accepted by Matthew and Luke. These questions cannot be adequately answered, and the inability to provide such inevitably raises doubt about the theory. In the absence of a better theory, however, it remains an option.

One possibility can at least be suggested. The Gospels are agreed that Jesus was honored (or reviled) as a miracle worker and healer. Even the opponents of Jesus acknowledge his power, though they ascribe it to Satan (Mark 3:22). Could there have been any link in the popular mind between miracle worker and Messiah? There are some pieces of Gospel tradition that may hint in this direction.

The demons whom Jesus accosts acclaim him to be a Son of God (e.g., Mark 3:11; 5:7). These admittedly seem to be from a divine-man tradition, but they certainly indicate that Jesus in his exorcisms was in touch with divine power. The Q story of the temptation also seems to ascribe miraculous power to Jesus as Son of God. A Q saying (Matt 12:28; Luke 11:20) relates Jesus' exorcistic power to the coming of the kingdom of God. No *Christos* title appears here, but the linkage between *Christos* and the kingdom is surely close. Also in Q is the question that the imprisoned John asks of Jesus, "Are you he who is to come?" (Matt 11:2-6; Luke 7:18-25). The response by Jesus is to catalogue miracles that he has performed.[44] It seems likely that the question is put in terms of the *Christos* expectation, to which Jesus responds by citing his miracles as implicit "proof" that he is indeed the "coming one."[45] Should this be the case, then the admission in Mark 3:22 that the scribes had quite a different interpretation of the miracles of Jesus can be seen in a new light. It becomes a tool in the controversy about Jesus' messiahship. Granted, declare the scribes, Jesus performs miracles, but he cannot be the Messiah, because he is actually in league with Satan.

Both Matthew and Luke at the compositional level are in touch with join-ing Messiah and miracle and, indeed, find it compatible with their thinking.[46] Matthew has the disciples respond to Jesus' walking on the water with an accla-mation of Jesus as Son of God (14:33). Luke enlarges the Markan summary of exorcisms and healings with both titles, Son of God and *Christos* (4:41). The author seems here to equate the two.[47] In Mark's story of the healing of Bar-timaeus, the blind man cries out to Jesus as son of David (10:47). Matthew finds this acceptable, has two stories of the healing of the blind, both of which have the men desiring healing cry out "son of David" (9:27; 20:30), and inserts the title into Mark's story of the Phoenician (in Matthew, Canaanite) woman (15:22). Matthew turns this title into an acclamation in the story of the entry into Jerusalem (21:9, 15). Surely for Matthew, then, the title "son of David" is a synonym for "Messiah."

Even in the Gospel of John there are traditions associated with the Messiah title that ascribe more than human powers to this figure. In one strand Jesus is acclaimed Messiah because he has powers of clairvoyance. Nathanael acclaims Jesus to be Son of God and King of Israel because Jesus says he "saw" him at a distance (1:49). The Samaritan woman ascribes to the concept of Messiah the ability to "show us all things," which probably means to reveal hidden secrets (4:25). Then she thinks Jesus may fulfill that criterion because Jesus "told me all that I ever did" (4:29). Another strand imputes miracles to the notion of Messiah. In a bitter controversy section, some of the people think he fulfills the criterion of the Messiah as a doer of miracles: "When the *Christos* comes, will he do more signs than this man has done?" (7:31). Even the conclusion of the original Gospel enlists Jesus' miracles as indication of his messiahship: "Now Jesus did many other signs in the presence of the disciples, but these are written that you may believe that Jesus is the *Christos*, the Son of God, and that believ-ing you may have life in his name" (20:30-31).[48] Most scholars think that the "true" Christology of John aims much higher than a simple affirmation that Jesus is Messiah. This probably means that the controversy with the synagogue about Jesus' messiahship reaches back into the community's past—and thus can be considered "tradition"—and yet its inclusion in such important ways into the Gospel itself suggests that that controversy is still raging, even if the syna-gogue has excluded Jewish believers in Jesus. Thus the Gospel of John suggests a decades-long association of *Christos* with miracle.

The evidence associating miracle and Messiah stretches from pre-Gospel tradition down through the composition of all of the Gospels—that is, from the emergence of the tradition (the 30s C.E.?) to the end of the century. Is it not conceivable that Jesus' reputation as healer, exorcist, and revealer could have triggered in some minds the possibility that he was the Messiah?[49] In fact, such a suggestion could have antedated the resurrection faith. How much stronger the

conviction that Jesus was indeed the Messiah would have become after the resurrection faith emerged! The resurrection enables the miracle worker to become
God's king, who will come to perform the final deeds of the Messiah (e.g., Acts
3:20-21), not as a military ruler but as God's exalted regent in the eschaton. I am
suggesting that linkage of Jesus' powerful thaumaturgy with messiahship makes
the resurrection faith in Jesus as Messiah more understandable.

Whatever the ultimate answer is about the emergence of "Messiah" as a
title for Jesus, it did obviously happen. At the same time it is clear that it never
became dominant in the communities that lay behind the canonical Gospels.
As I argued in the previous chapter, these communities primarily honored the
resurrected Jesus as the Son of Man. The question then must focus on the competition between the two perspectives, and why that of the Son of Man appealed
more to the Palestinian communities than did that of Messiah. I have already
made judgment about this competition in the previous chapter, but now it needs
more detailed description.

In chapter 2 I argued that the key difference between the two titles is that
between a "political" one (Messiah) and a "religious" one (Son of Man). "Messiah" as an heir to David's throne would have been primarily seen as a political-
military ruler. While this military sense could be spiritualized as a metaphorical
"arm of God," even such language is primarily that of an earthly ruler. And the
appropriation of the title by Bar Cochba shows that it maintained its meaning as
a human military ruler into the second century. Such language even finds its way
into the Lukan birth narratives: "He will be great, and will be called the Son of
the most high, and the Lord God will give to him the throne of his father David,
and he will reign over the house of Jacob forever; and of his kingdom there will
be no end" (1:32-33).[50] As I argued above, dispossessed peasants may not have
been optimistic that such a ruler would be more favorable to their miserable lot
than all the rulers, of whatever country, who had gone before and to whom the
peasants were currently subject.

I now have to insert the possibility that Jesus' reputation as thaumaturgist
may have contributed to the acclamation that Jesus was indeed the Messiah.
Surely this would have been a more popular and compatible perspective from
which the peasants could view Jesus! This must be acknowledged; it is even
conceivable that such belief would have been the factor that made the Messiah
title possible and acceptable in the first place. Jesus' power and his message for
the dispossessed seems likely to have been a powerful impetus to commitment
to the resurrected Jesus.

The belief that Jesus was Messiah by virtue of the resurrection (e.g., Rom
1:3-4) did not make inroads on the more popular acclamations that he was
Messiah-thaumaturgist or Son of Man. Jesus as exalted Messiah became one
among the various perspectives on Jesus, but not the only one, nor even the

dominant one. The continuing interest in Jesus as miracle worker is demonstrated even at the compositional level. It remained a powerful perspective.

The importance of the *Christos* title in the Palestinian communities may be due to its seemingly crucial role in arguments about Jesus with non-believing Jews. As I have tried to show, the primary functions of the *Christos* title are either to argue about who the Messiah is or should be (is Jesus or is he not?) or to acclaim him as, in fact, the Messiah. Both of these functions are closely related. The one acclaims; the other defends. That is, in controversy with non-believing Jews, the *Christos* title was the point of contention. Thus, even if within the believing communities there were other, more important titles and perspectives being developed to which one was committed, the inevitable controversy with non-believing Jews focused on *Christos* as the crucial title.

The Gospel of John shows this two-pronged Christology with clarity. Within, the community was raising the stakes about the person of Jesus to the status of divine Logos. Outside, there continued a bitter dispute with the synagogue about Jesus in terms of *Christos*. Judging from these sections of controversy, it does not seem certain to me that the Johannine community had the best arguments on its side. But at any rate, the community continued to affirm the reality of Jesus as *Christos*, if only because of the conflict with the synagogue. One can only wonder whether the title would have been of *any* importance had not the controversy been of importance.[51]

The same claim can be made, with more caution, about the communities represented by the Synoptic tradition. The *Christos* title functioned here also in controversy about the significance of Jesus, as if that title were the only point of contention between believing and non-believing communities. To a certain extent there was also controversy about Jesus' power as thaumaturgist. We have suggested, however, that this may also have been one way to argue about his messiahship. And when the title is used confessionally, it could well be the positive side of the argument. In contrast, the Son of Man title not only seems to have continued its dominance in the Palestinian communities but it escaped controversy—perhaps because it was an insiders' title, like that of the Johannine logos.

4 ——

THE FATE OF *CHRISTOS*
IN THE HELLENISTIC CHURCH

What could be more ironic than the fate of the term *Christos* in the early church? Beginning as a title in the Palestinian church (although of lesser significance than that of Son of Man), in the Greek-speaking church, where the translation is meaningless, it became so popular that it lost its significance as a title! In the Gospel traditions, even including the final authors, the titular meaning of *Christos* is maintained. What happened to it in the Hellenistic church?

A nearly equally ironic chuckle is caused by the chagrin of scholars. We do not know the answer to the question raised above. There is a gaping hole in our data. We know the history of the term in the Gospel tradition; we know that for Paul, our earliest reference to the Hellenistic church, the term has no apparent titular significance.[1] That Paul *knew* the titular meaning is hard to doubt.[2] That he uses *Christos* as a title in his own theological reflections is doubtful. We do not know explicitly how or why the term was transferred from the Palestinian context to the Greek or why there it became so popular, when reason militates against such popularity. As already mentioned, its primary functions in the Palestinian churches were (1) to denote a thaumaturgic person and (2) to be a tool in the argument with the non-believing Jews about the significance of Jesus. As we have already seen from the Cosmocrator trajectory, the Hellenistic church placed no emphasis upon the life of Jesus and there is no evidence it had the slightest interest in Jesus as a wonder-worker. Furthermore, there is little evidence (apart from Acts) that the Hellenistic church engaged in disputes with the synagogue using the term *Christos*. To that one could add the perplexity of a Greek in hearing the term itself. "Jesus the anointed" would have sounded quaint. Small wonder that an outsider could mistake the word for the more familiar *chrēstos*.[3]

The purpose of this chapter is not to attempt to replicate the labors of other scholars. The chasm caused by the lack of data cannot be crossed with any assurance. I do have at least a hunch and will explore that below. Nor will I assess the theological meaning of the term in the Hellenistic church, because that would mean dealing with the larger christological meanings assigned to the act of God in Jesus. In this instance, the meaning of a name is given by its bearer, not the reverse. I consider it primarily my responsibility to chronicle as briefly as possible the term's appearance and popularity throughout the Greek church and to explore the possibility that there is some possibility of understanding the perplexities. To return to the theme of irony: I will try to indicate how the title is *meaningless* because its use is so *ever present*.[4]

The Evidence

The word (I choose this term as a neutral one) *Christos* occurs in a bewildering variety of ways and combinations.[5] The order "Jesus Christ" is not as frequent as one might suppose, but it is obviously important. More frequent, especially in Paul, is the order "Christ Jesus," though perhaps determined by grammatical priorities.[6] "Christ" alone is even more popular. With some regularity the larger phrase "Lord Jesus Christ" is used, and, occasionally, other variants.[7] While scholars have struggled to assign meanings to these differences in usage, by and large, the judgment that the variations are stylistic rather than theological seems appropriate.[8]

To put the conventions of usage by the Hellenistic church into some perspective, one could ask, What happened to "Jesus" as a proper name? In general the church apparently found that "Jesus" without some accompanying word was not suitable. We find "Jesus" alone in Acts and in Hebrews, but only rarely elsewhere. The call on the name of Jesus in Philippians 2:10 is a dramatic exception. That Paul bears on his body the marks of Jesus is a well-known, but also rare exception. Why was the name Jesus without accompaniment not fitting? One can only speculate. The likelihood that seems to me at hand is the lack of interest in the earthly Jesus throughout the Hellenistic church. Just as it did not incorporate stories and sayings of the earthly Jesus, it seems to have felt that the earthly person, known by the simple name "Jesus," was not adequate as a pointer to their faith in the resurrected and enthroned Lord.[9]

The rejoinder immediately comes, however, that the name Jesus was not forgotten. It is safely and frequently enshrined in "Jesus Christ," "Christ Jesus," "Lord Jesus," and "Lord Jesus Christ." This means that, for example, "Jesus Christ" is an appropriate term for the resurrected one, but not "Jesus" alone. Were there that many "Jesuses" in the Hellenistic world that *Christos*, as a proper name, was necessary to denote which Jesus? That seems unlikely.[10] Is there some additional weight to *Christos* or *kyrios*, however dimly felt, that added the needed emphasis to make them an appropriate designation of the resurrected Lord? The logical answer to that question seems to be yes. What that weight might have been is not, alas, recoverable. We have the "fact" that *Christos*, originally a title, but meaningless in the Hellenistic world, becomes a name of the resurrected Lord—and yet a name that is more fitting than the "real" name, Jesus. Some reality lurks in this antinomy that needs to come to light. I do not think we have the data to resolve the difficulty. There are too many questions and not enough evidence.[11]

The Title in the Liturgies

First, a brief look at the use of *Christos* in the liturgical formulas is both needed and interesting. In general the formulas sit loose to any title or name. Frequently the fragments we have do not name Jesus or any "title"; the indication that the formula is speaking about Jesus has to be given by the author using the passage (e.g., 1 Tim 3:16). The major exception to this is the hymn in Philippians 2:6-11, where both the "name of Jesus" and the acclamation "Lord Jesus Christ" appear at the climax of the hymn. It is clearly the act of God in Jesus that gives meaning to the names and titles, not the reverse.

The appearance of *kyrios Iēsous Christos* in Philippians 2, however, does give us one sure anchor for that phrase. This sonorous combination, which occurs 30 times in the documents I have analyzed (cf. note 5 above), is clearly the fulsome acclamatory phrase given in the church to celebrate the significance of Jesus. As I explained in chapter 2, an acclamation was a phrase, repeated over and over, in a public setting to honor a god or goddess, a military hero, or emperor.[12] In the Philippians hymn, the acclamation is uttered by those doing obeisance to the resurrected Jesus—presumably the powers and principalities of the cosmos, now subordinated to the newly enthroned Lord. One could also suppose that the believers who sang the hymn also participated in the acclamation.

This same phrase appears often at the beginning and end of the epistolary documents and at places that are designed to recall the basic faith object of the church.[13] Since the acclamatory phrase almost always appears in this order, i.e., "Lord Jesus Christ," it seems certain that this was the standard order of the acclamation.[14] Its function in the documents is to recall the readers or hearers to their faith professed in the acclamation, most likely in a liturgical setting. In this traditional order, *kyrios* is probably the ruling term. That is, the "office" of Lord is filled by Jesus Christ. I argued above that the office is a cosmic one. The Lord denotes not simply the ruler of the church but more grandly the ruler of the cosmos. The person Jesus Christ now, by virtue of resurrection and enthronement, holds that office. Thus the title in the acclamation is *kyrios* not *Christos*; the latter is part of the name of the holder. The order gives a hint that the normal naming was "Jesus Christ," not "Christ Jesus," despite the frequency of the latter.

No one should doubt, however, that great variety is the rule rather than some universal conformity. As soon as the above paragraph is taken to be the "norm," a variance comes to mind. In the apparent formula in 1 Timothy 2:5 we hear, "one God, and one mediator between God and persons, the man Christ Jesus."[15] Here the order seems reversed and, indeed, to have influenced the author's use of the terms. He prefers "Christ Jesus" over "Jesus Christ" nine to one.

Evidence from Paul

The evidence in the liturgical fragments gives no support for belief that *Christos* bears titular significance in the Hellenistic environment. But what do the Pauline epistles suggest in support or in refutation of this supposition? The same variety of uses appears in Paul as in all the Hellenistic materials. There is no obvious difference between the Pauline letters and other documents in this regard. All—or almost all—of the Pauline writings are to be dated in the 50s. Even if 1 Thessalonians is earlier than the others, it is not by much. More importantly, there seems to be no difference between that writing and the other authentic letters.[15] We can thus start with a fairly firm judgment: *by the decade of the 50s, the usage in the Hellenistic churches seems to have been set.* The end of the trajectory, not some presumed middle stage, is exemplified in Paul. By the time of the 50s, *Christos* no longer functions as a title. What may have been the case earlier can only, perhaps, be gleaned from Acts, a suggestion to be discussed below.

What makes this hard to accept is awareness that Paul *had* to know that *Christos* was a title.[16] Scholars have thus often been unwilling to accept the likelihood that the word does not function titularly for him. That *Christos* has no functional significance as a title for Paul is clear, even if vestiges of an earlier titular meaning shine through in the Pauline syntax. Thus little is to be gained by seeking out possible vestiges. I will, however, follow Kramer in his discussion of some scholarly suggestions, just in order to indicate how the arguments run.[17]

1. In a brief aside Oscar Cullmann once said that the order *Christos Iēsous* indicated that Paul knew *Christos* as a title.[18] Paul thus speaks of Messiah Jesus. The statistics show that this order occurs more frequently in Paul than that of *Iēsous Christos*.[19] W. Kramer has reasonably argued, however, that Paul's usage is determined by a grammatical, not theological reason. The noun *Christos* is fully declinable, while *Iēsous* is not. The latter is spelled the same in genitive and dative cases. In order to make clear which case the phrase is in, Paul uses *Christos* first. The statistics

Kramer has marshaled seem convincing. The great majority of instances of the order *Christos Iēsous* are in genitive constructions and dative with prepositions.[20] Thus one cannot argue that *Christos Iēsous* has to be translated "Messiah Jesus."

2. A second argument begins from the observation that at times Paul uses *Christos* with the definite article, and at times not. Is it possible that the articular *Christos* is thus titular—as in "*the* Messiah"? Again Kramer shows that a grammatical reason may explain the difference.[21] He shows that in almost all instances of articular *Christos* in Paul, it is in relation to a determinative noun that has the article. In almost all instances of anarthrous *Christos*, it is in relation to a determinative noun that is also anarthrous. Thus the great majority of instances can be explained as Paul's sense that the nouns should agree, either as articular or as anarthrous.

How then does Kramer deal with the seven instances where articular *Christos* appears in the nominative?[22] Here there can be no grammatical rule to fall back on. His general argument is that, with the exception of Romans 9:5, there is nothing in the content that would indicate that *Christos* carries significance as "Messiah." Again, I would argue that the proof is in the *function*. If *Christos* were taken to be titular, would it change the meaning of the sentence? Kramer argues that it would not.

What conclusions can one draw? Kramer is clear: "In the Pauline period *Christ* was for Gentile Christians the name of him in whom the saving events, death and resurrection, took place."[23] The evidence forces me to agree with Kramer. There is no clear evidence, apart from Acts, that *Christos* ever is used as a title for Jesus in the Hellenistic church—at least one that might carry over from Jewish tradition. There is no evidence that the meaning of *Christos* as a title has been metamorphosed into a new reality. The simplest conclusion to draw is that in the documents we possess, *Christos* functions as a name, a word that points to the person in whom God has acted. And yet there is the uneasy feeling that the joining of *Iēsous* with *Christos* suggests that *Christos* gives weight to the name *Iēsous* that the latter name alone does not have. This may indeed point to some point of transfer from the Palestinian church to the Hellenistic.[24]

Why the word became so popular and pervasive in Hellenistic Christianity also has no answer that satisfies. Granted that it has no obvious titular significance, why did the word become so omnipresent as indication of the person in whom God acted? Was it simply the Greek insistence that a one-named person is not adequate? Once *Christos* is there for the taking, there is no inherent unlikeliness in such a process. That does not explain, however, the frequent use of *Christos* solo. Nor does the lack of a titular meaning take anything away from the church's confession of the act of God in the resurrected Lord. In whatever guise, any meaning the *Christos* title had was not appropriate for Jesus and was soon left behind. It is now the church's confession of the meaning of God's act that determines what is said about Jesus.

There is, however, a possibility that the lost stage of transmission is given us by the author of Acts. And it makes obvious sense. I have acknowledged that *Christos* has titular meaning in the Palestinian cultural environment. I have concluded that by the time we see evidence of its use in Gentile settings, it has no titular significance. That leaves one intervening stage: the Hellenistic synagogue. Our extant non-Gospel literature seems to be Gentile-oriented. We have no direct window to missionary activity to the Hellenistic synagogue. Could this be the location in which *Christos* as a title found its way into Hellenistic culture, there established itself, only to lose its titular significance when the Hellenistic church became largely Gentile? A careful inspection of Acts gives reason to think that this might have been the case—at least to think that the author of Acts presents such a scenario as what happened.

Acts

On the surface, *Christos* appears in the book of Acts in the same profusion of variety that is exhibited elsewhere.[25] A number of decades ago, however, H. Cadbury said that there were patterns discernible in the apparent profusions. He argued for two proposals: (1) that *Christos* was almost always titular in Acts, and (2) that its occurrences were mostly in what I shall call Jewish contexts rather than in Greek contexts.[26] Both of these proposals are, I think, accurate. Indeed, his second proposal turns out to be confirmed and even strengthened by my analyses.

Of the twenty-four instances of *Christos* in Acts, seventeen occur in Jewish contexts and seven in Gentile contexts. It is necessary first to look at the seven Gentile usages. Of the seven, five are formulaic. Three of these are the full acclamation, *kyrios Iēsous Christos*, which we find everywhere in the literature.[27] Two are "in the name of *Iēsous Christos*.[28] The remaining two are unusual.

In his speech at Cornelius's house Peter says the following: "You know the word that he [God] sent to Israel, preaching good news of peace by Jesus Christ (he is the Lord of all)." The phrase "preaching good news of peace" is itself remarkable, let alone the addition "by" (or "through"—the word is *dia*) Jesus Christ. What follows this sentence is a typical recap of Jesus' earthly ministry, death, and resurrection. How the notion of peace is associated with Jesus' ministry is unclear, but we can leave that unattended. The obviously added phrase "he is the Lord of all" is not to be questioned, but its function in the speech is unclear. Again, we can leave that aside.

The simple phrase "by Jesus Christ" is unusual both in the preposition and in the instance of "Jesus Christ" in a non-formulaic context. Here is one time I am not sure that *Christos* is titular; nothing in the surrounding text necessitates that.[29] But what is most important for our investigation is the question whether the phrase really belongs in a Gentile context. Peter is here recapping what was proclaimed to Israel—and what he has said in earlier speeches to a Jewish audience. In this sense the passage is not really a Gentile context at all. These verses have many interesting and perhaps important queries I must leave unaddressed. The key passage leaves much in ambiguity—most especially whether the context is really Gentile at all.

The second unusual instance appears in 24:24. Felix, the procurator, and his wife, Drusilla (specifically said here to be a Jew), call Paul and listen to him "speak upon [the] faith in *Christos Iēsous*." The textual problems are difficult.[30] If we accept the reading quoted above, it is the *only* instance in Acts of this order. The reading *Christos* alone has strong support and is more in line with other uses in Acts. Regardless of the textual decision, this verse instances *Christos*. In the narrative "(the) faith in Christ [Jesus]" is the author's shorthand way of alluding to the subject of the discussion among Felix, Drusilla, and Paul. Given the larger context (Felix is trying to understand the hostility of the Jews toward Paul) and the smaller one (one of the discussants is Jewish), Acts may intend us to assume that the discussion revolved around the debate in Jewish culture about whether Jesus was the Messiah or not.

Christos also appears in Jewish contexts. The few instances of *Christos* in Gentile contexts are either formulaic or have unusual features that preclude any sense that *Christos* had a particular meaning in the Gentile context. What is clear, however, is that Acts' use of *Christos* in Jewish contexts is specific and titular.

Two of the instances may be exceptions to the general preference. Both of them are healings. In 3:6 Peter heals the lame man "in the name of Jesus Christ the Nazarene." That the healing is done in the name of Jesus Christ is not unusual, but formulaic. Nor is it certain in this formula that *Christos* is titular. Suspicion about this is increased with the addition of "the Nazarene," which certainly refers back to Jesus. If *Christos* had titular force, the healing could have been done "in the name of Jesus Christ the resurrected"—or something similar indicating the force of *Christos*. In all likelihood, *Christos* is here a name. This instance may give a clue that all of the formulas involving the name of Jesus Christ are to be similarly interpreted. The second healing reads somewhat differently. Peter says to Aeneas, according to the context a Jewish believer in Jesus, "Jesus Christ heals you." While the "name" does not appear here, it seems likely that Peter's words are equivalent to "In the name of Jesus Christ."

All of the remaining occurrences in Jewish contexts are arguments or claims that Jesus is the Messiah. That is, the great majority of uses occur in debates, explicitly or implicitly, with Jews about the significance of Jesus—and these debates all focus around the title *Christos*, i.e., Messiah. Seven occur in actual speeches in debates with Jews.[31] Eight appear in summaries of debates.

- 5:42. They (in the context, "all the apostles") speak in the temple that "Jesus is the *Christos*."[32]

- 8:5. Philip preaches to the Samaritans "*ton Christon.*" It must be kept in mind that the Samaritans are in fact Jews.

- 8:12. The Samaritans believed Philip who preached to them about "the kingdom of God and the name of Jesus Christ." The phrase is unusual—kingdom of God rarely appears in Acts and the "name" is rarely the object of preaching. For the moment, however, one can acknowledge that Jesus Christ is the object of the preaching. That the occurrences of "in the name of Jesus Christ" are ambiguous as to the titular significance of *Christos* should give some pause about being too confident that *Christos* in 8:12 is titular. If it is, it is supportive of my general argument. If it isn't, it does not detract.

- 9:22. Paul argues with the Jews in Damascus that "*houtos estin ho Christos.*" The context supplies the antecedent of *houtos* as Jesus (although one has to go back to v. 20 to find it).

- 17:3 (twice). Paul is arguing in the synagogue in Thessalonica. He claims that the *Christos* had to suffer and that the *Christos* is the Jesus he is proclaiming.

- 18:5. Paul argues with the Jews in Corinth that "Jesus is the *Christos.*"

- 18:28. Apollos confronts the Jews in Corinth (?) with the claim that Jesus is the *Christos.*

The consistency of these speeches and summaries in the use of the title *Christos* is impressive. Apart from the formulaic use of *Christos* in Gentile contexts, virtually all of the uses of the term appear in either claims before Jews that Jesus *is* the Messiah, or in direct argument with Jews. The summaries make it clear that the Jews are arguing against the possibility that Jesus might have been the Messiah. The author of Acts seems well aware that the title functioned in actuality as a nodal point in argument with Jews—as I have attempted to show in the Gospel material. He relegates the *title* to the past, however, and does not use it as a central title of Jesus in the contemporary Gentile churches. Its role is limited to formularies. Is this a reason why in the Pauline literature, addressed mostly to Gentiles, that *Christos* as a title seems absent?

The Uses of *Kyrios Iēsous*

H. Cadbury also made another proposal that bears upon the location (in this case its absence) of *Christos*. He argued that *within* the believing community, the term was never *Christos*, but *kyrios Iēsous*. If this can be confirmed, then it demonstrates another boundary in the use of *Christos*. Not only is *Christos* used in dialogue with unbelieving Jews, it is not used as a term to refer to Jesus within the community itself. I believe Cadbury is basically correct in his claim, although there are a few instances where the boundary is not as clear as it might be.

Acts has fourteen, or possibly fifteen, occurrences of *kyrios Iēsous*.[33] All of the instances (with the exception of 20:21 and 7:59) use the words "the Lord Jesus" with the definite article and without a possessive modifier. In 7:59 Stephen sees the Son of Man in heaven and cries out in the vocative, "Lord Jesus, receive my spirit." This use is not unrelated to two occurrences in Paul in which the context is also acclamation and the title occurs without the definite article (Rom 10:9; 1 Cor 12:3).

Of these fourteen sure instances, all, with three exceptions, occur in contexts either within the community[34] or in missionizing situations.[35] The first exception I have already mentioned—that of Stephen's cry in 7:59. While the context is a hostile, Jewish one, Stephen's acclamation fits within the believing situation. The other two exceptions occur in the story of the seven itinerant Jewish exorcists. The actual phrase, *kyrios Iēsous*, occurs both times in the narrative. In v. 13 the narrator informs the reader that these exorcists were healing by "naming the name of the Lord Jesus." In the summary of the reaction of the city, both Jews and Greeks "magnify the name of the Lord Jesus." When the exorcists speak, however, they do not use the title "Lord Jesus" but rather that of "Jesus" alone (identified with the preaching of Paul).

We can be satisfied, I think, in concluding that in all instances in Acts, "*Christos*" occurs either in acclamations or in dialogue with unbelieving Jews, while "Lord Jesus" mostly is used within and on the lips of the believing community members. Clearly the author of Acts knows the difference and is faithful in his use of the terms.

The difficult question is how to assess any presumed historical information in Acts. The battle still rages as to whether Acts can be used to mine historical data or whether the book essentially presents the mind of the author, writing about 100 C.E. I myself have tended to dismiss serious claims that Acts is, even in part, a book of history. The author's political and theological tendencies have seemed to dominate the author descriptions.

And yet, what are we to make of the careful distinctions in terminology with regard to *Christos* that are clearly there in the text? I confess that they fit so perfectly with the other evidence I have presented that, in this area, the author seems to be accurate in his limitation of the term *Christos* to debates between believing missionaries and unbelieving Jews, both in Palestine and in the Diaspora synagogue. At the same time, it has to be admitted that his memory, if that is what it is, extends back for fifty to sixty years. Where did he obtain this information and why does he bother to follow the distinction so consistently? Does it serve his political and theological interests? I do not see that it does.

No one, I think, doubts that the author does have accurate information at many points, even if the basic thrust of the book's argument serves his sense of need at the end of the first century. The coherence of his use of *Christos* with the use I have seen in the Gospels leads me to conclude that here is another instance of accurate historical memory.

Colossians

Colossians, the next book in this "trench study," quite clearly has a different context from the Acts, and this may explain why the author's uses of *Christos* vary considerably from that of Acts. For the latter, Jesus was a human being who was vindicated by God and will return at the eschaton. For the author of Colossians, Jesus has been resurrected into a "cosmic" or "spatial" divine reality. Furthermore, Acts is well aware, as I have shown, of the early disputes with unbelieving Jews about the messiah. For Colossians such memories are not in view.

In Colossians, the name "Jesus" does not appear without an accompanying word. "Jesus Christ" does not occur. The word *Christos* alone has become the dominant name for Jesus (eighteen out of twenty-four occurrences).[36] None of these uses are in any context that might suggest debate with unbelieving Jews. Articular use outweighs anarthrous, but not in any significant measure (10 to 7, with 2:2 uncertain).

Christos is here the name for the exalted "spatial" reality of God. Believers are "in Christ"; they have died with Christ; they have been raised with Christ; they are hidden with Christ; Christ is the mystery of God; Christ bestows peace, has the word, is the true circumcision—to name most of the functions of this spatial reality in relation to the believer. The word "Christ" is the name for this unique reality, into which believers are incorporated and by which they are to live their lives on earth. Yes, this reality is also *kyrios*, but the simple name "Jesus" no longer fits this cosmic reality. The name *Christos* has been completely transformed from its original meaning of "messiah."

Hebrews

A first glance at the statistics might seem to place the usage of Hebrews in close relation to that of Colossians. There are twelve occurrences of *Christos* in the treatise, and nine of them occur without any other accompanying word.[37] This is comparable to the eighteen (out of twenty-four) solo appearances of *Christos* in Colossians. A second glance, however, highlights the difference between the two writers. While the author of Colossians never uses "Jesus" unaccompanied by another word, in Hebrews the single "Jesus" occurs eight times,[38] that is, virtually the same number of times as the solo *Christos*.

Is there, then, a distinction in the function of the two names for Jesus? Does "Jesus" occur when the earthly manifestation of God's agent is being described, with *Christos* reserved for the resurrected, exalted, high priest?[39] When one thinks of the most familiar phrases in the treatise, such a distinction might seem to hold. "But we see Jesus, who for a little while was made lower than the angels . . ." (2:9); "So Jesus also suffered outside the gate . . ." (13:12).

A close comparison of the functions of the two words, however, belies such a simple distinction. The usage is actually very fluid, and ultimately it does not seem to me that the author makes a clear distinction. Even in the passage first quoted above, Jesus was indeed made lower than the angels, but Jesus is immediately said to be crowned with glory and honor—obviously referring to the resurrection. One remembers also 12:2, where the author writes that Jesus endured the cross, but then is said to be seated at the right hand of God. Other comparisons bear out this fluidity. In 3:6 Christ is said to be Son of God; in 4:14, it is Jesus who is Son of God. In 9:14 it is the blood of Christ; in 10:19, the blood of Jesus. In 5:5 Christ is appointed high priest, and in 9:24 Christ entered the sanctuary. Yet in 6:20 it is Jesus who has entered the shrine, "having become a high priest forever after the order of Melchizedek." The interchangeability of the two words is illustrated by the passage 5:5-10, where both "*Christos*" and "Jesus" are used.

While there may be an inclination by the author to use "Jesus" when he begins with some description of the earthly life, the fluidity of the passing from earthly to resurrected functions and the interchangeability of the two words indicates that *Christos* is in this treatise a proper name. In fact, more clearly than in any document we have looked at so far, the treatise exhibits an author for whom *Christos* has no remaining titular significance.

First Timothy

The variety of expression exhibited above continues in 1 Timothy. *Christos* occurs fifteen times in the document. The author cites the full acclamation four times.[40] Once the word appears alone, in a rather strange expression.[41]

The author obviously prefers the term *Christos Iēsous*. Excluding the highly uncertain textual evidence for the order of the words in 1:16, all the remaining uses of *Christos* occur in the order "Christ Jesus" (eight times). All of the nine are completely anarthrous. Five are in the genitive, without preposition; two are governed by the preposition *en*; two are in the nominative. Clearly, "Christ Jesus" is the author's name for God's agent.[42] *Iēsous* does not appear in the epistle independently of *Christos*. There are no indications, as far as I can see, that *Christos* has any titular significance.

Of perhaps particular interest is the possible formula cited in 2:5:

> one God and one mediator between God and persons,
>   the person Christ Jesus,
>   who gave himself as a ransom for all.

For my purposes the interest lies in the order "Christ Jesus." If this is the order in the original formula, then it demonstrates a location in the early church where Christ Jesus was accepted, as the author of 1 Timothy does, as the order of the proper name. At any rate, by the beginning of the second century, there were many "locations" of early Christianity and seemingly as many choices made as to how to name God's agent.

First Peter

With this circular letter I have reached the end of my trench study of the uses of *Christos* in the non-Gospel literature. In addition to key documents of Paul, I looked carefully at Acts and made more cursory comments on Colossians, Hebrews, and 1 Timothy. First Peter is usually located toward the end of the first century in Asia Minor.[43] If this is the correct location, then it probably belongs in roughly the same time and space as 1 Timothy and Colossians. Written in the name of Peter, it reflects Pauline-school vocabulary and theological interests, as well as, in the judgment of many scholars, echoes and reflections of liturgical material. Thus it may represent a view of what Christianity in this time and space was becoming, or had become. In short, it may be a "consensus" document.

Its predilections for the use of *Christos* are startlingly clear. Only one appearance of the full acclamation exists (1:3). Otherwise the remaining twenty occurrences are divided into two categories: "Jesus Christ," eight times; "Christ" without an additional word, twelve times.[44]

Can any distinctions be made between these two ways of pointing to God's agent? One factor is striking. The majority of instances of "Jesus Christ" occur in the earlier part of the document (five out of eight in chap. 1), while the majority of occurrences of "Christ" solo are in chapters 3–5 (eight out of twelve). On the assumption that the document is heavily dependent on traditions, would the usage in 1 Peter reflect two different kinds of tradition?

It is also the case that six of the twelve uses of "Christ" alone refer in one way or another to the suffering of Jesus. For those who tend to identify the use of *Christos* for reference to Jesus' suffering and death, this is supportive evidence. The arguments are difficult whichever way one inclines.[45] One has to take seriously that fact that half of the uses of *Christos* solo do *not* relate to suffering. Thus I do not see any serious evidence that would indicate that *Christos* still had titular echoes in the document. The conclusion that seems most likely to me is that the author reflects both "Jesus Christ" and "Christ" solo as normal ways of referring to Jesus. That is, in the document *Christos* is a name, not a title.[46]

Conclusions

To say the least, any conclusions maintained must be tentative. Even worse, there are hardly any generalized conclusions possible; for every one stated, there is at least one document that shows such generalization not to be universal. I list below what seems *most often* the case, then will show exceptions.

The basic question is: what words does the early church use to signal that man, raised by God, who is believed to be God's agent of salvation? His human name is *Jesus* (of Nazareth). He was early on claimed by some Jewish believers to be the *Christos*. In Palestinian communities he was honored as *Son of Man*. He was confessed to be *kyrios*. My brief look at usages in Hellenistic Christianity shows that, with the exception of "Son of Man," all of the other words were used either solo or in some combination. Are there any patterns that emerge?

1. The actual name "Jesus" by itself does not seem to have been a term felt usable when speaking of God's powerful act. The exception is, of course, Hebrews, where "Jesus" occurs as frequently as "*Christos*," and not always in connection simply with his earthly life. Elsewhere "Jesus" obviously is felt usable in combinations with *Christos* and *kyrios*. The question I raised, but cannot answer, is whether this suggests that *Christos* still has lingering titular significance, such that believers felt it was appropriate to talk about God's agent as *Jesus Christos* or *Christos Jesus*, or *kyrios Jesus*, but not simply as *Jesus*.

2. The full acclamation, *kyrios Iēsous Christos,* occurs not frequently but consistently through most of the documents. That one finds it mostly at the beginning and end of documents suggests what is apparent, that it is a solemn phrase but perhaps too cumbersome to use in interior arguments and descriptions. This conclusion certainly holds for the Pauline documents themselves and 1 Timothy. Before one gets too comfortable, however, it should be pointed out that Colossians has only one instance, as does 1 Peter, while the acclamation is lacking altogether in Hebrews. Was it, for whatever reason, beginning to lose its function in later documents?

3. In all of the epistolary documents it does not seem to me that *Christos* functions as a title. Who can be sure of that? No one, of course, and Kramer is surely correct in pointing out Romans 9:5 as at least one instance where Paul shows he knows well the titular significance of *Christos*. But in general, whether the author prefers *Christos* solo, or *Iēsous Christos*, or *Christos Iēsous*, the function of the words seems to point to God's agent. Of course, the author attaches ultimate significance to this agent. The point is that the significance is denoted by what the author says God has done in and through this agent, not in the words themselves.

4. At the same time, it must be the case that all the authors in question know that *Christos* is, or was, a title, before it became a proper name. Paul is the obvious exemplar of such an author. It makes absolutely no sense to imagine that Paul was oblivious to the titular origin of *Christos*. Even without the evidence of Romans 9:5, our knowledge of Paul as a bilingual Jewish intellectual would have to mean that he knew the Hebrew origin of *Christos* and what that Hebrew signified. Paul, and the other authors in our trench study, thus must have known exactly what they give no evidence of knowing. They choose not to use *Christos* as a title, even though they know that that is what it was. The reason would seem to be that for the audience of Hellenistic Christianity, *Christos* as a title made little sense and had no significance.

In this regard there is an interesting comparison/contrast with "Son of Man." Both "Son of Man" and *Christos* are titles sensible to those embedded in Palestinian Jewish culture. They are useless in the Hellenistic missionary program of the churches. In the sense of function, both titles have equally been replaced. Yet Son of Man virtually completely disappears, while *Christos* retains presence as a name. How is this to be explained? One obvious explanation is that Son of Man can hardly function as a name.[47] *Christos* can, even if it must have sounded peculiar to Greek ears.

But the primary reason may lie in the situation narrated in the book of Acts. There we saw that *Christos* retained its titular sense precisely when we are shown instances of arguments between Jewish believers and unbelievers about the significance of Jesus. In these arguments the issue is whether Jesus is or is not the Messiah. Thus it is in this context that *Christos* retained its vitality and precisely as a title. The evidence in Acts also explains why *Christos* "translated" into Hellenistic Christianity while Son of Man did not. Acts shows that the arguments about the messiahship of Jesus occurred in Diaspora synagogues as well as in Palestinian Judaism. Acts doesn't say, but it seems reasonable to think that the title Son of Man was too esoteric and too embedded in Palestinian culture to have been known or worth arguing about in Greek culture. *Christos*, however, was another matter.

If I had to hazard a history of the word *Christos*, it would be something like the following. While "messiah" was not the primary title that moved Palestinian believers to believe that Jesus was (or would be) God's eschatological act, it did emerge as of some importance, perhaps because it had become linked in some way with thaumaturgic activity.

When arguments emerged between Jewish believers and their unbelieving co-religionists, the conflict seems to have revolved around the title *Christos* rather than that of Son of Man. The Gospel of John, as well as Acts, strongly suggests such a scenario. When the mission moves to Diaspora synagogues, the argument about messiahship continues and hence so does the title *Christos*.

The third stage occurs once the missionaries turn their attention to Gentiles. By now the title *Christos* has become a fixture in the argument with Hellenistic Jews. With Gentiles, however, the argument is not necessary or relevant and does not occur. Probably the title *kyrios* becomes the meaningful title carrying some of the freight of *Christos*. At any rate, *Christos* is not used by authors like Paul as a title because it is no longer necessary or functioning. That Paul knows the titular sense of *Christos* is hardly to be doubted. Probably after twenty years of using *Christos* in a non-titular manner, even someone like Paul does not think of it very often as a title. Even for Paul, *kyrios* has become the title of use.

Excursus: Justin's *Dialogue with Trypho*

While no New Testament text spells out the content of the argument with Jews about Jesus as *Christos*, there is one text in which the argument is so detailed as to elicit yawns from today's readers—the second-century "report" of a long discussion between the Christian Justin Martyr and the Jew Trypho. While it is difficult to think it is a report of an actual debate, supposedly in the late 130s,[48] the text does give us the kind of argument that Justin knows Christians used in the mid-second century to try to prove their case that Jesus is indeed the *Christos*. It serves, thus, as a text that reflects second-century ideas and should be used with great caution to fill in the gaps of such mentions in Acts, for example, of believers (in this case, Apollos) who "powerfully confuted the Jews in public, showing by the scriptures that the Christ was Jesus" (Acts 18:28). The arguments, for example, that the *Christos* was preexistent and could be called *theos* are probably much later than the mid-first century, reflecting later christological developments within Christian circles. Nevertheless, used with the appropriate caveats, this text may give us some idea of the kinds of arguments used at an earlier time than Justin himself.

In this excursus I will sketch the content of the arguments, without detailing the ingenuity that Justin uses to find support for his positions in Scripture. I am concerned here only with the kinds of argument adduced, and specifically those associated with the title *Christos* (and occasionally relating to Son of Man).[49] I will also follow the argument as it unfolds in the text. Justin has created a narrative, and one must assume that Justin lets the argument flow in the order acceptable to him.

Justin begins his christological argument in chapter 7. He initiates it with an appeal to the biblical prophets, who made known *Christos*, God's Son who was sent by God. Justin says that knowing the truths about God requires that God take the initiative in making himself "and his *Christos* known."[50] In chapter 8 Justin encourages Trypho to become a Christian. Trypho retorts that the proper way to God is through Torah. He speaks diffidently of the notion of *Christos*, maintaining that even if the *Christos* is alive, he does not know that he is and will not until Elijah anoints him. From Trypho's point of view, arguing the truth of religion by arguing about *Christos* is not important. What is important is following God's laws. It may not be accidental to the perspectives of both sides to see that it is the Christian who has introduced the notion of *Christos* into the discussion, not the Jew.

On the other hand, it is Trypho who raises the issue of Christians believing in a *crucified* man (chap. 10). Justin gladly accepts this challenge in chapter 11, even rubbing it in, perhaps, by calling Jesus *staurōthenton Christon*.

It is in chapter 14 that Justin introduces what amounts to his key weapon: the notion of the two appearances (*parousiai*) of the *Christos*. The first *parousia* is the *Christos* coming in lowliness and disgrace; the second, his coming in (eschatological) glory. With this ploy (which, so far as I see, Justin never derives from Scripture), Justin can now cover both fronts—the apparent disgrace of a crucified man and the claims of a resurrected glory for Jesus, especially at the eschaton. Some passages in the Scriptures "refer to the first coming [*parousia*] of *Christos*, in which he is described as coming in disgrace, obscurity, and mortality; other passages allude to his second coming, when he shall appear from the clouds in glory." With this theory, Justin can "explain" both the historical record of disgrace and the Christian claim of resurrection and future coming in power. He "explains" this, of course, by finding passages in Scripture that support both kinds of evidence.

The next chapters deal with topics ostensibly distinct (such as issues of Torah) from the christological debate up to chapter 14. But in chapter 30, Justin argues that the Christian *Christos* has power over demons and ties this up with the crucified Jesus. In chapter 31, he argues from the lesser to the greater: "If such power is shown to have accompanied and still now accompanies his passion, just think how great shall be his power at his glorious advent." Immediately (in chap. 31) he adduces Daniel 7: "He shall come on the clouds as the Son of Man, accompanied by his angels." Trypho takes the bait (chap. 32). He acknowledges that Daniel 7 makes one anticipate the coming of "that glorious and great one, who, as Son of Man, will receive the eternal kingdom from the ancient of days."[51] He then contrasts this glorious Son of Man with the Christian *Christos* who was cursed by crucifixion. Justin is, not surprisingly, ready to pounce on this distinction with his theory of the two comings, one in disgrace and one in glory. He refers to the resurrection claims of Christians. God has resurrected Jesus "and placed him at his right hand, until he makes his enemies his footstool" (Ps. 110, the favorite text of early Christian exegesis).

By chapter 36, Trypho, overwhelmed by bombardment of Scripture, is ready to concede the two-comings theory of Justin. His demand now becomes: Show us that "your Jesus"[52] "is the one about whom these prophecies were spoken." With this the argument should take a different direction, but Justin ignores the implication. Although he says more than once (cf. chap. 39) that he will answer Trypho's question, he never does (how could he or anyone?). Justin conveniently has his own agenda, which pushes Trypho's question aside.

After several further chapters of scriptural citations, both Justin and Trypho seem to have forgotten the question of chapters 36 and 39. In chapter 48, Trypho questions Christian claims that "the Christ" preexisted and was "God," then became human through a virgin birth. Such claims are "foolish" (*mōron*). Justin concedes that he may not be able to "prove" such claims—in part, perhaps, because he also has to acknowledge that not all Christians believe such doctrines either. He adamantly distinguishes between the basic claim that Jesus is God's *Christos* (*touton einai Christon tou theou*), which is not demolished even if he cannot prove the more esoteric doctrines.

In chapter 49, Trypho, not surprisingly, rejects any view of the *Christos* that is more than human. To this the Jew adds (repeating his first statement in chap. 8) that Elijah has to come to anoint him. The logic seems simple: since Elijah has not come, Jesus is not the *Christos*. By now the reader will anticipate Justin's reply. The coming of Elijah belongs to the second *parousia*; therefore, of course it hasn't happened yet.

In chapter 50 Trypho wants to hear Justin's arguments that there is "another God besides the creator of the world" (*allos theos para ton poiētēn tōn holōn*), and that the scripture predicts the virgin birth of the Messiah. Justin is in no hurry, however, and does not frontally consider the issue until chapter 61—again with esoteric scriptural arguments. First come arguments about divinity and preexistence. By chapter 63 Trypho professes to be convinced and now wants to hear arguments for the virgin birth. It is not necessary or possible to repeat Justin's "proofs" here. I do wish, however, to point to one glaring inconsistency in Justin's argument, primarily because it has to do with the Son of Man passage in Daniel 7 (chap. 76). The fact that Daniel's language is "*as* a Son of Man" indicates, Justin thinks, that he was like a human, but was not born of human seed.

Elsewhere Justin was forced to claim this passage belonged to the *second* coming; here, he uses it to refer to the *first*.

Although the *Dialogue* continues for many more pages, the christological argument at this point is, as far as I can see, completed. I want to try to sort out and summarize the views of both sides, insofar as I can.

Trypho

1. It is Justin who introduces the issue of *Christos*. Trypho himself seems to keep trying to direct the discussion to matters of Torah—interpretation and, especially, obedience. On the basis of the *Dialogue*, I would have to judge that, at least for Trypho, what separates the two communities is difference over Torah, not "Christology." Trypho is forced to listen to Justin about Christology and to make responses. But that issue does not seem to be of utmost importance for him.

2. Trypho is not disposed at first to accept Justin's imaginative exegesis, but, at least according to the *Dialogue*, gradually comes to accept most of what Justin argues from Scripture about *Christos*. Trypho comes to accept arguments that *Christos* has to suffer (whether crucifixion is appropriate is not so clear), that there are two "comings" of *Christos*, one in lowliness and one in glory, and that one can at least consider the divinity and preexistence of *Christos* (cf. Trypho's concession at the beginning of chap. 63). As far as I can tell, Trypho balks at the virgin birth. But it is, all in all, amazing that Trypho concedes as much as he does. Of course, it was not Trypho who wrote the treatise.

3. Trypho does not really seem to accept the possibility that the *Christos* is more than human. In fact, Trypho's beginning statement about the *Christos* (chap. 8), that even if the *Christos* now exists, he does not know that he is *Christos* nor has he any power until Elijah anoints him and thus reveals him "to all," shows the humanity (and even the lowliness?) of his view of *Christos*. Trypho then uses this as one argument to deny messianic status to Jesus, since Elijah has not himself yet appeared. Justin, as we have seen, uses the two-comings theory to defuse that point.

4. Trypho makes a distinction between scriptural "proofs" and the application of these proofs to Jesus of Nazareth. By such a distinction Trypho can concede to Justin's scriptural exegesis, when he wishes, without conceding that it is *Jesus of Nazareth* to whom the prophecies point. As noted above, this is a distinction Justin essentially ignores. The issue is important, however, since it can explain Trypho's willingness to accede to Justin's exegesis without becoming Christian.

Justin

1. Justin's view of Jesus as *Christos* is not remarkable, given the mid-second-century date. Jesus came in lowliness, was crucified, was resurrected to the right hand of God, from which place he will come at the eschatological day. Yet he was preexistent, could be called "God," and was born of a virgin. Thus there are two "comings," the first in the past in lowliness, the second in the future in glory. The Christian creed is already beginning to take shape.

2. Justin's command of Scripture is remarkable, both in his knowledge and in his imaginative exegesis of so many texts. The treatise is virtually a manual of Scriptural textual interpretation that can be used by believers in discussions with Jewish non-believers. Was this its purpose? While I do not need to get into a discussion about the purpose of the *Dialogue*, it seems to me one is confronted by a simple choice: either the purpose is to show off the author's exegetical pyrotechnics or it was designed to be useful in actual debate.

3. Justin is willing to take on Trypho with regard to matters of Torah, and this may be a secondary focus of the scriptural debate. It may be that when Jews took the initiative in debate, the primary issue was Torah; when Christians were the initiating partner, the primary issue was *Christos*.

Does the Dialogue Inform Our Understanding of Earlier Debates?

I do not think that the *Dialogue* tells us much we did not already know or suspect. First, it is necessary to eliminate topics that would likely not have been current in the mid-first century. On the surface, some would seem to be obvious: preexistence, divinity, and virgin birth. Caution is always needed, however, and decisions about what *could* have been current in the mid-first century are tricky.

Stories about the virgin birth are later rather than earlier. It is also true, I think, that there are no earlier hints about the claim earlier than the narratives themselves. Obviously, however, the narratives did not suddenly appear without some gestation period. What earlier suggestions may have accented and when they began to emerge is now lost to us. One curiosity needs to be mentioned. One of the issues in both birth narratives (Matthew's and Luke's) is that Jesus has to be born in Bethlehem; that is, it is specifically a defense of the claim that Jesus is *Christos*. In the *Dialogue*, however, as far as I can see, the argument for and against such a birth has now been separated from messianic claims by the Christians. The emphasis is on its support for the divinity of Jesus, not his messiahship.

Claims for preexistence are also difficult to date. In my judgment, the first clear reference is in the Colossians hymn (1:15-20), which is impossible to date securely. All one can reasonably say is that the hymn antedates the document itself—whenever that should be located (after 70 C.E.?). Some, of course, have found the idea already in Paul's time, specifically in the Philippians hymn (2:6-11), in a liturgically sounding sentence in 1 Corinthians 8:6, 2 Corinthians 8:9, and in the "sending" language, such as Galatians 4:4 and Romans 8:3. The documents in which these passages are found are mid-first century, and the liturgical nature of some of them might push the claims of preexistence back into the forties. Such an early date seems remarkable—but the rapid explosion of even the earliest Christology boggles the mind anyway. My guess is that claims of preexistence are at least as early as the Philippians hymn.

That the *Christos* is "divine" is another tricky issue. What counts as divine, and what are the terms used? Apart from uncertain places (Romans?), the clearest place to look is the Gospel of John. In a way more sophisticated than Justin, this text knows that the Logos is *theos*. *Theos* occurs not only in the prologue but also in debates with the Jews (e.g., 5:18; 10:31-36). Here, it is interesting to note, arguments about "divinity" do not occur in the contexts of debates about Jesus' messiahship but in terms of the Father/Son relationship.

On the other hand, someone who is preexistent and God's unique agent relating decisively to human history is not simply a human person. Would Paul have thought of the resurrected Jesus as "merely human," as Trypho wants to think about the messiah? It no doubt took a while for early believers to realize the implications of some of their claims, but it is hard to imagine opponents not picking up on the implications very quickly.

Thus, while these topics may seem in the *Dialogue* to be second-century add-ons to earlier arguments, they cannot be dismissed too easily as impossible in mid-first-century situations. *How* Justin and Trypho argue the points may be second-century, but the argument itself may indeed go back much earlier. If so, then the references in Acts to debates in the Hellenistic synagogues take on new meaning. Perhaps it was in such contexts that these topics became vivid issues for debate. Nor is a backdrop in terms of Hellenistic religions difficult to discern. Trypho's insistence that the *Christos* is merely human may have been a typical retort in the face of Hellenistic Jewish "Christians" who may seem to have sold out to Greek myths and superstitions.[53]

One issue dear to Trypho is that the *Christos* is not to suffer, especially in the manner of death, listed as a "curse" by Scripture. Surprisingly echoes of debate caused by this issue are not frequent in the New Testament. In general, these texts do not emphasize the crucifixion. Paul is an obvious exception (1 Cor 1:18-25), but even he is not as emphatic as is sometimes thought. When, however, he acknowledges that for Jews the crucifixion is a scandal, he shows knowledge of arguments over this issue. The Gospels tell the story, mostly without adornment, but there is little in the narratives that gives a clue about debate with Jews—the sarcasm by the onlookers watching Jesus die may hint at Jewish sensibilities. That the messiah does not suffer or die seems an obvious point of contention. It is surprising that there is not more suggestion of debate in the texts.

Absent from the *Dialogue*, as far as I can see, is the issue of miracle associated with *Christos*, from either side. The Gospel of John (e.g., 7:31) and other texts I have looked at suggest that in some quarters that was a debatable point. Also absent is the birth in Bethlehem as a necessary sign of messiahship (cf. John 7:41f.).

The New Testament texts, of course, were written for believers. One should not expect to find in any direct manner the struggles with the Jewish community about the significance of Jesus. I have argued that in the Gospels there is evidence of such quarrels, but it is not easy to extrapolate them, placed in the earthly life of Jesus, to the post-resurrection debate with the synagogue. The *Dialogue* may give certain clues about what were key issues, but the arguments here must be used with some caution. At the same time, they may help our imagination fill in the silence we are otherwise left with.

5

THE THREE TRAJECTORIES

What's at Stake for Believers

I am now at the end of the search for the earliest thinking about Jesus. Keep in mind that I have not so far looked at authorial theology, except as an author seems to continue the trajectory begun earlier. Authorial theology will be examined in the following sections. What has concerned me so far has been the hope of establishing contact with popular thinking about Jesus, insofar as that is possible.

I have tried to establish this contact with popular thinking through the slogans and titles the earliest believers chose from their familiar vocabulary to express the meaning Jesus had given to their lives. Once again, I want to emphasize that the titles are but the skeletons of believing responses, which were fleshed out with all the additional hopes, feelings, and ideas that the titles may have brought with them or, conversely, that the believers laid upon the titles. However it happened, what I call a trajectory is the entire package that carried the faith of believers. It has not been my purpose to attempt a complete structuring of each trajectory. That would involve too much detail and too much speculation. Each person's response was doubtlessly partial at best, and I do not wish to construct some ideal believer who had perfect faith. Suffice it to imagine the basic responses involved in the titles.

I will summarize here what seems to be such basic responses and to see what happened to them over time. It is the passing of time and change that makes a trajectory a trajectory. Although I began the search with what seemed to me the firmest foundation—the Cosmocrator trajectory—and worked backward to what may have been earlier or foundational—the Son of Man trajectory, here I shall reverse the order and try to put things in their historical order.

The Son of Man Trajectory

The mystery of this trajectory is its origin. We have no access to how the complex of meaning attached to "Son of Man" entered into the thinking of the first followers of Jesus. On the surface, the paucity of information as to its location in early Judaism suggests that it would have been an esoteric set of ideas, known only to certain insiders, intellectuals or otherwise. But it is precisely our lack of knowledge that should give us pause about making such a judgment. We can know that the complex was important to the followers of Jesus and was for them a popular notion. I have perhaps said too many times already that the Gospels provide the only real avenue into the minds of average Palestinian Jews in the first century. That the Son of Man concept was popular among these followers may well suggest that it was a popular notion among the peasants at large.

It is impossible also to know who introduced the trajectory into the earliest communities. Was it John the Baptist? Was it Jesus? Was it some nameless people attracted to Jesus who were jolted by the faith in his resurrection and began making the connection between the resurrected Jesus and his exaltation to Son of Man? We cannot know, and it ultimately makes little difference. What is important is *that*, not *how*, it happened.

The resurrected Jesus has been exalted to the "office" of Son of Man. Whether this is a proleptic or present event is of little importance, since the powerful deeds of the Son of Man will not be revealed until the eschaton. And these deeds are, first, the judgment of the world and, second, the establishment and leadership of the elect. The criterion for the judgment is not the Torah but Jesus' earthly teaching and person. Thus the traditions about the earthly Jesus are an essential part of the trajectory. And it is important that the teaching about the Son of Man is always done by Jesus himself, a fact that intensifies the significance of the teaching for the complex. I take it that this is the reason the Son of Man trajectory includes as a basic component the teaching of Jesus.

There is no hint that the miracles of Jesus play a role in this trajectory. They may rather belong to the *Christos* trajectory.

I have speculated that the Son of Man trajectory carried with it an elation and anticipation by the peasants that, finally, the right man was on their side. They expressed with this trajectory their confidence, perhaps enunciated first by Jesus himself, that God did indeed care for them and would make right their lowly position in the day of the Son of Man. They would, therefore, hear the teaching of Jesus as comfort and support, not as threat, and they would have looked forward to that day with anticipation, not dread.[1] Excluded from the kingdom by the elite (cf. Matt 23:4, 13), they felt included by the confidence that their leader was not the judge. This would have been a nonpolitical theology, different from that of the traditional view of the *Christos*, and perhaps preferred because the Messiah trajectory involved more politics, which might have been suspected of being just more of the same old—and therefore exclusive—politics. Thus what seems like an esoteric trajectory for insiders turns out to be a popular theology for the peasants.

While it had no ultimate future in the church, this trajectory did not die easily or quickly. This is indicated by the surprising tenacity the title held in the later stages of the Gospel-building process, including, apparently, the latest of the stages, the final author. In fact, whatever the origin of the "suffering Son of Man" theology, the author of Mark uses it as the center of his Christology. And whatever the origin of the final scene in Matthew, the climactic story is modeled on Daniel 7:13. Luke, also, shows that he knows and honors the trajectory by his use of the traditions, although he also knows that the title had never succeeded in being used in the Hellenistic church. Echoes of its use can also be seen in Hebrews and Revelation, the latter located in Asia Minor at the end of the century.

In the Hellenistic church, the trajectory, if only because of the strange title and the eschatology, could not be continued. That the resurrected Jesus is God's unique agent whose place is set in a cosmic framework could, however, be continued—and apparently was—in another trajectory, that of the Cosmocrator. Did the Son of Man trajectory give rise to its rebirth in other terms? Did Paul recognize the essential faith involved in the Son of Man trajectory but felt compelled for missionary reasons to transform it into that of the Cosmocrator? We do not know, but the possibility seems likely to me.

What is crucial, in any event, is to see the *structural* similarity of the two trajectories, Son of Man and Cosmocrator. The main difference between them lies in the eschatology, essential in one case and tacit in the other. Otherwise, they both affirm that Jesus, however named, is the ultimate criterion for world affairs and will include the faithful in his leadership.

The *Christos* Trajectory

This trajectory has a much stranger and even murkier path than that of the Son of Man. Evidence for its Jewish roots are about as opaque as for the Son of Man. Such evidence as we have suggests that "Messiah" is a royal title, denoting a reigning king, or hoped-to-be-reigning king. As (possibly) projected into the future, the Messiah was the hoped-for restorer of Jewish political and military independence, certainly linked with God and perhaps imbued with supernatural power to carry out God's will for the people.

While we find the title in the Gospel tradition, we find almost nothing of a political theology. Jesus is never portrayed as a political or military figure who does or will wield power, although the resurrected Jesus as *Christos* may wield power at the eschaton. As I have suggested, what we do find in the tradition is some linkage between Jesus as *Christos* and his thaumaturgic deeds. I have suggested that this may reflect a popular view in Judaism that Messiah and miracle worker are related. Again, as far as I know, our only source for this popular Judaism are the Gospels themselves.

Obviously not every miracle worker could be the Messiah, so why Jesus as thaumaturge evoked the further expectation remains a question for which we have insufficient evidence to answer. What we do have, however, may suggest an answer to the question so frequently asked, namely, Why is Jesus called Messiah but is not imbued with political or military traits? The answer would be that he is seen as Messiah not because he acts like a king but because he performs miracles. This would, again, represent a popular mentality, one that responded to reputations built upon the miraculous (especially if most of the miracles were healings), as well as one that was suspicious of political investitures. Was the Messiah as thaumaturge *also* a royal, political figure? From the evidence of the Gospels, the answer would have to be negative. Why then was the Messiah title invoked at all? Had the title in the popular mind already lost whatever political meaning it once possessed? I do not mean to avoid these hard questions; but I see no way of finding an answer. Practically speaking, our only data are found in the Gospel tradition itself.

Belief in the resurrection may have been the catalyst that elevated (if that is what it is) the thaumaturge Messiah into the royal one. Already imbued with the title, it now becomes the way believers could see his role as the resurrected one. Evidence that the resurrected Jesus was seen as Messiah is one thing; what this means is another, and the evidence shows no clear answer. What little evidence there is suggests that exercise of his power awaits the eschatological denouement. There is no evidence that the power is to be an earthly demonstration of military might. Presumably it is a coming in which the resurrected Jesus will enact God's decrees. In this sense, it is no longer clear how Jesus as the coming Messiah and Jesus as the coming Son of Man differ from each another. Has one trajectory influenced the other? There is no reason why there need be any influence of one on the other. Since, however, the eschatological coming of the Son of Man seems to have a sharper focus than that of the coming *Christos*, if there is influence, it is likely that of the former on the latter.

What little evidence we have, mostly from Acts, suggests that the *Christos* title entered the vocabulary of Hellenistic believers because of conflict in the synagogues. Just what was the substance of the debates there—that is, what was the meaning of *Christos* in those arguments—cannot be known. Presumably the title was related to the resurrection belief. It would have been the resurrected Jesus who was claimed to be *Christos*. Since there is no evidence that Hellenistic believers showed interest in the earthly Jesus, and certainly not in Jesus as thaumaturge, any original impetus toward seeing Jesus as Messiah because of his thaumaturgic ability could not have figured into the arguments in the Hellenistic synagogues.

If they are early traditions, Acts 2:36 and 3:19-21 may give hints. In 2:36 the resurrected Jesus as *Christos* is already linked with the title that would become standard, *kyrios*. Here both investitures are as a result of the claim that Jesus was raised from the dead. In 3:19-21 the resurrected Jesus as *Christos* will appear at the eschaton, but precisely what his function will be at the eschaton is not specified. The formulaic citation that Paul cites in Romans 1:3f. may also point in that same direction. There the so-called two-stage Christology has Jesus first as son of David and second as appointed Son of God—from the context, a resurrection event. Although *Christos* is not used, the context clearly implies that "Son of God" is tantamount to "Messiah." Alas, once again the function the office is to exercise is not clarified.

Dare one add to this discussion Paul's passionate argument in 1 Corinthians 15:20-28? There the resurrected Jesus reigns and does battle (surely against the heavenly powers and principalities) and finally presents the "kingdom" to God. Enmeshed in the argument is Paul's own contribution about the relation of resurrected Jesus and resurrected believer, but apart from that most of the claim could be a traditional argument about the messianic activity of the resurrected Jesus—even to the extent of using the term "kingdom."[2]

My suggestion, thus, is that *Christos* passed from Palestinian to Hellenistic culture through early arguments between Hellenistic Jewish believers in Jesus and the Hellenistic synagogues. Once the communities became largely Gentile, any titular significance to *Christos* disappeared. By the time we have texts (which are aimed at Gentile believers), *Christos* has become a name of Jesus, who is primarily defined as *kyrios*. The *Christos* trajectory has died a natural death.

As soon as one has made a generalization, one can always think of contrary evidence, which is conveniently labeled "exceptions." All four Gospels make it clear that *Christos* still lives, at least as a memory of the past. In none of the four is *Christos* the ruling title; yet all four use the term *as a title* without obviously rejecting it. Mark and John seem to prefer Son of Man. Matthew tends to lump all titles together. Luke, as in so many theological issues, remains ambiguous. Surely the idea that *Christos* must suffer is his own addition to the pre-Gospel tradition, even if it is probably a borrowing from Mark's Son of Man trajectory.[3] It may well be that the Gospel writers know that among Palestinian believers, the *Christos* trajectory was still alive, despite my disclaimer in the paragraph above. In Justin's *Dialogue with Trypho*, *Christos* certainly is titular in the arguments between the Christian and the Jew. While the discussion may no longer be a typical "event" by the time of its presumed happening (ca. 140 C.E.?),

Justin's investment in the scriptural arguments suggest that for him the debate was still meaningful. And in this debate the *Christos* title is still functional. The conclusion seems fair: in Gentile contexts, *Christos* is a name; in the context of the argument with the Jewish community, *Christos* remains a title.[4]

The Cosmocrator Trajectory

Just as we can see the death of the *Christos* trajectory but can only speculate about the process of the disease, so we can see the vitality of the Cosmocrator trajectory but must speculate about the process that brought it to life. By the time of our earliest evidence, the faith that the resurrected Jesus is Lord of the cosmos has already been enshrined in the liturgies of the communities. The cosmic scope accorded to Jesus of Nazareth is staggering, to the extent that he becomes the preexistent creator of the cosmos itself. How such a sweeping set of claims for Jesus could have come into existence in twenty years boggles the imagination, especially in the Gentile communities that were not conversant with the worldview in which the *Christos* and Son of Man trajectories were at home—and thus made sense.

The obvious question to ask is about possible influence. Did either of the Palestinian trajectories inform the perspective of the Hellenistic communities? I think it is impossible to judge. The linguistic evidence is not at hand. On the other hand, there are *structural* similarities, particularly between the Son of Man and Cosmocrator trajectories. In both, the resurrected Jesus is exalted to the status of world judge. In both he exercises (or will exercise) the authority of God. In both there is something ultimate about the change the world enjoys because of the new office Jesus holds. In both there is an audaciousness about the elevation of a crucified criminal to cosmic rulership. As already suggested, the eschatological basis of the Son of Man trajectory seems to have disappeared from the other view.

Since the structure itself of the *Christos* perspective is not clear, it is harder to judge similarities or differences. The implied cosmic scope of some passages in Acts might suggest a structural similarity, but as I speculated above, that may actually be influence from the Son of Man trajectory. On the other hand, at least the word *Christos* traveled from Palestinian to Hellenistic territory, while, by and large, the Son of Man title did not.

The anomaly is thus that the closest structural similarity of the Cosmocrator trajectory is with that of the Son of Man, but the vocabulary is closer to *Christos*. There is, however, another way of looking at the issue. Perhaps the question to ask is not about some intellectualist passing of traditions or change of words and concepts. Perhaps the question should be put to the *experience* underlying the trajectories of Cosmocrator and Son of Man. Does the continuity consist of experience rather than concepts and vocabulary?

Let's speculate. Could it be that in both trajectories there is a deep-seated concern that the world is in need of restoration to a place of meaning, peace, and harmony; that in both there is the affirmation that this restoration is tied to a person now raised to heaven, who carries out the will of God; that the community confesses its allegiance to this person and thereby has confidence that it is intimate with and dependent on the one who is righting the world; that therefore it is on God's side, or that God is on its side—and thus the community believes it is participating in a radical change of the world's reality and celebrates the new existence already manifest in the community itself? It is thus the change in the reality of individual and corporate existence that is in inseparable correlation with the conceptualization in the trajectories.

The difference in eschatological structure between the two trajectories might have produced different experiences. In that of the Son of Man, the final denouement is future but perfect; in that of the Cosmocrator, the denouement is present, but imperfect. In either case, there is change in the structure of the world and a correlated change in the experience of the community.

Structural similarity does not necessitate historical continuity; nor does experiential similarity necessitate continuity of conceptuality. One should at least consider that in this case the continuity lies in the experiential, which each cultural group has expressed in concepts that make sense to it and best express what may be the same experience.

In the Son of Man trajectory, the conceptuality emerges from the complex structure of an eschatological figure, now identified with the resurrected Jesus, who will right the world on behalf of God. In that of the Cosmocrator, perhaps based on the same experience as Son of Man, the conceptuality is transformed into notions of imperial rule and, perhaps, the cosmic scope of other Hellenistic deities. Some such background is required to understand such a huge transformation into the Cosmocrator trajectory. If there is historical continuity between the two trajectories, the seemingly enormous transformation of a human person into cosmic Lord has already been prepared for by the Son of Man trajectory.

A final, but not insignificant issue. I have argued that these trajectories express the view of reality that was held not only by the intellectuals but also the general member of the communities. But these ideas in the various mythic worlds are huge in scope and implication. Is it believable that such claims would have made sense and been responded to so positively by the Palestinian peasant or small, perhaps disenfranchised, person in a Greek city? There is perhaps a prejudice that "big" ideas are the property of the intellectuals, while the average person is too enmeshed in the struggle for existence to pay much attention to such ratiocinations.

Three considerations may help in understanding:

1. It seems to me that the evidence is clear that these trajectories do in fact belong to the general worlds of the early believers. *How* this could be the case may need explanation, but *that* these trajectories express the common faith of the believers does not seem questionable.

2. Believers already lived in the mythic worlds of these trajectories. For them the worlds themselves would have been ultimate reality. The trajectories express profound change, but they do so within the worlds already lived in by the communities. For us today as confirmed secularists, the worlds themselves may seem bizarre and thus the change they perceived, expressed in their claims about the resurrected Jesus, may appear more incredible to us than to them.

3. Who needs change, the intellectuals or the dispossessed? Who would experience change in the communities of these trajectories, the intellectuals or the dispossessed? When one looks at the transformation of Jesus into world ruler from this perspective, the investment of the average believer in the transformation may take on a new light. It is, in fact, such radical transformation of Jesus that would express their deep need and desire to have their own reality transformed. If, in their gatherings, they experienced a "community of significant others" who enjoyed the emotional release, however temporary and occasional, from their depressed conditions, then for them the claims about Jesus in the trajectories would have been liberating and believable.[5] Perhaps, then, we should change our own way of thinking. Perhaps it is, in fact, the rank-and-file members who sang and spoke the loudest when they affirmed in their liturgies that the resurrected Jesus was now in control of God's world, restoring it to a reality in which the members have a legitimate place and a confidence that their reality, at least as expressed within the communities, had been radically transformed, just as Jesus of Nazareth had been transformed to Lord of the world.

Part II

Jesus in the New Testament Writings

6 _____

THE SYNOPTIC GOSPELS
AND THE THREE TRAJECTORIES

It is one thing to archaeologize the traditions in the Gospels. It is quite another thing to imagine what the status of authorial perspectives was with regard to average believers. The prevailing view today is probably to assume an adverse relationship between what was current in the church of his time and the views held by an author. The author is thought to be writing against a view that is prevalent in the communities that he addresses. When the author advocates green, this means that the communities prefer blue.

At times, particularly in Paul's letters, this is obvious. In 1 Corinthians Paul is not happy with several of the views of the church there. Antoinette Wire has made a detailed study of this text and came up with a description of what she thinks the women in the church were saying.[1] It is obvious that in the letter to the Galatians Paul opposes a view that was threatening to become dominant among the believers. Closer to home, is authorial Mark opposing a triumphalist view of Jesus' power? To be sure, such interpretations of narratives are much more problematic than those of expository texts. Caution is in order.

To write a book collecting and organizing anti-authorial views would be both fascinating and exhausting. I must limit myself to the basic view of the three trajectories I analyze. Specifically, I want to ask whether the authorial views of the Synoptic authors continue, reflect, or vary from the views of the three trajectories identified in Part I. Obviously, the very fact that one thinks to be able to distinguish between popular and authorial traditions suggests that there is a difference. For my purposes, several questions are of importance. Do the authorial additions significantly alter the earlier, popular traditions? If so, what is the likelihood that they reflect a change in the traditional views themselves? Is there evidence that the authorial views came to be absorbed in the popular traditions?

The Gospel of Mark

The author of Mark remains firmly within the Son of Man trajectory. He is often credited with being the first to join the "kerygma" (proclamation) of the great church with the Jesus traditions. As such, he should rightly be considered the most influential theologian in the history of the church, since he brought together the two dimensions of Jesus, without which the church might not have been able to survive. What scholars mean by the "kerygma" of the great church, however, usually remains vague. It generally seems to mean a stress on the death and resurrection of Jesus, which is taken to be the heart of the kerygma (which basically seems to mean what I am here labeling the Cosmocrator trajectory). But the Cosmocrator trajectory is not found in Mark.[2]

This judgment may carry with it the acknowledgment that the "Jesus traditions" in and of themselves do not stress the death and resurrection of Jesus, but have other functions in the life of the earliest church. The classic form critics tended to assume that the justification of the life of the church was the bedrock of the function of the Jesus traditions. Thus, while death/resurrection might be implied in these materials, it did not form the subject of them.

My questions are two: (1) What does the "overlay" of authorial writing suggest is important to the author? By "overlay" I mean whatever the author seems to reveal as his perspective on Jesus. (2) What kinds of Jesus material did the author select to communicate his perspective? We can safely assume that there was much material the author chose *not* to use.

That Mark accepts the framework of the future, exalted Son of Man is clear from the materials I have surveyed in chapter 2 above. His elaborate enthronement scene in 13:24-27 shows this clearly. Here, vividly imagined is the mythic description of the eschatological coming of the Son of Man. I have already referred to the relationship of responses toward the earthly Jesus by the coming eschatological Son of Man (8:38), a saying that puts the coming of the Son of Man at the final judgment. I have also referred to 14:62, in which the accused Jesus looks forward to (himself as) the coming eschatological Son of Man. Thus Mark clearly accepts the structure of the coming Son of Man that is so explicitly inscribed in Q.

But Mark has made an addition to the Q structure that would prove fateful for the history of the church. He has *identified* Jesus with the Son of Man. This is stated in the three "passion predictions" (8:31; 9:31; and 10:33-34).[3] The label is partly inaccurate, however, since each of these three statements affirms that Jesus as Son of Man would rise after his death. Authorial Mark goes even further. The passion and resurrection predictions are carefully ordered in what I consider the key section of Mark's Gospel, 8:22—10:52. This section is crucial to understanding Mark's conception of true discipleship and perhaps even the main reason for his Christology. Mark interweaves the two together, affirming that one cannot have the one without the other!

There are three statements of the Christology-discipleship theme: 8:27—9:1; 9:31-37; and 10:33-45. This entire section is itself bracketed by two miracles of regaining sight: 8:22-26 and 10:46-52. Since Mark never otherwise includes two accounts of the same kind of healing, this repetition of the miracles of sight can hardly be accidental. While I think one must be cautious about ascribing symbolic significance to healing stories, in this instance it seems to me that Mark is telling the reader that to ponder this central section is to open one's theological eyes to the truth that Mark wishes to offer.

Each of these three sections is itself carefully organized into three blocks. First, there is the suffering and rising prediction (8:31; 9:31; 10:33-34). Then comes a rejection by a disciple or disciples of this as an inappropriate point of view (8:32; 9:33-34; 10:35-40). And this in turn is followed by Jesus insisting that not only is this suffering his own fate but that it is also the fate of a disciple who wishes truly to follow him (8:34-38; 9:35; 10:42-45). The third statement is the most elaborate and ends with an explicit affirmation of the "suffering Son of Man": "For the Son of Man also came not to be served but to serve and to give his life as a ransom for many" (10:45).[4]

One technique of Mark seems to be to absorb various other perspectives into his Son of Man structure. He does this with the *Christos* trajectory, as I will show below. But another instance is his treatment of the transfiguration story, a story that must have been important among the early followers of Jesus. Just *who* Jesus is in this story is unclear, besides the obvious: he is the supreme figure within Judaism.[5] Mark works hard, however, to turn the story into a proleptic epiphany of the Son of Man. Jesus warns the three disciples not to speak about the event "until the Son of Man should have risen from the dead" (9:9). In v. 12 Jesus mentions that, prior to resurrection, the Son of Man must suffer, similar to the passion predictions, only here in reverse order.

It is also here that Mark brings in John the Baptist and subordinates him to Jesus as the supreme suffering figure. This also makes it possible to see the initial comments about John in chapter 1 to be a similar technique. According to the Markan account, John is looking forward to Jesus. But the evidence suggests that the Johannine sect continued its reverence of John after John's death, perhaps honoring him as Elijah or even as the Messiah (cf. John 1:19-28; Luke 3:15). For Mark, John can be absorbed into the Jesus faith as Elijah (9:13), but not the supreme precursor of the eschaton. In fact, perhaps the most dangerous assault on Jesus' superiority over John lies in the logion he dares to cite in 6:14-16:

King Herod heard of it [of what?], for Jesus' name had become known. Some were saying, "John the Baptist has been raised from the dead;

that is why these powers are at work in him." But others said, "It is Elijah." And others said, "It is a prophet, like one of the prophets of old." But when Herod heard of it he said, "John, whom I beheaded, has been raised."

The judgment here is ultimately that Jesus is John *redivivus*. This makes Jesus' power (which is what I take the issue to be, even if nothing in our literature suggests that John was a thaumaturge) subordinate to that of John. The passage is obviously related to Peter's confession in chapter 8. In my judgment the "confession" is molded on 6:14-16. In chapter 8 authorial Mark replaces the notion of John *redivivus* with that of *Christos*, which in turn is replaced by that of Son of Man—and voilà, he is where he wants to be!

The treatment Mark gives the *Christos* trajectory is exceedingly complex, and some scholars have thought that this is his basic category for Jesus. There certainly are positive pointers in this direction. *Christos* occurs eight times, almost always titular (the heading in 1:1 is ambiguous). There is no instance where *in and of itself* it is used pejoratively. Interestingly, after 1:1 the term does not appear until that very section in which Mark begins to build his unique Son of Man structure.[6] The instances are scattered and are by no means unambiguously positive. Nevertheless, Mark's "overlay" does use the trajectory, but clearly subordinates it to his preferred trajectory, Son of Man.

This subordination occurs in two famous places in Mark. One is that movement from Peter's confession of Jesus as *Christos* to Jesus' initial teaching about the dying and rising of the Son of Man, a movement punctuated by Peter's implied rejection of the Son of Man as a suffering figure. The second occurs in the night trial, at the climax of which Jesus acknowledges that he is the *Christos*, but then immediately speaks of the exalted Son of Man.

The main question concerns what might have been the relation in the author's mind between these two trajectories. Either he has rejected the one in favor of the other, or he has subordinated the one to the other, or the two for him mean the same thing. Before facing this decision, it is helpful to ask whether any of the other traditions Mark chose to use reflect the *Christos* traditions. And this question is complicated by uncertainty (see chapter 3, above) about the meaning "Messiah" might have had in the popular mind. Was the Messiah a ruler or a miracle worker? With regard to the latter, what is the relation between Messiah and Son of God? There is so much miracle material in Mark that it is hard for me to doubt that the author valued Jesus highly as wonder worker. Some of the miracle narratives use terms such as "Son of God" or "Holy One of God." And these stories occur in the section prior to the appearance of the term *Christos* in 8:29. Only one miracle story probably specifically alludes to Jesus as Messiah, and even here the title *Christos* does not appear: in 10:46-52 Bartimaeus calls out to Jesus as "son of David." That is, while in the popular mind the Messiah seems to have been thought to be a thaumaturge, specific identification of Jesus' power with the *Christos* title is absent. The conclusion is that Mark wants Jesus to appear as a thaumaturge but that he is not interested in using the title *Christos* in relation to it.

There are, however, occurrences in which the term *Christos* seems to have a more royal meaning. Mark 12:35-37 cites Psalm 110:1 in relation to the idea of son of David. This enthronement psalm is usually associated in the Cosmocrator trajectory with the resurrection and enthronement of Jesus. The use of the material in Mark, however, is not in any relation to its use in the Cosmocrator trajectory. The Markan passage uses the psalm as a tool in the rejection of the notion that the Messiah has to be a son of David.[7] The Markan passage seems to reflect a debate with "the scribes." In the Markan account the people delight in Jesus getting the better of this learned class.

The only other clearly positive use of *Christos* in Mark, in my judgment, occurs in 9:41. Followers (missionaries?) of Jesus bear the name *Christos*. This suggests that some followers of Jesus, after his death, could continue to believe that he was the *Christos* (whatever that might mean for them), just as in Matthew 10:23 the missionaries clearly were spreading the idea of the imminent Son of Man, most likely already identified with Jesus. The Markan logion seems free-floating and not a Markan composition.

The two final uses are so ambivalent that they might in effect indicate that Mark rejects the use of the term. In 13:21 Jesus warns the disciples about people believing in a coming *Christos*. They are all "false Christs" who will indeed perform miracles, but whose purpose is to lead the elect astray. The question immediately arises: Are the false christs false because they are not the true Christ, or are they false because any christ is false? That the statement leads immediately into the intense prediction of the coming Son of Man (rather than *Christos*) suggests that the latter suggestion is more correct.

The passion narrative is, in my judgment, primarily pre-Markan, although there are likely Markan elements in it, elements that do not concern me here. The irony that Jesus is executed although or, more likely, because he may be the king of Israel is stated at the beginning, when Pilate queries Jesus if he is the "King of the Jews." The motif is repeated throughout the interrogation and execution. The title *Christos*, however, appears only at the end, when the Jewish officials, watching Jesus die, mock him by saying, "Let the *Christos*, the king of Israel, come down now from the cross that we may see and believe" (15:32). Here, for once, the title and the identification with the royal figure is made explicit. I suspect that all of this is pre-Markan—but in a text in which the notion of Jesus as Messiah is already rejected or at least in question. I also suspect that Mark, when he read this narrative, could use it without change, because he read the narrative from his own perspective of Jesus as the Son of Man. Jesus is falsely executed for a title that is not his.

The sum of the matter seems clear: The author of Mark prefers the Son of Man trajectory as dominant, but he is willing to bring in as a subordinate motif that of the *Christos*, especially if it implied stories of Jesus' power as thaumaturge.[8] What is strange is not the joining of the two trajectories as much as the positive acceptance of the miracle stories. Why does Mark value those, when he also wants to emphasize the earthly Jesus as the suffering Son of Man? We can speculate. Jesus as wonder worker seems to have been a popular motif among many early followers of Jesus. By incorporating popular motifs into his structure, the author can hope to attract them to his story. By absorbing these motifs into his dominant structure of the Son of Man, he can hope to neutralize any independent or conflicting point of view. For Mark, Jesus is a person of power *and* an obedient sufferer. There is no inherent conflict between the two images, and Mark obviously felt the two compatible, perhaps even complementary.

Mark created a Gospel not simply by having a view of Jesus; he put this view into story form. Thus it is important to note what kind of story he created, the kinds of material he chose. The answer in brief is that he chose primarily narrative ingredients. The passion account and the richness of miracle stories dominate. The specific *teaching* material is comparatively meager. Chapter 4 offers the parable of the seeds and its accompanying interpretations. Chapter 7 offers a significant discourse on what is or is not relevant in Torah and its oral interpretation (cf. 7:19, "Thus he declared all foods clean"). Other than that, the teaching is scattered within the narrative and is not very specific. Mark clearly wants to emphasize Jesus as the doer, not primarily the teacher.[9] Note that very little of the material he uses is specifically related to the Son of Man. With the exception of 8:38, that idea had not entered the teaching or the narrative tradition.

Mark is thus clearly centrally wedded to the Son of Man as his primary category. He knows of the eschatological figure who will judge, rule, and lead the elect. But he also knows of the earthly Jesus as the suffering Son of Man who will rise and become the eschatological Son of Man. Thus the earthly Jesus as the powerful and proleptic Son of Man becomes a focus of importance and interest.

Mark certainly takes seriously the idea that the Son of Man is a religious, rather than political, person. In fact, Mark has killed two birds with a single stone. By absorbing the *Christos* trajectory into that of the Son of Man, he nullifies the potential political dimension of the *Christos* trajectory. At the same time, by ignoring the Cosmocrator trajectory, he implicitly ignores the political implication of that trajectory.

Does authorial Mark signal the end of the Son of Man trajectory? In terms of an author's own perspectives, he clearly does. Yet, as I will show, there are evidences of a lively Son of Man expectation in Matthew and Luke, although their own views of Jesus have expanded into categories that are not among any our trajectories. The Cosmocrator trajectory never allowed the Son of Man trajectory any "space." Thus the Gospel of Mark represents the most intense expression of the Son of Man trajectory and also its authorial end. It was not with the Son of Man that the future of Christology lay. What is momentous is that Mark presents in narrative form the death and resurrection of Jesus, a narrative that proved useful, indeed, essential for the emerging church.

Matthew

Matthew has created a Christology that supersedes any single trajectory, although he uses "Son of Man" and *Christos* freely. For Matthew, Jesus is the true interpreter of the Torah, as the church becomes embroiled in conflict with the emerging synagogue leaders of the Jewish-Roman War. We cannot pursue the issue here, though it is a fascinating study in creativity. The question I raise is whether he integrates the trajectories into his Christology—and the answer seems to be negative. And yet, the trajectories appear abundantly.

Son of Man

By definition, Matthew contains all of the Q material. By general consensus, he also has access to Mark's Gospel and chooses to use virtually all of these Son of Man materials, although he changes the Markan material in sometimes interesting ways. Most striking, perhaps, is that Matthew includes fifteen Son of Man sayings unique to his Gospel.[10] But, with the use of both Q and Mark, Matthew has explicitly adopted the identification of the Son of Man with Jesus. He thus in one sense faithfully continues the Markan trajectory.

It is necessary only to mention briefly the sayings unique to Matthew, some of which I collected in chapter 2. I have already considered 10:23, the urgent mission activity of the believers in relation to the coming Son of Man. I remarked about the opening verse of the eschatological parable of the sheep and the goats, where the judge is the Son of Man. I have detailed the saying in 19:28, in which Jesus as the future Son of Man promises thrones for his disciples. In 13:41 the eschatological Son of Man sends his angels to remove iniquity from the world. Similarly, in 16:27 the Son of Man will come to repay humans for their deeds. These logia all look forward to the eschatological Son of Man. It is not clear that any of them originally was meant to refer to Jesus (19:28 being the most likely exception). But when Matthew took over the Markan identification, there can be no doubt about Matthew's understanding.

Most of the remaining Son of Man sayings unique to Matthew support the eschatological Son of Man trajectory. Into the Markan account of the eschatological Son of Man, Matthew adds the enigmatic comment about the "sign" of the Son of Man (24:30). In 24:37, 39 he warns about the suddenness of the Son of Man's coming. In a remarkable change of Markan language, he replaces Mark 9:1 with the statement, "Truly I say to you, there are some standing here who will not taste death before they see the Son of Man coming in his kingdom" (Matt 16:28).

A few occurrences of "Son of Man" in Matthew are sometimes taken to indicate that this title had become so widespread that it could be used as a synonym for Jesus, in much the same way that *Christos* became a proper name in that trajectory (cf. 12:40; 26:24, twice). It is also true that Matthew can change the Markan Son of Man saying into one of a personal reference (16:21, but cf. the reverse in 16:13).

There may be one final hint at the prominence of the Son of Man trajectory in Matthew in the Gospel's final scene. Jesus appears to the disciples and announces that "all authority in heaven and earth has been given to me" (28:18). This may reverberate with the enthronement passage in Daniel 7:14: "And authority was given to him [the Son of Man]."[11] Both passages mention the *ethnē*, the one in terms of ruling, the other in terms of incorporating into the church (an appropriate change for a Gospel that looks forward to a universal scope), and both affirm the eternity of the reign of the exalted figure. While there are differences in some of the language, Matthew's changes can be explained from his perspective. It does seem fair to think that Matthew's final scene announces the resurrected Jesus as the enthroned Son of Man.

Christos

Does Matthew use the *Christos* trajectory in a more positive way than Mark? I have referred to Mark absorbing the *Christos* trajectory. Matthew's seemingly less intentional usage suggests that for him the issue is both/and rather than subordination. Of course, the birth narrative places the *Christos* title in the forefront. Surprisingly, Matthew makes nothing of this story in the remainder of his Gospel.[12] The next occurrence is not until 11:2, considerably later on in the story. Matthew repeats most of the Markan usages, eliminating 9:41 (because he does not use the logion) and 15:32, the mocking by the Jewish authorities.[13] The confession of Peter (16:13-20), the question about the Messiah as son of David (22:42), the sayings about false messiahs (23:24), and the question of the high priest at the night trial are all taken from Mark. To this basic fund Matthew adds little (11:2, "the deeds of the Messiah"; 23:10, the community has only one teacher, the Messiah).

Two passages seem to be of importance, but they do not sit easily with each other. In the confession of Peter, after Peter acclaims Jesus as the *Christos*, Matthew changes Mark so that Jesus does not respond ambiguously about accepting this title: "Then he strictly charged the disciples to tell no one that he was the *Christos*." Matthew here has Jesus clearly accepting the validity of the title. Yet in the night trial scene, in the response to the high priest's question whether he is the *Christos*, Matthew changes Mark's robust "I am" to the more cryptic "You have said so" (*sy eipas*). It is difficult to read this as a positive response, although I cannot see a reason why Matthew would qualify here what he has affirmed in the story of Peter's confession.

Conclusion

Thus there are two trajectories in Matthew running merrily alongside of each other. Although that of the Son of Man is more prominent and pervasive, Matthew does not seem to wish to subordinate the one to the other, as Mark does. Nor does he reveal any need to integrate the two trajectories. Have we reached a point in time (ca. 90 C.E.) at which the two trajectories are beginning to lose their unique significance? What is true for authorial Matthew is not necessarily true for popular Christianity. The fact that Matthew accepts Jesus as *both* Son of Man and *Christos* may in fact suggest that believers in his churches still accepted the one or the other title.

The *Christos* title does not seem very dogmatically oriented; that is, it does not seem that Matthew has much concern to protect it. When he comes to the end of his Gospel and wants to show that the resurrected Jesus has cosmic authority, he seems to think in terms of the Son of Man. On the other hand, contrary to the use of the title in the Gospel of John, there seems to be no real controversy about the believers claiming the title. The only quarrel about the title in Matthew is that about son of David, a pronouncement story he takes directly from Mark.

Although there is much controversy with postwar Judaism evinced in Matthew, it primarily has to do with the interpretation of the Torah, not with any titles applied to Jesus. It seems enough for Matthew to argue that Jesus, in whatever role, is the true interpreter of God's will as expressed in the Torah. That is really the heart of his Christology. This role is not traditionally associated with either Son of Man or *Christos*, which might explain his diffidence.

Matthew writes in a postwar climate. It is not surprising that he might play down any political notions of the *Christos*. It would seem likely that he, like the Jewish reconstructionists after the war, is struggling to create a peaceful structure of his religion, so that it can be seen as no threat to the Romans. Perhaps this is one reason he is comfortable with the notion of Messiah as miracle worker (11:2). Had the Roman threat been less pronounced, perhaps the function of the *Christos* in Matthew would be more pronounced.

Luke

As with Matthew, so authorial Luke has a Christology that does not fit narrowly within the trajectories, although he is willing, as is Matthew, to use the building blocks of the traditions. For Luke, Jesus is the perfect, obedient Jew who fulfills the prophecies of the Hebrew Scriptures. As such, he is the founder of the true faith, the true Israel of God. He thus qualifies to be known as *Christos* and Son of Man, but his meaning is not exhausted by those titles.

Luke represents the "great church" at the beginning of the second century and is indebted to the Cosmocrator trajectory, although he is sometimes surprisingly quiescent about pushing that agenda. At any rate, we would suspect from the Acts to glean his basic christological perspective. Yet the author of Acts is more a political than a theological thinker, and his primary concern seems to be to write a version of the faith that will be sufficiently innocent to pass any objections of officials, whether civic or Roman. His Christology in the Gospel is designed to support his larger political views.

Since the title Son of Man is absent from the Cosmocrator trajectory, it is not surprising to see that the author of Acts never uses that title, with the important exception of Stephen's vision in 7:56. That it is nevertheless so prominent in the Gospel is something to consider below. Nor is it surprising to find the *Christos* title in Acts much more frequently than in the Gospel—a total of twenty-four times.[14] This number may actually seem surprisingly small. The main point is that, as in the great church at large, *Christos* has tended to become a proper name, and there is no title that satisfies the author as sufficient. In Acts, however, it does seem that the author uses his titles, including that of *Christos,* with accurate memory of earlier usages, a possibility to be explored in chapter 11 below.

I count twenty-four occurrences of "Son of Man" in Luke. By definition, all of the occurrences of Q are there (ten instances). Nine others are taken from the eleven instances in Mark. Thus Luke adds five occurrences of his own. It is clear that Luke favors the eschatological coming Son of Man (in Acts the eschatological figure is played down). Judging from the Gospel, the ultimate appearance of Jesus will be as the all-powerful, judging Son of Man. Not only does Luke cite Q and Mark, but he also adds future-oriented sayings such as 18:8, "When the Son of Man comes, will he find faith on earth?" and 21:36, "Watch at all times, praying that you may have strength to escape all these things that will take place, and to stand before the Son of Man."

Luke also leans on the sayings of Mark that depict Jesus as the present, suffering Son of Man who is to rise in glory. But can one detect a certain diffidence in his use of Mark? True, he does use the three Markan passion predictions. Luke follows the first Markan passage fairly faithfully (compare Mark 8:31 with Luke 9:22). Is it an unconscious twitch of language that he replaces Mark's idiosyncratic *meta treis hēmeras anastēnai* with the more traditional Cosmocrator terminology, *tē tritē hēmera egerthēnai*? At the second place (Mark 9:31; Luke 9:44), Luke omits any reference to the resurrection. Luke separates the third reference by his entire "travel section," which means that the staccato-like repetition in Mark is interrupted. Luke finally begins the third prediction at 18:31. There the ideas are reproduced faithfully, with Luke again using *kai tē hēmera tē tritē anastēsetai*. And while Luke moves, as does Mark, from the Messiah (more hesitantly affirmed than in Mark) to the Son of Man in the accusation of the high priest (Mark 14:62; Luke 22:68), Luke does remove the passage in Mark 10:42-45 about the serving Son of Man and replaces it with an "I" saying in 22:24-27. But to keep one from too easily assessing Luke's intent, one has to acknowledge a clearly Lukan addition to the announcement of the two angels in 24:7: "That the Son of Man must be delivered into the hands of sinful men, and be crucified and on the third day rise" (*tē tritē hēmera anastēnai*). Luke seems content with the Son of Man trajectory, but does it really determine his basic perspective?

Luke seems even less indebted to the *Christos* trajectory. Appearing far fewer times (twelve) than Son of Man, the instances are scattered throughout, with perhaps a slight emphasis in the latter part of the story. Twice the title appears in the birth narratives (2:11, 26). People wonder whether John is *Christos* (3:15). Luke comments that the demons know that Jesus is *Christos* (4:41). He reports two examples from Mark (9:20; 20:41). Three instances, however, cluster in the passion narrative (22:67; 23:2, 35). And perhaps the most interesting are the two statements the resurrected Jesus makes about the necessity of the *Christos* to suffer (24:26, 46). These are close parallels to the statement about the Son of Man in 24:7. When I put all of the material together, I judge that Luke is not essentially indebted to either one trajectory or another. Yes, *Christos* does not occur reasonably frequently, and most of the occurrences are unique to Luke, but I can detect no specific direction.

What ultimately determines Luke's Christology in the Gospel is Jesus as the fulfiller of the promises of God to Israel and as the innocent proclaimer of God's rule in the world. It is not accidental that when Luke rewrites Mark's story of the centurion's exclamation, "Truly this man was a son of God," he has the centurion say, "Truly this man was innocent" (23:47).[15] That seems to me to signal a dramatic shift in point of view. Yes, Jesus is *Christos* and Son of Man, but neither reveals the heart of Luke's faith.

Conclusion

I have argued that authorial Mark is our one true and only representative of an authorial perspective of Jesus as Son of Man. I have accepted the judgment that both Matthew and Luke go beyond any trajectory in their christological heart. Does this mean that popular Christianity went with them and that the titles *Christos* and Son of Man died in the communities? There is nothing in the evidence that would suggest this to be true, and there is much common sense to suggest otherwise. Although I would in no way wish to demean the intuitive thinking of the average believer, it is only reasonable to assume that popular mentality did not necessarily follow the more sophisticated thinking of the writers. It is particularly striking that so many Son of Man sayings are reported by both Matthew and Luke that are not from Mark or Q. The fact that authorial "sophistication" has gone beyond the simple ways of thinking in the trajectories says little about the vitality of the trajectories for the common believer. There is no way of knowing, but I strongly suspect that in the broad Palestinian environment, Son of Man and, to a lesser extent, *Christos* trajectories were still alive and well down to the last quarter of the first century.

7

PAUL AND THE COSMOCRATOR TRAJECTORY

Paul seems to be easily located within the Cosmocrator trajectory. Most of the liturgical evidence for this tradition comes from his letters or those of his disciples. Perhaps he is even a participant in creating the trajectory. In fact, he may be its classic exemplar. Yet I think it clear that the trajectory has, by the time of Paul's letters, come to have a life of its own, independently of Paul's own power, nor can it be assumed without reflection that Paul might have created the trajectory single-handedly. The trajectory exists independently of Paul, and this invites a question.

How did Paul, by all likelihood a rather "conservative" Hellenistic Jew with eschatological convictions, react to the Cosmocrator theology? Did he agree with it? Oppose it? Can we see in his letters attempts to blunt the edges of this perspective or bring it back to Jewish, eschatological views? One might thus ask, does Paul try to "Judaize" (or "re-Judaize") such perspectives? Although we may know better, there is nevertheless a tendency to assume that Paul acted to formulate the essentials of the Hellenistic theology of the time. May it not rather be that we see Paul react to a theology, which by the time of the 50s existed independently of his views, and over against which he had to respond? What does Paul do with the Christology of Christ as Cosmocrator?

Here I focus entirely on Paul's perspectives on Christ as Cosmocrator. His most creative and lasting contributions to Christian theology—justification by grace, the joining of the resurrection of Christ with that of the believer, and the reevaluation of power (i.e., the cross)—cannot be primary issues for discussion here, although they may implicitly intrude.[1]

First, it must be said that Paul agrees with the basic affirmation: *the* meaning of the resurrection is that Jesus has become Lord of the cosmos.[2] Paul shares with the enthronement Christology the lack of interest in the earthly Jesus. Preexistence, while marginally present in both the Hellenistic Christology and

Paul, is not crucial to the structure.[3] The present lordship is seen as activity of the enthroned Christ. Christ rules over the powers and principalities, or he fights them victoriously. Paul seems to agree with the perspective of the statement in 1 Peter (the enthroned Christ is victorious over hostile powers) rather than that of Colossians (reconciliation instead of subjugation).

> Then comes the end, when he delivers the kingdom to God the Father after destroying every rule and every authority and power. For he must reign until he has put all his enemies under his feet. The last enemy to be destroyed is death. "For God has put all things in subjection under his feet." (1 Cor 15:24-27a)

In the final analysis that difference may be minor. In either case, the world is ruled by a benign Cosmocrator who is on our side.

Paul also agrees with the lack of emphasis in this Christology on reference to the death of Jesus as sacrificial. Of course in these materials the death is almost never mentioned and has no significance in the theological structure.[4] For the Cosmocrator Christology, no death is needed, except to provide the point for the exaltation to heaven. Sin is not *the* problem. The problem is bondage to hostile powers that unjustly determine human life. As Rudolf Bultmann pointed out, Paul also does not use the sacrificial metaphor to describe his own basic view of the significance of the death. Allusions to the sacrificial metaphor in Paul are citations of traditions.[5] Paul certainly does find the death significant. But since for Paul as for the Cosmocrator Christology sin is not the primary problem, the metaphor he chooses to describe the death is not that of sacrifice (and it is not certain that the sacrificial metaphor always has to do with sin anyway).

I suggest that Paul makes two, for him, significant modifications in the Cosmocrator Christology as contoured by the Hellenistic church. This does not mean that Paul had not always had these beliefs firmly in his theology. But since the Hellenistic church had gone its own independent direction, it was inevitable that now Paul put the Cosmocrator Christology within his own framework. Nor do I want to imply that these "reassertions" are anything but familiar terrain in the Pauline theological landscape. Seen in the perspective I suggest, however, his statements may take on new significance for later church theology. That the later church "voted" for Paul was decisive for what would become "orthodox" church theology.[6]

The Eschatological Dimension of Christology

The first modification that Paul makes to the Cosmocrator Christology is that *Paul reasserts an eschatological dimension for Christology.* Imagine the scenario of history presented by the political, non-eschatological Cosmocrator Christology. Jesus has been enthroned as rightful Lord of the cosmos, over both earthly and supernatural powers. This is a reality that provokes joy in the communities who are aware of the significance of this event—joy because the world has been restored to a benign ruler who has liberated humans from the fateful tyranny of the hostile powers and principalities. Similarly to the accession of a benign emperor, the event leads one to be optimistic about present and future. But it does not mean that one anticipates a final event in which a utopian and eternal social reality will occur. It is not even certain whether all such believers anticipated a reality others called "eternal life."[7] It is hardly accidental that none of the liturgical materials say anything about the believers' life after death! History continues (forever?) under this benign ruler. Living conditions, so to speak, in the cosmos are changed for the better, but evil continues and in history nothing will ever be perfect. For those who believed in life after death, continued existence was conceived as a blessed condition in "heaven" (?). There would be, however, no eschatological finis and no present perfection in this life, on this earth.

As suggested above, Paul would agree with much (and perhaps all?) of what was affirmed in this Christology about the *present* changed reality in history due to the enthronement of Christ. Paul, however, refuses to give up the eschatological finality of God's victory in Christ—obvious to all readers of the apostle. The issue is what this eschatological finality adds, or subtracts, from the non-eschatological framework of the Hellenistic church.

In the first place, Paul's eschatology does not seem to alter views about the reality and quality of present, historical existence maintained in the Hellenistic church, as far as the limited evidence seems to suggest. For those who believe in God's act in Christ, life in the church is guided and empowered by divine actors, God, Christ, Spirit. That outside, "secular" history is improved is not, as far as I know, claimed by Paul.[8] Paul's eschatology is frequently said to be "now-but-not-yet." This "eschatological reservation" is maintained by Paul to temper the kind of enthusiasm, supposedly visible in some of his churches, in which the "now" takes precedence over the "not yet." This point of view is taken from the presumed enthusiasm of the Corinthian church, which I have already suggested may not be eschatological at all.[9] Since it is Paul who envisages an eschatological utopia, it may be Paul who is the enthusiast!

In the second place, Paul's eschatology does not envisage a continued life upon a perfected earth, any more than does the Hellenistic Christology. The scenario for the future involves those who believe in Jesus. There seems to be no hell for those who do not believe. They will simply no longer exist.[10] The emphasis that Paul gives to this noncorporeal future in 1 Corinthians 15 is almost surprising.

> I tell you this, believers: flesh and blood cannot inherit the kingdom of God, nor does the perishable inherit the imperishable. Lo! I tell you a mystery. We shall not all sleep, but we shall all be changed, in a moment, in the twinkling of an eye, at the last trumpet. For the trumpet will sound, and the dead will be raised imperishable, and we shall be changed. For this perishable nature must put on the imperishable, and this mortal nature must put on immortality. (1 Cor 15:50-53, mostly RSV)

Eternal life will not be on earth, but presumably in heaven (the third heaven?—cf. 2 Cor 12:2-3). Thus Paul, no more than the Hellenistic church, believes in a perfected rule on earth.[11]

Paul nevertheless clings to his eschatological utopia. But how does his eschatology change the theological horizon of the Hellenistic church? This is a more difficult question to answer than one might assume. For most of us today any notion of future eschatology is unreal. The church has lived by the framework of the Hellenistic Christology. That is, over the centuries, Christianity has in effect not anticipated the end of the world and has relegated eschatology to footnotes.[12] We simply do not think as Paul thought. We are content to live with some perhaps vague understanding of God-Christ-Spirit as Lord over the cosmos. We pray that God will affect the life of the church. We also pray as if God can affect the life of the larger world—whether there is much confidence in such prayer depends, I suppose, on the individual petitioner. Many, I am sure, do not think God is really in control of the world (much less the cosmos, which means, of course, something vastly different from what it did in the first century).

But for Paul, hope in an eschatological utopia protects a view of God-in-Christ as ultimately in covenantal control of the world. The Christology of the Hellenistic church does not affirm the view of the victorious God that Paul and all apocalyptically oriented Jews fervently knew to be true. Since, however, eschatology emerges out of conviction that the God of covenant will ultimately triumph, nothing less than the hope of a final, victorious establishment of God's people can sustain belief in God itself. I suspect that, for Paul, God would not be the God of Israel without expectation of an eschatological victory that would be the ultimate establishment of covenant with God's people (including now, of course, Gentile as well as Jew).

Without the eschatological utopia, eternal life in Christ might also be called into question. Bultmann argued many years ago that Paul had two great enemies, personified as Sin and Death. The power of sin leads inevitably to death. Since all desire to live, death is the ultimate enemy ("The last enemy to be destroyed is death").[13] Sin becomes personified only because sin leads to death. It is true, obviously, that for most Jews of the time, belief in eternal life could be sustained without any belief in Jesus as God's ultimate agent. Paul, however, has so linked the resurrection with the living Christ that without his belief in the consummation as the ultimate victory of the warrior Christ over the final enemy, death, he would have to have feared that his life might be less secure (cf. 1 Cor 15:19).

Perhaps the most intense future-oriented statement, and at the same time the one filled with the most pathos, occurs in Philippians 3:8-21. Here Paul's yearning and forward-looking desires are manifested in his goals for the future. He wants to "gain" Christ; he hopes to "attain" the resurrection; he is "straining forward to what lies ahead." The climax occurs in verses 20-21: "But our commonwealth is in heaven, and from it we await a Savior, the Lord Jesus Christ, who will change our lowly body to be like his glorious body, by the power which enables him to subject all things to himself" (RSV).

Whether Paul has the hymn he has cited in 2:6-11 in mind (and I think it almost certain he does), the yearning in chapter 3 serves as a perfect correction to the non-eschatological Cosmocrator Christology so beautifully expressed in that hymn.[14] The apostle's gaze is toward the future consummation, and central is the expectation of his personal resurrection. Even the "commonwealth" (a political term, referring to a legal entity) exists in heaven, not on earth.[15]

The Priority of God in the Eschatological Drama

The second of Paul's modifications to the Cosmocrator Christology is that *Paul insists on the ultimate priority of God over Christ in the eschatological drama.* The distinction here must be made with care. I need to repeat that there is no thought in the Hellenistic communities of a usurpation by the enthroned Christ. The replacement of Yahweh by the victorious Christ is not so much a theoretical change in the heavenly pantheon as it is a reflection of a new and vital experience that expresses itself in implied theological nuances. If Paul emphasizes more the ultimate priority of Yahweh than the Cosmocrator Christology, does this then mean he is operating out of a different experience?

First, that Paul insists on the ultimate priority of God is well demonstrated by 1 Corinthians 15:27-28. When the eschatological victory is complete, "then the Son himself will also be subjected to him who put all things under him, that God may be everything to everyone" (RSV).[16] The curtain falls on the eschatological drama, leaving God alone on stage. If, as most scholars believe, "to the glory of God the Father" at the end of the Philippians hymn is a Pauline addition, then this surely counts as Paul's insistence on God as the ultimate actor.

Second, despite the apparent theological innocence of the replacement theme, Paul may have feared it could lead to a new religion with a structure independent of the God of Israel. As many have insisted in recent years, so far from Paul being the creator of a new religion called "Christianity," he saw himself as the apostle of the God of Israel to the Gentiles.[17] He considered himself a true servant of Yahweh and would have been horrified to think he were participating in a new paganism, even with a "Christ" as the god. The potential proto-Marcionite tendencies in the Cosmocrator Christology would have been reason enough for Paul to have denied any separation between creation and redemption.[18]

But, third, does Paul's refusal to separate Christ as Cosmocrator from the God of Israel imply a difference in the experience of new reality? Does Paul retreat from the new meaning structure implied in such Christology? Does Paul move from the enthusiasm of the Hellenistic churches back to a more somber emphasis upon the cross of Christ? This is a crucially important question; at the same time, one difficult to answer. Contrary to the view that Ernst Käsemann made popular (cf. note 9), I suggest the perhaps surprising conclusion that Paul's experience is actually more heightened and ultimately more optimistic than the "political" perspective of the Cosmocrator Christology.

Paul uses the language of "new creation" to describe the new reality present in this world (2 Cor 5:17; Gal 6:15). I have elsewhere argued that Paul's eschatological framework was indebted to Jewish (especially early rabbinic) equation of the Edenic situation before Adam's sin with future, eschatological delights.[19] When Paul speaks of the new creation as a present reality, he brings future into present. God's eschatological gifts are already present now to those who believe in the God of grace. It is interesting to see how instinctively he uses language that ties in creation and redemption. The importance of the presence of the Spirit of God as indication of eschatological reality (e.g., the "first fruits" of Rom 8:23) shows equally well that Paul understands the present time as a time of celebration of eschatological gifts. Paul affirms strongly that all those in Christ now live in eschatological reality. Even here, Paul's eschatological framework nuances how he interprets the liberation brought by the enthronement of Christ as Cosmocrator. Enthronement is not just a political change; it is the ultimate (eschatological) victory already manifested in the present. The ground for celebration has a solidity (at least for Paul) that a "political" enthronement cannot produce.

Nevertheless, Paul's catalogue of hardships in 2 Corinthians 11:21—12:10 is impressive indication that the apostle is not a fool. This world can still run amok and live by rules not controlled by Christ the Cosmocrator. Despite his celebration of the presence of the new creation, he knows that the old world is still all too present as well. How does Paul deal with these conflicted realities? It is here that his so-called theology of the cross emerges as an interpretive principle. The issue is complicated and I can only suggest the results of my earlier research.[20]

The cross is the revelation of who the God of Israel truly is—a God who gives life by grace, who does not rule the cosmos by domination and power. The cross reveals the new world controlled by a new definition of power. The cross thus is not a sign of weakness or suffering for its own sake. The cross is the revelation of eschatological reality and is guidance for all who must live in two worlds at the same time, the world of love as power and the world of domination as power. The perspective of the cross helps Paul understand his catalogue of hardships—and he thus can sum up his list by putting himself on the side of love as power: "For when I am weak, then I am strong" (2 Cor 12:10). Thus his sometime emphasis upon the cross is not a retreat from celebration of eschatological presence. It is, in fact, a description of what that eschatological presence looks like in the face of the world not yet under control of the God of Israel. It is a demonstration that eschatological existence is a reality even in the face of the hatred and self-seeking of the false world.

Paul did not win all his theological battles. Indeed, the most important one he lost. The radical gospel of justification by grace has always been too hot to handle. A walk through church history shows tragically how for every hero of justification by grace, five seem to have arisen who deflected the radicality and turned the interpretation of Paul into a safe place where the more comfortable justification by works, in some form or the other, became what Paul is supposed to have said.

But Paul did not lose all his battles. The two alterations he made in the Cosmocrator Christology—an ultimate eschatological victory by God and the subordination of the agent Jesus to Yahweh—became church teaching. Today these alterations are commonplaces in our theological textbooks (even if not always held with passion). Eschatological denouement is affirmed but rarely embraced; and the subordination of the resurrected Jesus to Yahweh is camouflaged under the doctrines of the Trinity. During his lifetime, however, the issues were not commonplace, and the prominence of the liturgical materials shows that another outcome must have been possible. Who is to say that the other point of view would have been disastrous? It could have been. And who is to say that Paul won the battle single-handedly? Of course he did not. His contributions in this direction were, however, immense.

8 _____

THE COSMOCRATOR TRAJECTORY
IN COLOSSIANS AND EPHESIANS

Colossians and Ephesians, in some ways so closely related to each other, exhibit key characteristics of the Cosmocrator trajectory. In Colossians 1:15-20 is found one of the kingpin liturgical foundations of the trajectory. Colossians 2:11-15, perhaps echoing a formula, climaxes in the cry of victory over powers and principalities (although the hymn itself speaks of reconciliation). The acclamation of the resurrected Jesus occurs four times (1:3, 10; 2:6; 3:17). Clearly, God's power is channeled through the exalted Lord.

The same features mark Ephesians. A clear liturgical echo of the enthronement of the resurrected Jesus over powers and principalities occurs in 1:20-23. Yet, in 6:12 the victory is said to be incomplete, with the war still ensuing with the evil powers in heaven—an unusual juxtaposition of the "now but not yet."[1] Acclamations of the exalted Jesus occur seven times with the title *kyrios*.[2] Again it is clear that power emerges from the exalted Jesus, a power that determines the fate of the world.

In neither document is eschatology a very real part of the scheme. The hymn in Colossians does not look beyond the exaltation of the resurrected Jesus. And it could be said that the liturgical echo in Ephesians does not look beyond the time of the church. True, in Ephesians 6:12 the battle between good and evil goes on, but there is nothing said about an ultimate victory.

In neither treatise does the earthly Jesus play any role. In fact, these two treatises, if anything, move away from earth to heaven, so that any earthly Jesus appears an irrelevant shadow[3] with little reality. Perhaps the authors would deny such a suggestion; the fact remains that the earthly Jesus has no function in the theological schemes of the authors. Colossians 1:20 will require discussion below.

The two documents, however, both, in some concert, move the simple trajectory into seemingly unique directions—although one would hardly say that the directions contradict the basic trajectory. While one can imagine these movements surprising the singers of the hymn in Philippians 2, the ultimate question is whether these changes in wording are so much changes in content as in metaphor. Those spearheading the new movements would surely have defended the "innovations" as implicit but necessary affirmations that brought out the full force of the trajectory.

These directions focus around three issues, and I will deal briefly with each. One should keep in mind that two of these issues are "spatial" in character (*plērōma* and being seated at the right hand of God). The second is temporal, the play on the word *mystērion*. The question is ultimately how these spatial and temporal movements work and fuse together. Since the scholarly consensus is that Ephesians is not only the later document but is closely indebted to the text of Colossians, I will in each instance first discuss the meaning in Colossians.[4]

Plērōma in Colossians

The Cosmocrator trajectory affirms that the resurrected Jesus is exalted to be Lord of all the cosmos and sits at the right hand of God. There seems to have been little speculation about what that meant about the relation of God to the resurrected Lord. The most likely conclusions are that they thought of the two as discreet entities, however much they were related in form and with the metaphor of family as Father/Son.[5]

The framer(s) of the hymn in Colossians 1:15-20 have thought about the relation between God and Jesus and have come up with a particular vocabulary to express their understanding. The Greek reads: *hoti en autō eudokēsen pan to plērōma katoikēsai* (19a). The meaning is not entirely clear, but the direction is. Scholarly consensus seems to agree that the subject of the sentence is *plērōma*, although God could be the implied subject. Whether that grammatical conundrum matters much is doubtful, since the fullness is taken to be the fullness of God. The basic meaning then seems to be that all of God's reality dwells in Jesus. This statement comes in the post-resurrection segment of the hymn, so that the first inclination is to say that it is as a result of the resurrection that Jesus is filled with the reality of God, and thus is God in a "complete" form.[6] Surely we are not yet in a Nicene world. But which world are we in?

In 1:15 Jesus is the image of God. In 1:19 he is the *plērōma* of God. Does image say less than fullness? Probably it does; thus the hymn is consonant with the basic Cosmocrator view of the resurrection of Jesus, which makes a status for him that did not exist prior to the resurrection. One is brought short, however, by what is an apparent insertion by the author of Colossians into the hymn, "making peace through the blood of his cross" (*dia tou haimatos tou staurou autou*, v. 20a). The hymn seems to speak of resurrection and fullness being the vehicle of reconciliation of the cosmos. The pointer to the cross threatens to change things dramatically. For the issue at hand, it raises the question whether the Jesus—presumably the earthly Jesus—of the cross is already filled with the reality of God. Or is the cross here a cosmic event not specifically tied with the earthly Jesus? The hymn itself remains so far above earthly realities that one is tempted to accept the latter possibility. But if the phrase is an insertion of the author of the book itself, one has to be cautious. The cross is mentioned one other time in Colossians (1:14-15), where it seems to function as a victory over the hostile powers. The two metaphors function in radically different ways. Yet the cross in 2:14-15 is itself a cosmic event, however much the theology touches earth ever so briefly. It would be my best guess that the insertion of the cross motif in 1:20 does not really affect the meaning of *plērōma* in the hymn.

The author uses the term *plērōma* only once on his own, in 2:9: *Hoti en autō katoikei pan to plērōma tēs theotētos sōmatikōs*, "For in him all the fullness of the godhead[7] dwells in reality." The sentence is in the context of disagreement with an opposing point of view, and presumably what the author of Colossians says he thinks is in opposition to a view of the opponents. The sentence echoes the hymn in its use of "dwell" and clarifies, perhaps, the temporal meaning of v. 19, with its use of the present tense of "dwell." The real problem concerns his use of the word *sōmatikōs*. Could this possibly mean "bodily" in a corporeal sense? This hardly seems possible, since the assumption is that the author conceives of God in a noncorporeal, spiritual way. Thus the meaning must be that of "reality."[8] Thus here the author's comment on the hymn is to declare that the fullness is the *present* reality of the exalted Jesus. Thus, as far as we can learn from the author, he pushes the meaning of the exalted Jesus in the direction of identification with God. Yet he does not seem to think of such a complete identification that the exalted Jesus is completely incorporated into the godhead or that the term "God" loses any significance. But the hymn framers and the author of Colossians, following suit, are beginning to think that the exaltation of Christ means not just cosmic authority but also the complete reality of God indwelling in him. Instead of the danger of the resurrected Jesus becoming a second god, the problem might become how closely the resurrected is absorbed into the godhead.

Plērōma in Ephesians

The author of Ephesians substitutes for the Colossians hymn a fragment from the Cosmocrator trajectory that begins, at least, in the familiar language of that trajectory (1:10-21). God has raised Christ, seated him at the right hand above all powers and principalities, and put all things under his feet.[9] Then the passage takes a stranger turn (vv. 22-23). "And has made him the head (*kephalē*) over all things *tē ekklēsia*, which is his body, the fullness of all things in all things filled up."

I first bracket the phrase *tē ekklēsia*, which I argue below is an authorial gloss. Apart from that, the passage seems to say that God has made Christ the head over the *plērōma*, which now is not the divine reality, as in Colossians, but the cosmic reality. We have a picture of the cosmos with a head, Christ, and a body, which is under the head. What the relationship between the head and the body might be is not stated, but the implication clearly seems to be that the head is superior to the body, just as the general tenor of the fragment is that God has made Christ above all other realities. This new formulation translates the typical Cosmocrator language in 1:20-21 into that of the *plērōma*. The direction is now not toward the relationship within the godhead but within the cosmos. This is hardly what the hymn in Colossians means by *plērōma*! Yet one could argue that the statement (so far) in Ephesians is actually closer to the basic affirmation of the Cosmocrator trajectory than is the direction taken by the hymn in Colossians. As it stands, the assertion seems to mean that the entire cosmos is in relation and subordination to the resurrected Jesus. There seems to be some relation to the Colossians hymn at 1:17, although Ephesians specifically identifies the union of Lord and cosmos with the resurrection event.

What creates difficulty is the phrase *tē ekklēsia*. This insertion seems to me to disturb the meaning in two ways, neither of which is compatible with the other. (1) What sense does it make to say that God has given Christ, as head over all things, to the church? Is this an honorific assignment? Christ is now the servant of the church, although he is head over all things. How can he be servant if he is head? (2) What sense does it make to identify the church with the body of Christ, which is then immediately said to be the *plērōma* of all things? The phrase causes such self-contradictions in the adjacent phrases that I find it hard to think that it would not have been smoothed out in a liturgical statement. Verse 23 makes sense apart from the words *tē ekklēsia* and little sense with it (if those words were part of the original statement). I therefore think that the phrase is an insertion by the author of the final text, for whom the church is such a central concern.

When "the church" is inserted—by the author of Ephesians, I argue—into the context, the thought changes remarkably, however self-contradictory it may be. First, it seems to imply that God made Christ the head over the *plērōma* for the sake of the church. But, second, even more striking, the *plērōma* now *is* the church. Christ is now head over the church. This is not in itself an unusual idea, although it does go beyond Paul's use of the metaphor. But the insertion limits the headship of Christ to the church. What has happened to the cosmos? I have to conclude that the author of Ephesians is so focused on the church (as a universal, even cosmic body) that he forsakes the fairly clear meaning of the *plērōma* in the passage. Even the question of the intention of the author is uncertain. Has he no real interest in the cosmos? Does he insert the church because that is his overriding concern? The passage itself cannot solve the issue of the meaning of *plērōma*. It is necessary first to look at the author's other uses of *plērōma*, which may not reflect the sense of the term in the hymn fragment.

The second use of *plērōma* occurs in 3:19. In a prayer the author makes in the name of Paul, "Paul" wants the believers "to know the love of Christ, which surpasses knowledge, that you may be filled with all the fullness of God." This moves in a remarkably different direction from 1:23. There the fullness is from Christ to the cosmos (or church). Here the direction is from believer to God. But just what this direction entails is uncertain: *hina plērōthēte eis pan to plērōma tou theou*. The use of *eis* suggests a process, as would seem appropriate, since the believers are still on earth. But does being filled with the *plērōma* of God mean absorption into the godhead? Is this the ultimate goal? What has happened to Christ as the *plērōma*? Is the idea here compatible with the notion of the church as the *plērōma*? The passage also seems to ignore the claim that believers are already raised with Christ into heaven (e.g., 2:6). We seem to have different languages or metaphors to talk about the same reality of union between believers and God. Forgetting the resurrection as a present reality for the moment, it has to be that either 3:19 proposes a metaphysical idea or the use of *plērōma* has become a metaphor for a close relation to and dependence on God. Either of these seems possible.

The final instance of *plērōma* (4:13) creates even greater difficulties and resists an easy interpretation, even though the passage is important for understanding our author. The reference occurs in a long section, beginning with spiritual gifts given to some leaders who are to be directed to improving the church members at large, using various metaphors to point to "spiritual growth." The immediately preceding metaphor describes the work as the "building up of the body of Christ" (v. 12)—a hint of a hashed metaphor? But the notion of body seems to dominate the following phrases. The work is described as attaining unity of faith and knowledge of the Son of God. Then comes the phrase *eis andra teleion, eis metron hēlikias tou plērōmatos tou Christou*. One must look immediately at the following contrast in order to get some sense of the metaphors the author is playing with. In v. 14 the reverse of the intent expressed above is that we may no longer be children (*nēpioi*). Thus the primary metaphor must be seen as one of growth into maturity for members of the church. The ruling verb is *katantaō*, "to reach, arrive at." The leaders are to help the members to arrive *eis andra teleion*. *Teleios* and the root *telos* can have many meanings. One could translate the words in question as "perfect man."

With the contrast of children in the next sentence, however, *teleios* surely must be taken as "mature," especially as modifying the male *andros*. Thus we "reach the mature male" (an awkward phrase in today's culture). That leaves us with the final phrase, *eis metron hēlikias tou plērōmatos tou Christou*, literally: "(reach) toward the measure of the stature of the fullness of Christ." The Greek *hēlikia* normally has a temporal meaning—age of various sorts, including the age of maturity. It can also have a spatial meaning—stature (of a person). Since the word here is followed by *metros*, which mostly is a measure of quality, *hēlikia* most likely assumes a spatial rather than a temporal meaning. Thus we have "measure of stature"—a tautologous phrase that can be shortened to "size." The phrase thus reads: "(reach) toward the size of the fullness of Christ."

In this context *plērōma* has to be part of the giant and somewhat awkward metaphor of participation in the perfection of Christ. It cannot be taken literally as some indication of the "size" of the spiritual greatness of the Christ. Believers are to be led to grow to (reach) the desired relation with Christ.[10] In the following sentence, the attaining of the fullness of Christ will keep believers from continuing to be children, "tossed to and fro and carried about with every wind of doctrine." The author then makes a return to the desired goal: Believers are to "grow up in every way into him who is the head, into Christ" (vv. 14-15). The following verse then details the bodily growth image, in which believers are to be in healthy and harmonious relation with Christ. Yet in this restatement, *plērōma* is not used. The author wants to use physiological images (why?) to depict the correct relation with Christ. In the frequent metaphorical uses by the author, *plērōma* takes its place and becomes, at least in this instance, a physiological word. At any rate, we have two apparently parallel clauses: (1) "(Attain) to the size of the fullness of Christ" (v. 13); (2) "Grow up in every way into him who is the head, into Christ" (v. 15). I do not see any significant difference between these two metaphors. The basic point seems to be to exhort believers to move toward a spiritual reality or maturity that the author thinks to find in the resurrected Christ.

Thus there are three usages of *plērōma* relevant to my theme.[11] In relation to the occurrences in Colossians, the difference in meaning is remarkable. We have a change from an "ontological" use in Colossians to more of a metaphorical or mystical function in Ephesians. In the hymn in Colossians, *plērōma* is used to indicate an ontological similarity between the godhead and the resurrected Christ. The author's only other use of the term (2:9), while creating difficulties, certainly stays with the ontological meaning of the hymn.

The author of Ephesians clearly goes into another direction. He does not seem interested in the cosmos, despite the hymn fragment in 1:23. In 1:22-23 he reduces the cosmos to the church, although here he may be thinking of the church as a spatial *plērōma*, under Christ as head. The other three uses—1:23; 3:19; 4:13—seem to me to move in the direction of metaphors, denoting the spiritual perfection of and participation in the godhead, however named. As such, they lose their ontological status that was maintained in Colossians. The author of Ephesians does not preserve for the term *plērōma* the ontological significance found in Colossians.

Seated in Heaven

A second change in the language of the Cosmocrator trajectory occurs when both Colossians and Ephesians write about believers already being raised to heaven, sitting in the heavenly places. In the Cosmocrator trajectory, the believer is destined for such places but must await a future time before this can happen (if there is to be such a time). Actually, in this instance the language of Colossians is more restrained than that in Ephesians. The author of Colossians uses the word *synegeirō* twice, in 2:12 and 3:1, and *syzōopoieō* in 2:13. In what seems like a liturgical fragment (2:11-12) the author lists the steps the believer has undergone: a fleshless circumcision, baptism *en hō kai synēgerthēte*; while in verse 13 the further statement is made that Christ *synezōopoiēsen hymas syn autō*. The aorists in this section clearly point to an already achieved event. The resurrection of believers as a present event is part of the lists of salvational events in 2:10-15. In language that echoes 1 John 3:2, he writes that "You have died and your life is hid with Christ in God. When Christ, who is our life, appears, then you also will appear with him in glory" (3:3). This may rest on baptismal assurance, as the author writes in 1:13: "He [God] has delivered us from the dominion of darkness and transferred us to the kingdom of his beloved Son."

Other language, however, suggests the "not yet" that is traditional in the Cosmocrator trajectory. In 2:20, "If with Christ you died to the elemental spirits of the universe, why do you live as if you still belonged to the world?" "Since then (*ei oun*) you have been raised with Christ, seek the things that are above, where Christ is. . . . Set your minds on things that are above, not on things that are on earth" (3:1-2). Even though the believer has been raised with Christ, it is possible for him or her to live on earth instead. Thus there is some ambiguity. The author writes of a presence in heaven with more confidence than does, say, a Paul. He still has room for eschatological reservations. All is not settled, in heaven!

The language of Ephesians is at first even more startling. First the author repeats a term from Colossians in 2:5: "And although we were dead in our trespasses he made [us] alive with Christ" (*synezōopoiēsen*). Then, to top it all, he adds: *synēgeiren kai synekathisen en tois epouraniois en Christō Iēsou*, "and resurrected and sat us with him in the heavenlies in Christ Jesus" (v. 6).[12] Although startling, this is the only occurrence that suggests that believers now exist in heaven. Believers have been made alive, but it is hard to imagine the author of Ephesians thinking literally that believers exist spatially in heaven. After all, in the household tables they are definitely on earth—and in a fight against the evil powers (6:10-16).

The notion of being raised to the heavens certainly goes beyond the more cautionary note of a Paul. Ernst Käsemann would call it triumphalism, and in its own language it comes close to the mysticism of the Gospel of John. Certain dimensions of early Christian theology are moving toward an idea of a present eternal life (cf. the attack on it in 2 Tim 2:17). Colossians and Ephesians, as well as the Gospel of John, point in that direction, but they still constrain their readers who live on earth and must still struggle with imperfection. Thus these three documents take a present eternal life seriously, although I do not see any linguistic links of Colossians and Ephesians with the Gospel of John.

Mystērion

A third key term that emerges in Colossians and Ephesians is not new to the Pauline corpus. The word *mystērion* occurs occasionally in Paul, and Paul is dependent on its functions in apocalyptic literature.[13] For Paul the word in the singular alludes to a specific bit of apocalyptic "scenery," the general scheme of which he keeps hidden. For example, in 1 Corinthians 15:51 he tells the Corinthians a *mystērion*: at the eschaton, those alive will be transformed into resurrection existence. The *mystērion* in Romans 11:25 reveals the ultimate salvation of Israel. The eschatological bent of the word is also apparent in 1 Corinthians 2:7: "We speak wisdom of God in *mystērion*, that which has been hidden, which God decreed before the ages for our glorification." Paul here looks forward to the ultimate glorification of believers as the culmination of God's eternal decree for humanity. The apostle probably plays on this idea in 1 Corinthians 4:1, when he speaks of the apostles as being stewards of the *mystērion* of God.[14] Paul thus thinks in terms of an overarching, eschatological plan of God, which will culminate in the final end of history (cf. 1 Cor 15).

Mystērion *in Colossians*

The word "mystery" occurs four times in Colossians. The first appearance, in 1:26-27, is perhaps the most consistent with Paul's use of the term, but even here the fulsomeness of the rhetoric illuminates a decisive shift. The term *mystērion* seems to be identical with the *logos* of God. The Word is "the mystery hidden for ages and generations, but now revealed to his saints, to whom God wished to make known the richness of his glory of this mystery among the Gentiles, which is Christ in us, the hope of glory." The mystery is the eternal plan God has determined for believers, who are now Gentiles. The eschatological plan, once focused on Jews, now involves Gentiles, and since Gentiles now constitute the primary body of believers, the mystery centers on what Gentiles receive. The almost ecstatic rhetoric seems to exult in the idea that Gentiles now are part of God's plan—indeed, *are* the plan! The Gentile church is heir of God's ultimate plan for humans. And what is the ultimate goal? "Christ in you, the hope of glory." But here we come to the heart of the ambiguity in Colossians. Is the ultimate goal the union of Christ and believer, or is it the eschatological future? Certainly, the author wishes to affirm that one cannot have the latter without first having the former. Ethical preparation has been replaced with mystical union.

The word is repeated shortly thereafter, in 2:2-3. Again the language is fulsome. The term *mystērion* is associated in the immediate context with richness (*ploutos*), assured understanding (*plērophoria*), understanding (*synesis*), and knowledge (*epignōsis*). It is difficult to know whether these words should be carefully distinguished from one another or whether they simply form a giant web of eulogistic praises. The author is still not done, however. The mystery is equated with Christ, and to this is added, "in whom are hidden all the treasures of wisdom and knowledge." I do not think one can attempt to be precise about the words chosen. The intellective terms are clear throughout. The author seems to want to say that *mystērion* engulfs all given wisdom. That the author has in mind any particular set of philosophical systems seems unlikely. It is also unlikely that he has in mind any eschatological scheme. The present *mystērion* is the generic term for God's perfect plan that culminates in the Gentile believer's participation in Christ. The eschatological temporal goal is close to being replaced by a present participation in God's ultimate wisdom. The final occurrence is Colossians 4:3. Once again *mystērion* is equated with *logos*. In fact, in this context the term "mystery" seems tantamount to "gospel."

In Colossians, then, *mystērion* has become a central term for God's plan for the Gentiles. But the author emphasizes a reality in the present, in which Gentiles may participate, and in that participation reach the relation with Christ that is the ultimate salvation for believers.

Mystērion *in Ephesians*

The author sets the basic meaning in the first occurrence—a meaning similar to that in Colossians, but yet with a distinctive difference. "For he has made known to us in all wisdom and insight the mystery of his will, according to his purpose which he set forth in [Christ], as a plan [*oikonomian*] for the fullness of

the times, to unite all things in Christ, things in heaven and things on earth."
Here, with the same overindulging of wisdom words as in Colossians 2:2, the
author portrays God's *mystērion* as God's plan executed through Christ. Now,
however, the goal is stated differently from Colossians. The goal is not that of
uniting with Christ but the "historical" achievement of uniting (*anakephalaioō*)
all things on earth and heaven. This is remarkably similar to the language of
the hymn in Colossians (v. 20), except that the word there is *apokatalassō*. The
idea is also consonant with the liturgical fragment in Ephesians 1:20-23, even
vv. 22-23, excluding the mention of the church as an insertion into the fragment.[15] It should also be noted that Ephesians 1:10 is completely compatible
with the Cosmocrator trajectory.

In the next occurrences (3:3-4) we learn only that the mystery had been
hidden from all history until now, when it has been revealed to apostles and
prophets through the Spirit.[16] The author continues to emphasize that the mystery is a "plan" hidden for all times (again, the emphasis is on, at least tacitly,
that which is now revealed to the Gentiles). In 3:9 this idea is continued. The
plan (*oikonomia*), which is the mystery, has been hidden until the present time.

What is startlingly new is the addition, "That through the church the mani-
fold wisdom of God might now be made known to the principalities and powers
in the heavenly places" (*tais archais kai tais exousiais en tois epouraniois*, v. 10).
The *mystērion* has been hidden from all reality until the event of the Christ,
through whom the divine plan of uniting all things has been made known to
the church. Yet, until the advent of the church, the *mystērion* has not been made
known to the powers and principalities. Since the mystery was hidden in God (v.
9), it is clear *nobody* knew of it except God. Nor is it surprising that, if the powers
and principalities are hostile to God's plan (as I think the authorial view has it),
God did not disclose the *mystērion* to them.

How the church revealed the mystery to the powers is part of the mystery!
The most likely suggestion is that of A. Lincoln: Just by its very existence, the
church manifests to the powers the outcome of God's plan.[17] Apart from a peculiar use in 5:32, a reference to a *mystērion* in the relation of husband and wife, the
last occurrence of *mystērion* in Ephesians is 6:19. Here we have an explicit identification of *euangelion* and *mystērion*—an identification possible also in Colossians 4:3. I think it clear, however, that in Ephesians the ruling term is *mystērion*
rather than *euangelion*.

The use in Colossians and Ephesians differs significantly. Both begin by
extolling God's *mystērion* as if it were an eschatological plan, hidden for ages, now
revealed in the event of Christ. At this point, however, the two authors diverge.
For Colossians the consummation of the mystery is the joining of believer to
Christ. For Ephesians it is the cosmic plan of uniting, of bringing into existence
the new reality. Yet neither author carries through on the usual eschatological

end-time denouement. For Colossians the goal of the mystery is the relationship with Christ. And while Ephesians could more easily look forward to a historical consummation, the author does not seem to want to go that far. The divine reality is realized in the present. True to the Cosmocrator trajectory, what is being realized does not mean ultimate perfection. Nothing the author says makes us look forward to an end of the historical order.

Excursus: The Powers and Principalities

Are the powers and principalities hostile to God's plan? There is no simple answer to this question. Colossians and Ephesians go their own ways and present their own difficulties.

Colossians

The powers occur only in two places in Colossians, and each of these suggests different solutions. The first and most obvious place is the hymn in 1:15-20. The powers were created by the one who is the image of God (v. 16) and they thus belong under his rule. The consummation of the divine act is the reconciliation of all powers in him who has made peace. While there is a dark hint of rebellion, the ultimate result is reconciliation. Whatever had been the case, the cosmos is now unified under the firstborn from the dead. Since this event is tacitly linked with the resurrection, it must be the case that the believers do not now have to fight against negative forces outside the historical realm.

But there is another passage, also replete with liturgical echoes, that goes its own, different metaphorical way, although the outcome may be the same as in the hymn. In the fulsome passage 2:10-15, a different set of metaphors dominates. Verse 10 begins by affirming that Christ is the head of the powers. Then follows a description of the events of Gentile incorporation into the church: a spiritual circumcision, baptism, and resurrection; being dead in sin, made alive with Christ, having had sins forgiven. Then follows v. 14, an extremely difficult verse.[18] Whatever is the negative evidence held against humans, God (most exegetes assume that God is the subject of vv. 14-15) has nailed such claims to the cross (i.e., the crucified Jesus has taken these claims upon himself). Verse 15 is the crucial and climactic moment. In God's act of the cross, God has "stripped the powers and principalities, made a public example of them by leading them in a triumphal procession behind him." The metaphor is of a victory procession in which the captured enemy, humiliated by nakedness, is forced to follow the victorious ruler—in this case, Christ.[19]

Whatever the details may ultimately be, it is clear that the powers are seen as hostile to God's intent for humanity and that they are ultimately defeated in the cross. Nothing could be further from the metaphor than the notion of reconciliation—the key word in the hymn in 1:15-20. The effect may be the same: Christ is head of the powers; but the metaphors are strikingly different. It suggests that these two passages originate from different "places" in the theological reflection of the church, the origins of which are beyond our reach.

What holds the two passages together is the confidence that the powers no longer hold sway over humans. It is interesting to note that there is no passage in Colossians like Ephesians 6:10-13. There are continuing sins among believers, but the author of Colossians does not attribute them to powers other than human volition.

Ephesians

At first glance, the decision here seems simple. In Ephesians 6:11-17 the author uses a long metaphor of armor to highlight how vigilantly the church must fight, not against human realities, but "against the principalities, against the powers, against the world rulers of the present darkness, against the spiritual powers in the heavens" (v. 12). Fight against the devil has been mentioned earlier, and this battle takes place in the context of the evil day and the evil one. There is no fiercer description in the New Testament of the participation of the church in this heavenly war. That there is opposition is not the issue; the only question is the outcome of the battle. To this I shall return.

An earlier reference to the powers and principalities is more ambiguous. In 3:10 it is the church's duty to make known God's *mystērion* to the principalities and powers in the heavens. In and of itself, it would be difficult to determine whether the disclosure has the purpose of enabling these powers to participate in the mystery or whether the disclosure is a sign of victory over these powers. If one reads 4:9 out of 6:12, then disclosure is victory. But that is not the only way to read the passage.

The first reference to the powers and principalities in the letter occurs at 1:20-23. Here, in what I have suggested is a fragment from a confession, the usual Cosmocrator trajectory affirmation of the resurrection as enthronement over all previous rulers is affirmed. As so often happens, however, it is not clear whether the enthronement is victory over opposition, or reconciliation, or restoration, or reunification into a harmonious whole. The fragment itself does not give itself away. True, the idea of the use of Psalm 8 might suggest the victory. On the other hand, the head/body language in v. 23 might suggest harmony. The announced purpose of uniting all things in 1:10 certainly could suggest reconciliation or harmony.[20] Certainly, there is nothing of the *Sturm und Drang* of the passage in 6:12, and the difference in tone is striking.

Thus we have one passage (6:12) in which the powers and principalities are evil. We have two passages (1:10; 1:20-23) in which the simplest interpretation is to see the powers as at least neutral, and perhaps not at all hostile. We have one passage (3:10) that could be read either way. Is there a solution? If we look at the forms, what do we see? There is one fragment, surely pre-authorial, in which the easiest reading is "neutral." We have one passage of admonition stating a continuing war. Although the details of this admonition are perhaps traditional, it is surely appropriate to see the author's intentions at work. It is also important to see that this war is a continuing one, even after the enthronement of Christ.

I think it thus likely that the pre-authorial stratum of the material worked from a view that the cosmos was harmonious with the enthronement of the Christ; the author, however, saw the situation differently. For him, the powers and principalities were evil and were continuing to oppose God's mystery (cf. also 2:2). This is the author who inserted *tē ekklēsia* into 1:22, which minimized (or opposed) the harmonious relationship of head and body as a cosmic reality. He is also the one who vaunts the church as the vehicle of disclosure of the mystery to the powers and principalities—and at this point we can concede that this disclosure is probably a cry of victory rather than one of incorporation.

The final question concerns whether the warfare in the author's mind will continue or whether there is an eschatological denouement, an end of the historical reality. In general, the author seems to live with the assurance of God's victory (as he would put it), which assures the ultimate safety of the believers (already seated in heaven). There is opposition lurking to upset this safety (e.g., 2:2). There is encouragement to fight the battle (6:11-17). But is the ultimate end of the battle an eschatological denouement? I see no strong suggestion that this is in the author's mind. The believers are encouraged to fight *hina dynēthēte antistēnai en tē hēmera tē ponēra kai apanta katergasamenoi stēnai*, "so that you may be able to withstand on that evil day, and having done everything, to stand firm" (v. 13). Presumably, the final exhortation is "to stand," that is, not to surrender. Nothing is said about ultimate victory. The battle seems to be a continuous one, which the church must for all time continue to endure.

The author of Colossians also does not emphasize an end of the historical process, although he does acknowledge a future reality. The ultimate goal of history is the relationship between the believer and God.

Summary and Conclusion

1. Both Colossians and Ephesians remain within the basic Cosmocrator trajectory, however much some of the metaphors they use show novel perspectives. As so often happens, different metaphors do not necessarily mean different perspectives.

2. Both documents have absorbed into their thinking the notion of the *plērōma*. What source or sources there may have been for this term is not clear. The use does suggest a way of thinking that we might call "spatial," a way of uniting realities into wholes. The two documents, however, use the term in different ways. In Colossians, the *plērōma* is the union of the godhead. In Ephesians, on the one hand, it is the union of the cosmos; on the other, it is the unity of the believer with the godhead. This spatial thinking has tended to replace the temporal direction of Jewish thought.

3. This spatial thinking has enabled both authors to think in terms of believers already being in heaven because of their relation to God and Christ. If believers have been raised, it seems logical to think of their presence in heaven. One must be careful to see, however, that spatial thinking can be as metaphorical as temporal.

4. There is still temporal thinking on the part of these authors. It manifests itself in the divine plan, the *mystērion*. This is God's intent for humanity, conceived from eternity, but hidden from all until the advent of the Christ. In effect, for these authors it is a plan for the salvation of Gentiles, now incorporated into the story of God's people. Focus on a future denouement of history, however, seems absent in Ephesians and downplayed in Colossians. The plan culminates and completes itself in the relation of believers to the godhead. The culmination of the plan is the ultimate relationship, variously expressed in the texts.

Let me try to compare and contrast what I consider the views expressed here with what I will call a "typical" perspective in the earlier Cosmocrator trajectory. In the earlier trajectory the resurrected Christ was viewed as a supreme ruler. One lived in society under the now benign Lord, anticipating that the world would be different and better because the new ruler is the divinely appointed one. One did not look forward to an eschatological denouement, but did expect the present society to be improved because of the change of lordships. Believers were now free to live out their authentic lives under God.

In the alteration given by our present documents, one still honors the Cosmocrator trajectory's belief in the resurrected Jesus as supreme Lord. One also has no view of an eschatological future. Instead of a societal expectation, however, the present documents urge incorporation into the godhead. I have avoided the term "mysticism" because I am not sure it is appropriate. Nothing is said about experiential dimensions, although I do think one can talk about mysticism without experiential dimensions—as I believe the Gospel of John does. There is, I think, a tendency toward a relation that one could call "objective." That is, it exists when and if the believer lives and believes so that she and he are incorporated into the divine reality. The language of *plērōma* and *mystērion* is used to point in this direction. At any rate, the ultimate goal is not a future denouement but the present salvational relationship with Christ and God that is sometimes (not always) expressed in substantival ways.

The outside world no longer seems important. Colossians and Ephesians concentrate more on the inward reality of church and relationship with God. The political and social dimension of the Cosmocrator trajectory no longer is the focus of the victory of the resurrected Lord. Instead, one moves "indoors" into the church and upward to the salvational relationship with God.

9 ─────────────────────────────────────

Hebrews and the Cosmocrator Trajectory

The brilliance and ambiguities of this document have long been known and chronicled. It is generally agreed that the document is rhetorically shaped; that is, it is either a record of a speech or a treatise composed in the shape of a speech. It is not a letter, such as we find in the specifically directed ones of Paul. The author obviously knows something about his addressees and speaks to their present and past situation. Mostly these references are general and past-oriented. Only in chapter 13 does he tell them what he thinks they should do—and even this is veiled in a metaphorical system.

There is no consensus either as to dating or to addressees. On the one hand, the author writes as if the temple system in Jerusalem is still in effect. On the other, the references to some sort of persecution in the past and the encouragement to cease claiming Judaism as a parent suggests a post-70 date, perhaps even a late first-century date.[1] Early Rabbinic discussions about the temple as if it were still standing, although it had clearly been destroyed by that time, make a pre-70 date less compelling. There is a difference, however, between the moods and modes of the two kinds of materials. In Hebrews the temple is set up to be argued against: it is this against that. One wonders if this kind of argumentation would have been seen as necessary or helpful in a post-70 Diaspora environment.

Are the addressees Jewish, Gentile, or mixed? The author writes as if the audience is versed in the regulations for the temple. The author also writes in the most literate Greek of the New Testament. Presumably this means his addressees are Hellenistic in culture. But where in Hellenistic culture, either Diaspora Judaism or Gentile, would one find a community or communities knowledgeable about this system? For that matter, how does the author know what he knows? Is he Jewish? And if the audience is Hellenistic, why is there no reference to pagan sacrificial systems, which would have been much more obvious to a Hellenistic setting than a temple across the sea, standing or otherwise? In other words, since the upshot of the document is to abolish *any* sacrificial system, why is there not some attention to pagan practices, which would have been so obvious, perhaps painfully so, to a believer in Jesus, whether Jewish or Gentile? Alas, we cannot answer our own questions.

The question that does press, however, is whether in a theological analysis, the usual decisions about introductory matters are crucial. In my judgment, a theological analysis can proceed cautiously without knowing the answers to these questions, although I wish we were able to settle these issues more than we can. For whatever it is worth, I will give my hunches about location and dating, even though these hunches do not determine the judgments I make about the theological stance of the author. It seems to me most likely that the document is late-first century (emphasizing the call in chapter 13 to separate from the synagogue) and that it was addressed to a Hellenistic audience, which was, at time of writing, largely Gentile, though informed by a view of faith that stressed its Jewish origins. That the author details so much about the temple system does not, in my judgment, prove that the audience is knowledgeable about these matters, any more than one could be confident that Paul's Galatian believers were versed enough in the Jewish legal system to understand all he said in his letter to them. The audience in Hebrews may have been more overwhelmed by the bombardment of the author than knowledgeably convinced by the arguments. I am suspicious of the view that the knowledge of addressees can be read out of the level of the author's presentation; at least, one has to be cautious about making a one-to-one correlation. It is also the case that an author may be writing to an "audience behind the audience"—as I believe Paul was in his letter to the Galatians. I rather doubt that those Galatian Gentiles could easily follow Paul's logic. I am sure that the missionaries Paul was opposing could, and did, make sense of his logic (no doubt to disagree with it). Just so, in Hebrews there is an assumed backdrop of people who believed the church should fit within the walls of the Jewish system. If the author expects to be understood at his level, it is perhaps this audience behind the audience that he is really addressing.

Hebrews and the Cosmocrator Trajectory

At first glance the theology of Hebrews seems firmly set within the Cosmocrator trajectory. In the elegant exordium (1:1-4) the author claims that the revelatory actor, the Son, is the agent of creation, exists in (or at least close to) the "nature" of deity, and has sat down "at the right hand of the Majesty on high." Sitting at the right hand is repeated several times in the document (8:1; 10:12; 12:2), all clearly referring to the resurrected, glorified Jesus. Reference to battle with enemies is explicitly mentioned in reference to Psalm 110:1 in 1:13 and 10:13 and a curious dancing around the motif of subjection of "everything" occurs in 2:8f., in reference to Psalm 8.

Nevertheless, a careful look at the language shows a number of important differences from the Cosmocrator trajectory, which indicate that the author has in a major way altered the basic trajectory. Chief among these is the absence of any language about the subjection of the powers and principalities to the resurrected Jesus. In fact, terms used elsewhere in the Cosmocrator trajectory to indicate the past rulers of the cosmos do not appear in the vocabulary of Hebrews.

The political model of rulership is thus absent. Consonant with the absence of rulership language is the absence of the dominant acclamation, *kyrios Iēsous Christos*, in the document, which in the Cosmocrator trajectory can be associated with the rulership motif (as in Philippians 2:11). The closest the author comes to that language is in 13:20, in the final benediction, with an appeal to the resurrection of "our Lord Jesus." The rarity of *kyrios* language in Hebrews to refer to Jesus may suggest that this passage echoes a formula from the tradition.

Furthermore, the language of subjection, referring to the present lordship of Jesus, is seen to be inappropriate. Commenting on Psalm 8:7 (LXX)—"all things [God] subjecting under his feet"—the author admits: "Now we do not yet see all things subjected to him" (Heb 2:8).[2] That is, a key platform of the Cosmocrator trajectory is rejected. The world continues as it is; no change occurs within it because of the exaltation of the resurrected Jesus. What we can be confident in, continues the author, is that we "see" the resurrected Jesus glorified (v. 9). The author's eschatology forces the subjugation into the future.

With this in mind it is interesting to see how the author handles the phrase in Psalm 110:1, "until I make your enemies your footstool." While the Psalm clearly implies that God is the actor causing the subjection of the enemies, in the Cosmocrator tradition, the resurrected Lord tends to take a more active role. The implication in some materials is even that the subjugation has already occurred. Indeed, Paul in 1 Corinthians 15:25 explicitly assigns the active role to the reigning, exalted Jesus. In Hebrews, however, the text makes it clear that God is the actor, performing the subjugation. The role of the exalted Jesus is simply to "wait" until God completes the work. "He sat down at the right hand of God, then to wait until his enemies should be made a stool for his feet" (10:13). Between the resurrection and the denouement of the second coming, the exalted Jesus plays no royal role.

In fact, at the denouement the "coming" Jesus (whatever that means) will not come as the judge but as savior. In a sentence that seems ambiguous but which offers little likelihood for an alternate reading, the author says: "Thus Christ . . . will appear a second [time] not to deal with sin but to offer salvation for those expecting him" (9:28).[3] Does this mean that there is no judgment of the evil along with the good, as we may indeed find in Paul? No, because the author is clear that God remains the judge. "Eternal judgment" is listed in 6:2 as one of the elementary doctrines. The author assumes its reality and feels no need to devote attention to it. That it is part of his theological structure, however, can be noted in 10:26, where he rather luridly warns of "a fearful prospect of judgment" for those to reject the faith, once having accepted it. But if it is not the returning Jesus who exercises eschatological judgment, who can it be? The obvious answer is God—which seems to be stated in 12:23, with a reference to God as judge. The context of the passage hovers between eschatological or present description. Even if God is judge in the present, or if it is here primarily an honorific title, the implication would seem to be that, if there is an eschatological judgment, it is acted out by God. At any rate, such judgment is not the prerogative of the exalted Jesus.

In sum, all royal roles have carefully and explicitly been removed from the Cosmocrator structure. The exalted Jesus is not the reigning Lord; he is not the ruler over the powers and principalities; they are not subjected to him; when he comes again, it is not to exercise the royal role of final judge. God remains the actor who exercises authority and power over the cosmos.

What then is the function of the resurrected and exalted Jesus? He is the heavenly high priest. "We have such a high priest who is seated at the right hand of the majesty in heaven" (8:1). Here the royal motif of being seated at the right hand is explicitly assigned to the one who is the high priest. In 4:14 the author points to this high priest who has "passed through the heavens," and is named "Jesus, the Son of God." The notion of passing through the heavens is unique to New Testament vocabulary, although the author of Ephesians claims that the exalted Christ has risen above all the heavens (4:10). Presumably the passage in Hebrews implies that the exalted high priest is not just in the heavenly arena but at the highest point, where God is. That there is no specific cosmic geography in mind is suggested by the language in 9:24, where in contrast to the earthly temple, Christ has "entered heaven itself."

God, it will be recalled, exercises the royal functions, otherwise ascribed to the Cosmocrator, and the exalted Jesus "waits" until God has completed this work. As heavenly high priest, however, the exalted Jesus has a crucial function. His priesthood, in effect, begins with his resurrection and entry into the heavenly temple. In contrast to the earthly priesthood, the resurrected Jesus has an eternal existence; "Consequently he is able for all time to save those who draw near through him to God, always living to make intercession on their behalf" (7:25). The same idea seems to be repeated, in different words, in 9:24: The resurrected high priest has entered into heaven, thus now able "to appear before God on our behalf."

The imagery demands the scene of a priest making intercessory prayers to the deity on behalf of a people or individual. The deity is pictured as having the final authority of decision. In the case of the resurrected Jesus, however, he is himself in the presence of God and thus can speak directly with God on behalf of—whom? In 9:24 the image seems to be that those interceded for are already believers, already in the church. Why then does the heavenly high priest need to intercede? Have they sinned since becoming believers?[4] In 7:25, on the other hand, the heavenly high priest seems to present to God the names of the new faithful, asking God to enroll them in the book of the saved. If the phrase *eis to panteles* in 7:25 means "for all time," then the idea seems clearly that of beseeching God to add new members to the list of the saved. If the phrase means "completely," "entirely," then it is not so clear that 7:25 says anything different from 9:24.[5] Unless the eschatology of Hebrews is purely artificial, then "for all time" would seem to indicate a temporal perspective foreign to a genuine eschatology.

It is interesting to see Paul using the idea of Hebrews 7:25 in Romans 8:34. In his metaphorical system, however, the context is a legal one, the heavenly court, in which the resurrected Jesus plays the role of a legal witness (or defense attorney). Paul, no more than the author of Hebrews, feels the need to get specific about what the nature of the intercession is. In both cases, the bottom line seems to be the assurance the idea brings to the believer. The believer can be confident of her or his salvation because, as Luther well put it, "the right man is on our side." Thus what really matters is not which metaphorical system is "better," but which captures best the confidence of the believer. Obviously for the author of Hebrews, the priestly metaphor speaks best to him.

The Earthly Jesus

Closely related to the work of the high priest is, of course, at least in the author's mind, that of Jesus as the sacrifice. While the work of the high priest is focused on present intercessory activity of the exalted Jesus, that of the sacrifice seems to be tied in with the death of the earthly Jesus. This raises an even more difficult issue than that of the exalted Jesus. Just what is the function of the earthly Jesus, and how does that relate to the inclination in the Cosmocrator trajectory to pay little attention to that side of Jesus, except perhaps with some reference to his death? True to that trajectory's general lack of interest in the earthly Jesus, the author of Hebrews says nothing (or very little) about the teaching of Jesus and nothing (or very little) about his miraculous activity.[6] Why, then, does he take the pains to emphasize certain other dimensions? It is reasonable to discuss the author's judgments under three headings: humiliation, overcoming of death, and sacrifice for sin.

Humiliation. That the earthly Jesus suffered has almost a romantic ring to it, and certainly the words depicting this are the most memorable—at least the most remembered—in the document. The author mentions the "suffering of death" (3:9), the perfection that comes through suffering (2:10; 5:8f.), the human temptations (4:15), the uttering of cries to be saved from death (5:7), the despising of the shame of crucifixion, the suffering outside the gate (13:12). The hard question remains: What is the function of this motif?

More than one function is detectable. The first is paraenetic: As Jesus was willing to suffer, so we should accept whatever shame and abuse is heaped upon one because of commitment to Jesus. A telling statement is made in 13:13: we should accept the same shame or abuse (*oneidismon*) he endured. The same word is used in 10:33 of believers' suffering. Our leader has suffered; thus we should be willing to do the same. Even more: "Because he himself has suffered and been tempted, he is able to help those who are tempted" (2:19).

The second function is christological. The earthly Jesus is completely human (e.g., 2:11, 14) and he has to be made "perfect" (e.g., 2:10; 5:7) through suffering. He has to be perfected so that he can be the requisite high priest (e.g., 5:9). This old Wisdom motif is here put into the service of Christology, but in a curious way. If perfection is necessary so that the exalted Jesus can function properly, then this motif of the earthly Jesus really serves as a preparation for his role as exalted high priest. Then the question nags: Since Jesus has been exalted, why does perfection tied to earthly existence matter? Clearly, the author is sensitive to the need for a perfected, earthly Jesus. His statement that Jesus was sinless (4:15)[7] communicates that clearly. But again the question nags: if Jesus was sinless, was he not already perfected? What does the author of Hebrews want to communicate by his emphasis on perfection through suffering, if "perfection" is not primarily a moral category (i.e., not about sin)?[8] Suffering is something the Son must go through to be qualified to function in his heavenly office. Since perfection comes after suffering and is the moment of qualification for heavenly duties, it denotes, in effect, the resurrection of Jesus itself. The offering that then perfects those being sanctified (10:14) might then, in effect, relate Jesus' perfection with that of the believers. That is, the resurrection of Jesus effects that of the believers.

Overcoming of death. In one remarkable passage, the author ascribes to Jesus' death the moment of victory over death (2:14-15): "That through death he might destroy him who has the power of death, that is, the devil, and deliver all those who through fear of death were subject to lifelong bondage." This is remarkable because it is both like and unlike statements made elsewhere in the New Testament. The picture behind the imagery implies that Satan is the cause of death for mortals. It also suggests that the fear of death is a genuine enslavement for humans.

This fits in well with the general Cosmocrator emphasis upon Jesus as the victor over powers and principalities. The author deviates from the usual view by (a) introducing the name "devil" as the power involved and by (b) identifying this victory with Jesus' death rather than resurrection. Paul, of course, writes of Jesus' victory over death (1 Cor 15:26), but for Paul this is the "last" victory, certainly associated with the eschatological denouement and not in any explicit way related to the devil. It is also true that in Colossians 2:13-15 the author associates the disarming of the powers and principalities with God's victory over them in the cross—and here victory over death is stated as part of that disarming. This passage, however, associates victory over death with the annulling of the demands, presumably of the Torah, not of some Satanic figure. Thus the death of Jesus functions as a liberating event, also a motif of the Cosmocrator trajectory, though rarely associated with death rather than exaltation. The author shows by his reworking of the story how variegated could be the general idea of Jesus as God's victory over the powers and principalities. It may not be accidental that this is another example of the author's removal of the victory motif from the resurrection of Jesus per se.

Sacrifice for sin. This motif is stated in the exordium ("having made purification for sins," 1:3), but is not iterated until the author expounds the notion of Jesus as high priest in chapters 9 and 10. In these later passages, the motif is mentioned, almost in passing, and does not receive the kind of detailed exposition of the high priest. It is also of note that the author refers to the effective death of Jesus with various terms. In 9:12, the death achieves an "eternal redemption" (*aiōnian lytrōsin*); in 9:14 it purifies the conscience; in 9:15 it redeems from sins of the first covenant; in 9:26 it abolishes sin; in 10:12 the death is a sacrifice for sins; in 10:14 it "has perfected for all time those who are sanctified." The idea is referred to again in passing in 12:24 and 13:12.

But what does the author intend to say by this series of references? Such an apparently simple question becomes complex and difficult to answer, once the evidence is stacked together. Notions of sacrifice, redemption, purification, perfection—all these jostle for attention. The very variety of metaphors and their insertion into a larger discussion (of Jesus as high priest) suggest that the author's attention is primarily focused on the high priest, while the notion of the effective death of Jesus is scattered throughout the larger discussion, perhaps because it is a traditional theme. Only once is the link between the two themes made explicit (9:12).

The idea of perfection might seem to be the author's own contribution to the meaning of Jesus' death, but even that is shrouded in mistiness. In 5:8f., there seems to be a chain that progresses from obedience through suffering to becoming perfect to being the source for salvation for others. In 10:14 the perfection extends to believers, because of the death. Clearly the perfection is not a moral category. Nor does it seem to be cultic. Does it relate to the religious sense of "initiation"—that is, of Jesus and then believers being initiated into the new covenant? Attridge suggests it might mean "a vocational process by which he is made complete or fit for his office." Jesus thus becomes "the perfect model."[9] The ambiguity of its possible meaning may thus suggest that all the terms essentially say the same thing, but even what the "same thing" might mean is uncertain.

The ambiguity can best be pointed to by asking just what sin or sins Jesus' death does away with. The author is surprisingly vague about what he takes sin to be, considering that he refers to the death of Jesus as frequently as he does. One could compare Paul's letters (even the vice catalogues are absent in Hebrews), or the deutero-Pauline letters that focus on what the Gentiles do or did. Nothing of that specificity emerges in our document.[10] In one place the author explicitly identifies sin as that occurring under the first covenant (9:15). But is his view of sin simply retrospective and related to Jews only? And if that is his basic meaning, is his audience primarily, or only, Jewish believers in Jesus? Or does the reference in verse 15 to "the called" refer to all those who live after the first covenant is taken care of? That is, is the idea that, whether for Jews or Gentiles, the new covenant cannot become effective without a death that abolishes the old? If the author wanted to be specific, why is he not clearer?

Before I try to put together these various and not always consistent strains, there is still another passage, not yet discussed, that seems to belong under the rubric of the earthly Jesus.

> For if the message (*logos*) declared by angels was valid, and every transgression or disobedience received a just retribution, how shall we escape if we neglect such a great salvation? It (*hētis*) was declared at first by the Lord, and it was attested to us by those who heard, God witnessing also by signs and wonders and various miracles and by gifts of the Holy Spirit distributed according to his will. (2:2-4)

This passage is difficult and is susceptible to more than one interpretation. The beginning seems clear enough. The author compares the legal demands of the law with "salvation."[11] That he means the message of salvation seems logical (to make the comparison work) and is supported by the following phrase, which points to speech, declared by "the Lord." What we seem to have here is a three-stage, or three-level process: first, speech, then attestation by others, and finally miracles, whose purpose is to corroborate the legitimacy of the speech and the attestation.

It seems to me that we have three options for locating this process. (1) It may refer to Old Testament prophecies, which are seen to be independent of the Torah delivered by the angels. (2) It may refer to the message of the earthly Jesus, passed on by the original disciples and corroborated by the miracles of Jesus or those of the disciples, or both. (3) It may refer to the speech of the resurrected, exalted Jesus, the miracles then referring to those in the early church. Each of these options has attractive, as well as problematic features, but I cannot here go into adequate detail.

One key issue is to whom "the Lord" refers. Is it God, the earthly Jesus, or the resurrected Jesus? The term *kyrios* occurs in Hebrews sixteen times. It is certain that eleven of these occurrences refer to God.[12] Of these eleven, ten are in Scriptural citations (the exception is 8:2). The term certainly refers to Jesus in three places: 1:10 (also an Old Testament citation), 13:20 ("our Lord Jesus"), and 7:14. The reference in 12:14 could be to either Jesus or God. Since the scriptural citations are givens, they may be discounted as far as reading the author's preferences. Once discounted, *kyrios* actually refers to Jesus more than to God, but these statistics do not help us with the passage at hand. For what it is worth, the certain *kyrios* references to Jesus are evenly divided in "location." Hebrews 1:10 refers to preexistence; 7:14, to the earthly Jesus; and 13:28, to the exalted Jesus. In my judgment, the referent of *kyrios* in 2:3 has to be determined by the context. Alas, there are three possible contexts.

A perhaps helpful exercise is to ask where else in the New Testament would we find a similar context? There are three options.

1. Old Testament predictions. That certain prophets or prophecies in the Old Testament were inspired and were references to the coming final revelation of Jesus is not, of course, an unusual idea. It is certainly present in Hebrews itself. The exordium begins with such references, and the scriptural catena uses Old Testament texts to show that Jesus is the person meant by the citations. That Jesus and the church are the fulfillment of Scripture is a constant theme of the author of Luke-Acts, and Paul's use of Scripture constantly assumes this common point of view in the early church.

2. The earthly Jesus. Here the ground becomes less certain. That Jesus taught is, of course, a common feature of the Gospel tradition—although that he proclaimed "salvation" would be a matter of interpretation.[13] To my knowledge, nowhere else in the non-Gospel literature, in documents that might count as belonging to the Cosmocrator trajectory, is there any similar tradition about Jesus' proclamation of salvation—not even in the book of Acts, where one might expect to find such a tradition. In the epistolary literature, any proclamation of salvation involves the message *about* Jesus, not the message of Jesus himself. This is true of Acts 4:12 as well ("There is salvation in no one else. . ."). On the other hand, that the miracles mentioned in Hebrews could refer to those done by Jesus

is reflected in Acts 2:22, where similar terms are used and the deeds are specifically stated to be done by God. It needs to be emphasized, however, that Acts 2:22 is itself unique (unless Heb 2:3 is parallel) to the Cosmocrator trajectory. Thus while the words in Hebrews can make sense with the earthly Jesus as the context, it certainly would be unique, not only in the Cosmocrator trajectory but in the Son of Man trajectory as well.

3. The resurrected Jesus. This context would suggest, I take it, that the resurrected Jesus proclaimed, in some way, salvation and that the miracles referred to were those done by charismatic figures in the early church. Again the problem is that there is hardly any other place in the New Testament tradition where a similar assertion is made. True, in Acts the resurrected Jesus appears to his disciples and teaches them "about the kingdom of God." I know of no other parallel. Some have suggested that Hebrews 2:3 possibly reflects a church tradition.[14] I agree that the passage with its listing sounds that way; I do not see how one can be confident of its traditional origin when one can find no other unit that says the same thing. The Cosmocrator trajectory certainly is silent about such things, and this militates against an easy agreement regarding its traditional status.

In the presence of so many uncertainties, I think it precarious to pronounce a sure decision about the matter. What the author wants to impress upon his hearers is essentially clear and simple, regardless of the conundrums that beset the scholar: It is essential to adhere to the faith that Jesus is the bringer of "salvation" and to trust the proclamation that the author and others like him make, since they stand in a firm, attested tradition.

Alas, we want to know too much: in this case, which tradition the author had in mind. For all who are concerned with mapping the terrain of the earthly Jesus in Hebrews, this question is, nevertheless, important, if unanswerable. I think it most likely that the tradition assumed is that of Old Testament prophecy. Since, however, the weight of the scholarly tradition lies against this and for the earthly Jesus interpretation, I can only acknowledge my deviation from the preferred context and bow to the scholarly preference. In the summary that follows, I will include both "contexts" to show how the general picture of the earthly Jesus might be slightly different, depending upon the option chosen.

Summary. True to the Cosmocrator trajectory, the author of Hebrews puts all the weight of the earthly Jesus in the significance of his death. A different nuance, however, seems to shimmer through the language. In most of the Cosmocrator trajectory the death of Jesus is seen from the perspective of God's act. In Hebrews, the language seems to suggest that the author thinks of the event more as something that Jesus does. The difference may be minor—certainly both God's will and the obedience of the earthly Jesus are always seen together—or at least assumed everywhere in the Cosmocrator trajectory.

True to the Cosmocrator trajectory, there is nothing said about the teaching or miracles of the earthly Jesus. Even if 2:3f. does, as is widely thought, refer to the earthly Jesus, this is a passing, perhaps traditional, statement that does not seem to bear theological weight or purpose.

What does Jesus accomplish by his death? At least four things. (1) By his willing acceptance of suffering Jesus becomes a model for the believer—a model the author seems to think his audience needs to emulate more than it seems willing to do.[15] (2) By his death Jesus destroyed the devil and thus death itself, freeing humankind from a bondage that the fear of death enforces. (3) As sacrifice, his death absolves from sin, although the author does not get specific about what that means. (4) Jesus by his willing suffering becomes perfected, thus enabling his access to heaven as the perfect high priest, there to make intercession for believers.

Thus the earthly Jesus stands tall in the theology of Hebrews. Without his efficacious death, salvation would not be possible. In this sense Hebrews is unique in the Cosmocrator trajectory in the emphasis it places on the earthly Jesus as agent. Yet it is not the Jesus of the Gospels either, since teaching and miracle are not the focus. That makes it difficult to see Hebrews as a beginning bridge between the two trajectories. It rather remains what it is, unique and determined to portray Jesus its own way.

The Christology of Hebrews

The christological thrust of Hebrews is two-pronged. The one is the exalted Jesus, shorn of any political traits and functions. Here his function seems to be that of an intercessory priest for the faithful. The other is the earthly Jesus who does what is necessary to make a believing community possible: he does away with sin and death and becomes perfected so that he can enter into the heavenly temple. To try to put together the puzzle of the theology of Hebrews is to ask whether these two distinctive motifs can be put together in an integrated way.

One has to start with what I take to be a clear intention to denude the exalted Jesus of any political significance. It is not as if the author had an additional metaphor—that of the high priest—which he added to the traditional political metaphor of the Cosmocrator. He ruthlessly replaces the one with the other. But why does he wish to do that? I do not think any definite answer is possible. It could be that the political metaphor is perceived as dangerous. It could be that the realities of the situation have raised skepticism that any sort of transformation of the cosmos is possible; thus the metaphor is less believable and effective. At any rate, the replacement is too complete to be unintentional.

By the use of the priestly metaphor, he effectively takes the work of God out of the political, social, economic order and limits it to the church. The church is now not the place where the cosmic design of God is manifest but the only community to which God devotes attention. Furthermore, the work of God in the community seems to be that of preparing it for eternal life. Granted, the members have "tasted the heavenly gift and become partakers of the Holy Spirit" and "the goodness of the word of God and the powers of the age to come" (6:5f.). Here we have at least a strong residue of the sense of present transformation. In general, however, the community seems to be looking to the future to be joined to the exalted Jesus, who is to come to accept them into eternal life. For some in the Cosmocrator trajectory, this might seem a complete sell-out to an internalized and self-serving understanding of the scope of God's actions in Jesus. Our ignorance of the circumstances, however, means that we can hardly make judgments on the issue.

The picture of the earthly Jesus is, if anything, even stranger. While there is more stress on the person of Jesus than in any other Cosmocrator trajectory document in the New Testament, he is certainly not the overpowering strong man of the Gospels, outwitting his opponents with his clever stratagems, causing the audience (friends and enemies) to be awed by his profound teaching and powerful miracles of healing and nature.[16] No, the Jesus of Hebrews is a willing sufferer, facing and enduring death—with salvational results for believers. He is weak and has to call upon God for deliverance.[17]

What is going on? Why such an image? Granted, the death does have beneficial results, but that could have been affirmed without emphasis upon weakness. There are two possibilities.

Paraenetic: This is clearly an issue for the author. "For we have not a high priest who is unable to sympathize with our weaknesses, but one who in every respect has been tempted as we are, yet without sin" (4:15; cf. also 2:18; 13:13). Here the sufferings of Jesus are presented as an act of strength that the believer needs to emulate. Leaning on the wisdom tradition, suffering is presented as a path to maturity and ultimate achievement.

Anti-imperial: A second possibility is admittedly purely speculative; there is no positive support for it in the text. Could it be that the weakness of Jesus describes a person the opposite of the powerful emperor? Just as the exalted Jesus is denuded of imperial functions, so the earthly Jesus lives a life of weakness, not one of strength, power, and pomp. The attractiveness of this possibility is that it fits so neatly with the anti-imperial description of the exalted Jesus. The author may be fearful of any suggestion that Christianity is in competition with Rome. His sensitivity in chapter 13 to late-first-century issues of the separation of church and synagogue, and the political ramifications of such separation, might suggest he is casting an anxious eye to Rome and its increasing suspicion of the Christian enclaves.[18] One can certainly read the treatise as a statement of Christian political innocence, and the move toward a priestly metaphor as a direction toward political quietism. Whatever the intent, the result was to alter radically the original thrust of the Cosmocrator trajectory.

Another result was certainly in the author's mind. Ironically, the thrust of the document is anti-sacrificial. For the Greek or Roman, sacrifices were those of flesh and blood, immolations in the temples. But for the author of Hebrews what Jesus has done is effectively to end any sacrificial cult, whether Jewish or Greco-Roman. His "once for all" is the act that abolishes every sacrificial cultus. Thus with one stroke the author has distanced Christianity from both the political and the cultic arenas. What is then left? A proto-pietistic-Protestantism?

THEOLOGY AND POLITICS

Acts and Revelation

Not many New Testament documents have overt political messages. I suppose most, perhaps all, of these books have at one time or the other suggested to readers implications for attitudes toward government. Certainly implications are there; the problem is that they are covert and leave room for dispute. Most agree, however, that the book of Revelation carries an explicit political message. The apocalyptic enemies are, or are at least allied with, political figures, most likely Roman. Thus the Roman government assumes an adversarial position toward the true church.[1] It is also true that in chapter 18, the author laments the economic practices of the wealthy. Obviously such practices are broader than Roman and are temporally not bound by the times of the empire. Nevertheless, I believe that most scholars take the lament, which is also a prophecy of doom, to be directed explicitly toward Roman practices in his day. That is, in chapter 18 he has the Romans in mind.

While not everyone might agree, I think the book of Acts is equally explicitly political. On the surface, no two books in the New Testament are further apart. Revelation is a fantastic and a-historical portrait of the final end of the world. Acts, on the other hand, purports to be a historical account of the growth of the early church in its mostly mundane interaction with nonbelievers. Yet the word "mundane" is exactly the point. The way the author describes these interactions reveals his political concerns, fears, and hopes for the church at the beginning of the second century—surely not too far from the time of writing of Revelation.[2]

Yet how different are these fears and hopes from that of Revelation! For Revelation the fear is of cooperation with and capitulation to Rome; the author's hope is a church that will oppose the empire, even if that leads to martyrdom (as he thinks it surely will). The author of Acts, on the other hand, wants to convince his readers[3] that the church has nothing to fear from civic and Roman government, that the church and Rome are compatible. Thus the author's fear is that of unnecessary opposition between government and church; his hope is for a mutual understanding that will allow the church to grow and expand without opposition or persecution by government structures.[4]

The question that concerns me here is the relation between the theological and political positions of the authors. Is there something different in the theological stance that inevitably leads to their so different political attitudes? Or is it the case that the theological is controlled by the political agendas? These questions may ultimately be unanswerable, but I will confront the issue. First, I look at each one's theological structure, then compare the two, and finally raise the issue of the relation between theological and political.

The Theological Structure of Acts

Acts seems solidly anchored in the Cosmocrator trajectory.[5] The full acclamation, *Iēsous Christos kyrios*, occurs four times. Association of the name Jesus with the name or title *Christos* occurs frequently. Interest in what the earthly Jesus did is almost entirely tacit.[6] The author focuses on the death of Jesus as an evil act, not as salvatory, and on the resurrection. There are two issues, however, that affect how one views the theology of Acts, especially in relation to its consonance with the Cosmocrator trajectory. (1) Eschatology: In general the Cosmocrator trajectory minimizes the eschatological dimension of God's *oikonomia*, the eternal/temporal working out of God's purpose for history. The documents acknowledge the formal framework of an eschatological denouement, but as often as not, place emphasis upon the present consummation. For Paul, of course, the future remains vital. How does Acts fit into this perspective? (2) The meaning of the resurrection of Jesus: For the Cosmocrator trajectory, the resurrection of Jesus is modeled on a political structure—enthronement and rulership over the cosmos. As we shall see, for Acts the resurrection of Jesus is a variegated landscape.

The Issue of Eschatology

Whether there is a serious interest on the part of Luke-Acts in the coming end of the world in God's eschatological judgment has been disputed. One would think that the context of the various speeches in Acts would give clues—the more obvious future-oriented statements being in speeches before a Jewish audience.[7] This position is hard to sustain, however. One could read Peter's speech at Pentecost easily in a non-eschatological way. The most explicit future-oriented statement occurs in Peter's next speech. "Repent . . . that he [God] may send the Christ appointed for you, Jesus, whom heaven must receive until the time for establishing all that God spoke by the mouth of his holy prophets" (Acts 3:19-21). Even here nothing is said explicitly about future judgment and life in heaven. In 4:12 "salvation" is restricted to God through Jesus Christ—but it is not said specifically what that word means. Stephen's speech has no eschatological overtones at all. Peter's speech to the Gentile Cornelius and associates (presumably Gentile) refers explicitly to the expectation that the resurrected Jesus "is the one ordained by God to be judge of the living and the dead" (10:42). Since this is the first speech in Acts directed explicitly to Gentiles, the incorporation of future judgment in the oratory seems at first hearing to be surprising.

We await with eagerness what Paul will say! He makes his first speech to Hellenistic Jews (and God-fearers) at the synagogue in Antioch of Pisidia. But any explicit statement of an eschatological position is absent. Jesus is "Savior" (13:23), but this is not said in an eschatological context. The emphasis is all on the resurrection of Jesus, seen as the fulfillment of promise, the result of which is forgiveness of sin and release from Torah obligations.[8] Yet in the following speech to the philosophers at Athens, which is very Hellenistically oriented, Paul does, in fact, make the only explicit reference in his speeches to the day of judgment (17:31). The speech to the elders from Ephesus puts us back into ambiguity again. Before a presumably Gentile audience, Paul declares that his message was "of repentance to God and of faith in our Lord Jesus Christ" (20:21),[9] that he was "preaching the kingdom (20:25),[10] and that it consisted in "declaring to you the whole counsel [*boulē*] of God" (20:27).[11] Nothing here suggests even what Acts 17:31 did, a future set of events. Yet the author reports in 24:25, before the Gentile Felix, that Paul debated the issues of "justice [*dikaiosynē*], self-control, and future judgment [*tou krimatos tou mellontos*]."

There are echoes of a future orientation before Jewish audiences in the speeches made after Paul's arrest. In the first speech (22:3-21) there is no hint of such a topic. In the second (23:1-6) Paul claims to stand on the Pharisaic view of the resurrection of the dead. In the speech before Felix (and Jewish accusers), Paul acknowledges that he has a "hope in God, which these themselves [the accusers] accept, that there will be a resurrection of both the just and the unjust" (24:15).[12] Paul begins his final speech, before Festus, Agrippa, and Bernice, with a claim to belief in the resurrection of the dead (26:8). But then the language becomes more general. The purpose of Paul's mission is "to open their [Gentiles'] eyes, that they may turn from darkness to light and from the power of Satan to God,[13] that they may receive forgiveness of sins and a place among those who are sanctified by faith in me" (26:18; Jesus is speaking; cf. also v. 23).

The author's position is thus complicated. He stresses that to follow "the Way" means forgiveness of sins, enlightenment, and present correct behavior, as made possible through Jesus, an agent of God, for whom God has vouched by raising him from the dead. Equally clearly, the author knows the motif of the future, eschatological judgment, which he can introduce at will, and to Gentile hearers as well as Jewish.[14] His structure is that of a typical future eschatology, like other Cosmocrator trajectory treatises. But he does not stress the nearness of the final denouement; rather he emphasizes the present result of God's act in Jesus and all peoples' responsibility to respond in the present. This kind of both/and is not uncommon in the Cosmocrator trajectory, but the issue can be spelled out more fully in Acts than in some of the other literature, because of its length and nature. There is thus more nuance to the eschatological portrait than we find, for instance, in Colossians and Ephesians. My best judgment is that the author is committed to a future denouement, just as Paul is. Yet the sense of urgency is absent. Since this disappearance of urgency is typical of other, later Cosmocrator trajectory treatises, Acts fits in compatibly with the trajectory.

The Resurrection of Jesus[15]

There is a more serious obstacle to including Acts simply as a typical representative of the Cosmocrator trajectory, and this is the author's varied position on the resurrection of Jesus. In the Cosmocrator trajectory the resurrection means exaltation to heaven, and, by one metaphor or another, power over the cosmos. Acts begins as if it intends to follow directly in that direction. In 2:34-36, Peter climaxes his Pentecost speech with the citation from Psalm 110:1 and with the interpretative words: "Let all the house of Israel therefore know assuredly that God has made him both Lord and Christ, this Jesus whom you crucified" (2:36). The use of the title *kyrios*, typical of its function in the Cosmocrator trajectory, indicates some sort of regal power, as does, in this context, the title *Christos*. While I think it likely that 2:36 is old tradition, it is utilized by the author of Acts and placed in a dramatically prominent position.

That the prominent position of 2:32-36 is intentional is clearly shown by the fact that the statement is one of a kind in Acts, and is the only citation of Psalm 110:1 in the document. Nowhere else does the author as clearly show his allegiance with the trajectory, although there is at least one echo. Peter asserts to the Sanhedrin: "This man [Jesus] God exalted [*hypsōsen*] to his right [hand] as Leader [*archēgon*] and Savior" (5:31).[16] To this one should add that the full acclamation, *kyrios Iēsous Christos,* occurs four times, while the title (if that is what it is) *kyrios Iēsous* is used probably fifteen times,[17] in a variety of locations and contexts. Five of these uses occur in the phrase, "In the name of the Lord

Jesus." *Kyrios Iēsous* seems to be the name used in the churches with which Acts is familiar. At any rate, the variety of contexts in which this title appears suggests that *kyrios* has lost, if not its titular sense, at least any identification with a particular theological motif.

Apart from these admittedly clear indications of Cosmocrator theology, the other places in Acts where the author refers to the resurrection of Jesus move in different, sometimes seemingly strange directions. The passages are as interesting in what they do not say as in what they do. None of them gives hint of exaltation or enthronement. Not all of them are even clear in their intent.

In the second speech of Peter the Jews are said to have killed the *archēgon* of life, whom God raised from the dead (3:15). It is neither certain that the phrase "*archēgon* of life" refers to the earthly Jesus or the resurrected, or whether it matters, nor what *archēgon* means.[18] As the first to be raised, Jesus is at least the pathfinder (some would say the eponymous ancestor) of all believers. There seems to be more rhetorical play than substance in the wording. The Jews have killed the one who is the source of life. To derive more than that from the sentence seems speculative. At the end of the same speech the apostle may refer again to the resurrection of Jesus, but if so, in a unique way. Speaking to the Jews, he says: "God, raising up his servant, sent him first to you, blessing you when you turn from your evil ways" (Acts 3:26). While many commentators take "raising up" (*anastēsas*) to refer to the resurrection, it hardly makes sense to think of God sending the resurrected Jesus first to the Jews. Thus, with others, I think it makes more sense to think of "raising up" to refer to God establishing the earthly Jesus as a messenger to his people. In this case, the verse says nothing about the resurrected Jesus. If it does, then the thought must be that God sent the resurrected Jesus first to the Jews, through his apostles—an unusual idea not, to my knowledge, replicated elsewhere.

Three places relate the resurrection with the forgiveness of sins. In 5:31 Peter claims before the Sanhedrin that the purpose of the resurrection was "to give repentance and forgiveness of sins to Israel." In a looser connection, Peter, in his speech to the Gentiles whom Cornelius has collected, says that everyone who believes in the resurrected Jesus "receives forgiveness of sins through his name" (10:43). Finally, Paul joins the chorus in his first speech to the synagogue audience at Pisidian Antioch: "Let it be known to you . . . that through this one [the resurrected Jesus] forgiveness of sins is proclaimed to you." In what sense the resurrected Jesus enables forgiveness to occur is not stated. Presumably, if people believe in the resurrected Jesus, they repent and receive forgiveness. That is, the connection is purely formal and external.

In two passages the resurrection is tied, in some way, with future judgment. Peter, in his speech to Cornelius, says that the resurrected Jesus commanded the apostles to proclaim to the people (*laos*) that he is the one appointed by God to be judge of the living and the dead. The connection is rather loose, but it is probably important to note that it is the instruction of the resurrected, not the earthly Jesus that is the basis of the proclamation. Paul, in his speech to the Athenians, draws the relation closer. There is to be a day of divine judgment by a man (*andros*); God has given assurance, proof, pledge that this will happen by raising him from the dead (*anastēsas auton ek nekrōn*). Here at least one purpose of the resurrection is to provide warning and assurance that the final judgment will, in fact, occur.

We are still not through the catalogue. To return to Paul's speech at Antioch, the promise to the forefathers is said to be fulfilled by the resurrection of Jesus (13:32). And in Paul's speech to Agrippa, the result of the resurrection is that the resurrected Jesus proclaims light to both Jew and Gentile (26:23). The meaning of this statement is unclear. If one is guided by what Paul has said earlier (v. 18), where Paul's ministry is to lead to "light," then the proclamation by the resurrected Jesus would be in the form of words. This is difficult to imagine, and the author may mean that the event of the resurrection itself is the proclamation.

What is to be made of this strange development? The strong enthronement motif at the climax of the Pentecost speech has disappeared and been replaced by topics much closer to Jewish thought forms: fulfillment of promise, final judgment, forgiveness of sins, illumination to all the world. The resurrection has been altered from a cosmic claim of rulership to an in-house Jewish catalogue. Given this dramatic change, the wonder is that the Cosmocrator theology appears at all! The author seems to desire to shy away from such claims and to "hide" the resurrection of Jesus inside the Jewish matrix. I think it is the politics of the author that determines this decision.

Christology

Let me try to sum up the theology of Acts by looking at the author's Christology. It is easy to say that the author is interested in the resurrected Jesus, not the earthly. It is not easy to say exactly how the resurrected Jesus functions in Acts. As we have just seen, even the function of the resurrection itself is so varied as to be difficult to summarize. Jesus is not the Cosmocrator (always excepting Acts 2:24-36). He is at least the coming world judge (10:42; 17:31). The resurrected Jesus also is the fulfillment of God's promise to Israel, a beloved theme of the author. The resurrection of Jesus is the proof (if that is not too strong a word) that the "Way" is the fulfillment and continuation of Israel. The author seems to look back and to the future to find the significance for the resurrected Jesus. At present Jesus remains in heaven, waiting until the eschatological denouement, at which point he begins to function (3:10-21).[19]

Thus one looks back to the Jewish theme of fulfillment and forward to the Jewish theme of final judgment. For the present, Jesus apparently has no functions; that is, he is not proclaimed as a present ruler who fights against cosmic (or human) rulers. Thus Jesus in Acts is a neutral, even "safe" Jesus for one to preach in the face of suspicious civic and Roman authorities.

The Theological Structure of the Revelation to John

The book we call the Revelation of (or to) John contains few uses of Cosmocrator trajectory language. There are no full acclamations (i.e., *Iēsous Christos kyrios*). In fact, there are few acclamations directed to the resurrected Jesus at all. The clearest is certainly old tradition, the Eucharistic prayer in 22:20: "Come, Lord Jesus."[20] This shortened acclamation is repeated in the benediction (22:21). Twice he is described with an acclamation, seemingly in the context, more appropriate for God: Lord of Lords and King of Kings (17:14; 19:16, in reverse order). Acclamations are mostly directed toward God in this treatise. The term *kyrios* almost always refers to God, not the resurrected Jesus. Apart from the acclamations just mentioned, only Revelation 11:8 refers to Jesus as *kyrios*, interestingly enough in relation to the crucifixion (this use of *stauroō* is the only occurrence in Revelation of either this verb or the noun).[21]

The word *Christos* occurs only seven times. Three of these times are in the opening verses, where *Iēsous Christos* seems clearly a proper name. Twice we have a reference to God "and his Christ."[22] The phrase, probably dependent ultimately on Psalm 2:2 (LXX: *kata tou kyriou kai kata tou christou autou*), implies a closer connection between the ultimate authority of God and the Messiah as his agent than is usually the case in the Cosmocrator tradition.[23] Clearly, *Christos* is not a key term in Revelation, even as a proper name. Nevertheless the author assumes that Jesus comes from the line of David: "The lion of the tribe of Judah, the root of David, has conquered" (Rev 5:5; cf. also Rev 22:16).

The resurrected Jesus is never said to be elevated to the right hand of God (Ps 110:1 is not cited or alluded to). Nor is it ever said that the resurrected Jesus sits on a throne. In most instances there seems to be only one throne for the deity, although in 22:1, 3 there seems to be a single throne for both God and the Lamb. What the meaning of this might be is uncertain.[24] The twenty-four elders, however, have their own thrones (11:16).

The powers and principalities are not mentioned in Revelation. The enemy is the devil, Satan. Arrayed on one side are Michael and his angels; on the other side, the dragon and his angels. The dragon is "that ancient serpent, who is called the devil and Satan, the deceiver of the whole world" (Rev 12:9).[25] These figures are more active in their pursuit of the righteous than is stated about the powers and principalities in the Cosmocrator trajectory.

Language from the Son of Man trajectory occurs occasionally. In 1:12-20 there is a description of the exalted Son of Man, perhaps taken, I have suspected, from pagan images. At any rate, he holds the seven stars in his hand, which may imply rulership over fate. He speaks to John. That this Son of Man is the same as described in Daniel 7:13 is assured by the citation of that verse just prior to the description (1:7). The passage makes it clear that the coming with the clouds is the eschatological coming for judgment.

In 14:14 one like a son of man appears, this time riding *on* a cloud. Whether this is a reference to the Son of Man is uncertain. In the following verse, "another angel" orders the rider on the clouds to put in his sickle and harvest. On the one hand, the one like a son of man is on a cloud, perhaps alluding to Daniel 7:13. The use of the sickle for harvest could be one way of speaking of the judgment of the Son of Man, although in the plot of Revelation, the judgment at this point in the drama would seem to be at best a preliminary one. On the other hand, would the Son of Man receive orders from an angel? Is the one like a son of man an angel? The following verse speaks of "another angel," as if he might be. Yet the "another angel" could be in sequence with the angels mentioned in the earlier part of the section: 14:6, 8, 9. Scholars are divided about the issue. If this passage is a reference to *the* Son of Man, it would reflect tradition not otherwise witnessed in the Son of Man trajectory. At best, we have three references to the Son of Man. This suggests that the author of Revelation knew of the Son of Man perspective and indeed thought of Jesus in this eschatological manner. Whether it has seriously influenced his picture of Jesus is not certain.

God and Jesus in the book of Revelation

If we can withdraw from the narrative of the book all the action and look for places where the author expresses, perhaps off-hand, his views of God and Jesus, can we draw a portrait of these two protagonists?

God. Given its apocalyptic context, the formal description of God does not seem to be remarkable. Only once is it said that God is creator (14:7), but that could be assumed even if there had been no reference at all.[26] Not surprising also is the absence of remarks about God's past or pre-eschatological activity. All emphasis is placed on what is now beginning—eschatological judgment and salvation. For examples, the elders cry out, "We give thanks to you, Lord God Almighty, who are and who were, that you have taken your great power and begun to reign" (Rev 11:17). And the reign means judgment and salvation. Similar ideas are expressed in 12:10 and, by implication, in 19:2. There are two places in which someone says that he is coming soon. In both contexts, the most obvious speaker is God. In 16:15, in the context of "the great day of God the almighty," someone says, "Lo, I am coming soon." And in 22:7 the angel says, "And the Lord, the God of the spirits of the prophets, has sent his angel to show his servants what must soon take place. And behold, I am coming soon." Commentaries with great assurance assume that both of these words are those of the resurrected Jesus.[27] I do not see why God could not be the speaker. The late prophets speak of the coming of the day of the Lord.[28] Given the theocentric direction of the book, it certainly seems possible, even likely, that God is seen as performing the final act. In the final vision, God alone is needed, and only God appears.[29]

The imponderable is the question: Is God a God of love or of wrath and destruction? The author presents a succession of violent acts that still boggles the mind. And he does this with a naturalness of description, such that he has to assume they are appropriate actions. If God is a God of love, it is love only for the saints. And the violence is universal. That is, it is not limited only toward those who have persecuted the believers. It seems indiscriminate. Such divine violence, prior to the final judgment, is not typical of other Jewish apocalypses.[30]

The Resurrected Jesus. If the theology of Revelation is relatively simple, the Christology is, in contrast, complex and opaque—at least at first overlook. In fact, the Christology seems almost like an appendage to the description of God and God's acts.[31] This gives us a key question: what does the Christology add to the thought of the book that couldn't have been the case without it? But first the basic data.

As already said, the book seems little influenced by either the Cosmocrator trajectory or the *Christos* trajectory. There are a few more attachments to the Son of Man trajectory, but not enough to place Revelation within that category.

The name *Iēsous* appears solo eight times. Once the resurrected Jesus speaks (*egō Iēsous*) in 22:16. Once appeal is made to *pistin Iēsou* (14:12).[32] All of the remaining uses, six instances, are in direct connection with one or another form of the term *martyria*.[33] There are two problems here. (1) What does *martyria* mean in these contexts? (2) Why is it consistent that *martyria* is tied with the name Jesus (in 1:2 with Jesus Christ)? *Martys* in 17:6 seems to have the meaning of having shed blood because of testimony given. The other occurrences, all *martyria*, are ambiguous enough so that each could be interpreted in more than one way. The *martyria Iēsous* could mean "witness to or about Jesus," or "witness by Jesus," which itself could be variously interpreted (witness by Jesus in his death or by Jesus to truth). Since in Revelation Jesus is not described as a teacher or proclaimer of truth but is the one who dies, I think it likely that any "witness by Jesus" is a reference to his death. Otherwise, I find it impossible to distinguish between the basic alternatives. It seems likely that the phrase is inclusive of both meanings. Believers witness to Jesus in the sense that they acknowledge his self-giving death, which surely implies, in the theology of Revelation, that they are also called to be such witnesses as Jesus was. That is, the phrase plays on the ambiguity in Greek between an objective genitive (testimony to Jesus) and a subjective (testimony by Jesus).[34]

Perhaps more important is the association of the word *martyria* with the name "Jesus."[35] It is not just that most of the appearances of *martyria* are related to the name Jesus; it is also the fact that the majority of uses of the name Jesus occur in relation to *martyria*. While the title "Lamb," *arnion*, occurs more frequently than the name Jesus, only one use of *martyria* is connected with that title. There is clearly some association in the author's mind between "Jesus" and *martyria* that does not exist with the title "Lamb," even though this title is certainly associated in the author's mind with the death of Jesus. But what could it be? First let us look at the title "Lamb."

Clearly, the predominant title for Jesus in Revelation is "Lamb," *arnion* (thirty-eight times).[36] This is unique usage. The word occurs only once elsewhere in the New Testament, in John 21:5, referring to believers, not Jesus.[37] In Revelation the term refers most explicitly, but not always, to the slain Jesus, who has conquered death. Whether the Lamb has been slain due to murder or to priestly sacrifice is not clear. Certainly it is not the usual word for a sacrificial lamb in the LXX.[38]

One must admit that many, perhaps even the majority, of occurrences of *arnion* read either like additions to an original *theos* (or similar) or just the title for Jesus that most often comes to mind. That is, although there is no evidence for it, *arnion* must have been a traditional term for the resurrected Jesus in the mind of the author. "Lamb" is used when the author wants to speak about the resurrected Jesus, in whatever function.[39] There are, however, three major exceptions, where the functions become clear. The first is the initial appearance of the Lamb. The second is a recognizable cluster of sayings. The third is the martyr's death of Jesus.

The Lamb Enthroned. The first mention of the Lamb occurs in a dizzying description of what amounts to an enthronement scene. Chapter 5 opens with the lament that there is no one "worthy" (*axios*) to open the scroll.[40] A heavenly angel comforts John: "Weep not; lo, the Lion of the tribe of Judah, the Root of David, has conquered, so that he can open the scroll and its seven seals" (v. 5). Here, obviously, is a reference to the victorious one, described in messianic terms, although it may be significant that the title *Christos* does not occur.[41]

The animal image, however, changes abruptly. John sees by (before? near?) God's throne a lamb, standing, one who has been slaughtered (murdered? sacrificed?). He has seven horns and eyes.[42] The seven horns are not interpreted; the eyes are said to be "the seven spirits of God sent out into all the earth" (v. 6). Does this indicate that through the Lamb God is omniscient? Since the Lamb will prove to be a warrior figure, it is hardly the case that the Lamb is to be seen in contrast to the Lion. They are different images for the same conquering figure, mostly described henceforth as the Lamb.

The four creatures and the twenty-four elders then prostrate themselves before the Lamb and they "sing a new song."

> Worthy are you to take the scroll and to open its seals,
> for you were slain and by your blood you ransomed[43] people for God
> from every tribe and tongue and people and nation
> and made them a kingdom and priests to our God
> and they shall reign[44] on earth. (5:9-10)

Here is an ecstatic acclamation offered by the prostrated heavenly figures. As we have seen in the Cosmocrator trajectory, acclamations were offered in homage to divine and human leaders, and certainly at enthronements. In the hymn in Philippians 2 the acclamation is clearly part of the enthronement ceremony. It is interesting in Revelation that the acclamation is not in terms of who the honored one is but in terms of what the honored one has done.

Then follows a second acclamation, this time clearly belonging to an enthronement ceremony. The host of angels joins the elders and the living creatures to acclaim the Lamb as worthy of cosmic rulership.

> Worthy is the Lamb who was slain,
> to receive power and wealth and wisdom and might
> and honor and glory and blessing.
> To him who sits upon the throne and to the Lamb[45]
> be blessing and honor and glory and might for ever and ever.[46]

The elders prostrate themselves and do obeisance. Those making this acclamation of lordship include those in heaven and on earth and under the earth (v. 13). The similarity with Philippians 2:10 is striking, although the words differ.

What we have in this scene is an enthronement ceremony of the Lamb. He is exalted to heaven, perhaps as a result of his slaughter by which he ransoms people and makes them into a kingdom for God. He is acclaimed by all heaven as worthy of receiving cosmic power. But he remains a Lamb, not a king or Messiah. Nor does he reign in the stead of God. The author of Revelation constantly makes it clear that at best the Lamb reigns with God. The Lamb does not even have his own throne.[47] Nevertheless, he is a royal figure without a royal title and exercises rulership, although at present perhaps only over the faithful who are at the moment the kingdom of God and the Lamb.

This is clearly an enthronement ceremony. But out of which trajectory? In the Cosmocrator trajectory, enthronement occurs as the resurrection event. In the Son of Man trajectory, it occurs as an eschatological event. Which is this scene? In one sense everything that happens in heaven is eschatological—time sequences are probably not to be taken literally. If one took such sequences literally, however, the enthronement would be pre-eschatological. And what does one do with the fact that the only reference to any of the three trajectories is an oblique one to the *Christos* trajectory? I do not think there are any obvious lines of relationship.

The cluster of sayings, although not a single description as the enthronement described above, points to the relationship between the Lamb and the believers.[48] Perhaps the most remarkable (even bizarre) metaphor occurs in 7:17. The believers are pictured as being before the throne of God and serving him (v. 15). Then follows a description of the life of the blessed, with a pastiche of scriptural citations and allusions, into which the Lamb is inserted. "For the Lamb in the midst of the throne will be their shepherd, and he will guide them to springs of living water" (v. 17). The Lamb will himself be a shepherd! Underlying what was doubtlessly an intentionally wrenching metaphor is the idea that the resurrected Jesus will function as the leader of the believers in heaven.[49] Perhaps continuing the motif of shepherding, Rev 14:4 states that the believers "follow the Lamb wherever he goes."[50]

The author then uses marriage imagery. The Lamb has a bride and is to be married (19:7). It becomes clear that the bride is the community of the redeemed. Then follows a beatitude: "Blessed are those who are invited to the marriage supper of the Lamb" (19:9).[51] In Revelation 21:2, the New Jerusalem is described as "a bride adorned for her husband." The context would indicate that the husband is God. In Revelation 21:9, however, the bride is the "wife of the Lamb." Whatever the original metaphor, in its present form it is another way of affirming the intimate relation between the Lamb and the heavenly redeemed.

Thus the primary meanings assigned the Lamb are (1) that he is enthroned to be ruler in heaven and (2) that he is the leader of the redeemed in heaven.

The reader may be surprised to learn that the phrase "blood of the Lamb" occurs only twice in the document, at 7:14 and 12:11. The other two passages in which the blood of Jesus is mentioned are 5:9, in a context where Lamb is clearly meant, and in 1:5, the nearest name to which is Jesus Christ in the same verse (but in a different sentence). The verbs associated with the blood of Jesus in these four passages are also varied: freed from sins (1:5); ransom for God (5:9); robes washed white (7:11); conquered the evil one (12:11).

While the references to the "blood," i.e., the death, of Jesus are fewer and more stereotypical than one often thinks, it is crucial to ask, To what does the blood refer? Is it a sacrificial death or is it a martyr's death? Indications point to the death of the martyr as being most congenial to the author. Believers are (or should be, he thinks) facing their own martyrdom. A Jesus who was martyred is the ideal model for his to use. Only Revelation 1:5, with its references to releasing from sin, might suggest a sacrificial death. In some Jewish traditions, however, the death of the martyr is said to atone, and it seems consistent with the author's point of view to read 1:5 as referring to the effect of the martyr's death. We can then add this motif to the ones listed above. Jesus died a martyr's death and by this wins benefits for believers (as well as being a model). To this should be added the close association between the name Jesus and *martyria*. Jesus made his witness and died a martyr's death.

Summary

My attempt here has been to look at the underlying structure of the author's theology. Certainly it has not been to follow the plot with its electrifying images and violent scenes. One could imagine the structure with an entirely different plot and set of images. It is doubtlessly the plot and images, rather than the structure, that has stimulated and intrigued readers for two thousand years.

The structure itself bears resemblance to those we have looked at earlier in this book. Linguistically it has little to do with the Cosmocrator or the *Christos* trajectories. The author clearly knows the Son of Man trajectory and uses it on occasion. Yet he goes his own way, at least linguistically, although structurally he seems to remain close to the trajectory of the Son of Man, if one gives an eschatological interpretation to all "events" in the book, including that of the enthronement.

What is intriguing is to ask what exactly God and the Lamb do, in relation to the plot. Does God cause the events to unfold? When the Lamb opens the seals does he cause the scenes that follow? Or do they just somehow happen? One can legitimately argue that ultimately God is responsible for the violence. But does it explicitly say that? There seems to be a certain distance placed between God and Lamb, and the events, for once; let us look at the action as it unfolds.

The first set of violent actions are instigated by the "four living creatures" (6:1-7). Whatever the origin of these creatures, in Revelation they function as divine actors—that is, like angels, whether called so or not.[52] The next set of actions is instigated by angels blowing trumpets (8:7—9:21). Up to this point, the violence is indiscriminate; that is, it is not directed toward people identified as evil but toward humankind in general.

Beginning in chapter 12, however, the violence is directed toward evil—either divine or human. In chapter 12, Michael and the devil square off against each other, each with their cohorts of angels. In chapter 13, the beast begins to assume center stage. In general the beast represents forces of human evil, most explicitly that of Roman emperors and their power. With chapter 15, we again have angels performing violence. In general these acts are also indiscriminate, although the author makes some effort to tie them in with attacks on evil people who do not repent (cf. 16:2, 9, 11).

The resurrected Jesus finally appears as a warrior in 19:11-16. He rides a white horse, leading the armies of heaven also astride white horses.[53] He is victorious over the nations, "with the fury of the wrath of God the Cosmocrator" (*pantokratōr*).[54] Thus God and the resurrected Jesus do not escape being described as active forces in the horrendous battle described. Nevertheless, that such a majority of the actions are assigned to angels, and that in these the act of God and the Lamb are tacit, suggests to me that the author is reticent, perhaps unconsciously, directly to involve God and the Lamb in most of the violence. The author may delight in the violence, but he may also dimly sense that there is something theologically wrong with a God of violence.

At any rate, in the structure itself, God seems to take a more pro-active role. The Lamb is enthroned, yet he has no throne of his own. There are acclamations to God alone that have no parallel in the other trajectories. The Lamb is acclaimed as having power, but he seems almost as much a spectator of the unfolding events as does John himself. The author seems trapped between his knowledge of Christian tradition, in which the resurrected Jesus has some active role to play, and the Jewish apocalyptic tradition in which God is the only actor needed. Even the rather vague references to the eschatological judgments in Rev 20:4, 11-15 are ill-defined as to who the judge is. Presumably, it is God (v. 11), but if so, one of the chief functions of the Son of Man has been taken away. John has wedded Jewish apocalyptic tradition to early Christian traditions about Jesus, changed his name to an apocalyptic animal, and given him whatever roles to play as seem possible, most notably the arrival, after the carnage is mostly over, as the millennial ruler over the nations. This is still a penultimate event, since the final one is God's presence in the New Jerusalem, a presence that does not speak of a conquering hero.

Comparisons

To compare such disparate books is, no doubt, an audacious task, one fraught with danger, and perhaps doomed to ultimate failure. May I remind the reader that I am not trying to compare the "historical" writing, per se, with the "imaginative." I want to look at the theologies implied, or even stated, by the authors, theologies that, presumably, lie behind their creative tasks, that are expressed in the historical and the imaginative. If this is kept in mind, the task is easier and the compatibilities surprising.

1. Both Acts and Revelation begin with the resurrection of Jesus. The beginning is both narratival and structural. Acts 1 pictures the resurrected Jesus in his forty-day fellowship with the disciples. Revelation 1 portrays the exalted Son of Man. Structurally, the emphasis is upon the situation after the death, although Revelation lays an implied emphasis upon the death that is absent in Acts.

2. Both Acts and Revelation at the beginning emphasize the resurrection of Jesus as enthronement to rulership. This happens in Acts 2:34-36, the climax of Peter's Pentecost speech, and in Revelation 5, at the first mention of Jesus as the Lamb—the Lamb is an enthroned Lamb. Again, the difference is that the Lamb is closely linked with God in this act, so that the acclamation is to both Lamb and God at the same time (5:13). Yet neither uses the Cosmocrator trajectory's terms for the powers and principalities. Revelation sticks with the Jewish Satan (and to a lesser extent the devil). The enthronement is acted out completely in the context of Jewish apocalypticism. Acts occasionally uses Satan and *diabolos*, but in general the author never seems to think that the enthronement entails assumption of power over other forces. This must be interpreted in relation to the disappearance of the enthronement motif after 2:34-36. The author of Acts does not emphasize the present power of the resurrected Jesus.

3. Both seem to express ambiguity with regard to the present activity of the resurrected Jesus. As I have suggested, in Revelation there seems to be a distance between both the activity and intent of God and the Lamb and the unfolding drama. True, the Lamb opens the seals, which sets off the violence, but it is not said that the Lamb desires the violence to occur. The Lamb seems more a spectator than actor, with the exception of 17:14, where a war between the Lamb and the enemy (in human form) is mentioned, and the triumphal procession of the rider on the white horse at the end of the events. In Acts, believers are exhorted to look to the day of judgment, but nothing in Acts suggests that the resurrected Jesus has a present function. Nor does his future function seem imminent. This result is surely tied to the retreat of the author of Acts from any reference to the enthronement of Jesus after the first speech.

4. Both, each in its own way, see the unfolding drama, whether historical or imaginative, in Jewish categories. Acts uses the promise/fulfillment motif; Revelation, the eschatological.

5. Can these two authors be so similar? Surely the radically different tones mean or imply some radical difference! Or are the differences primarily one of temperament? I find these questions difficult to answer. One cannot simply say

that the author of Acts is interested in the historical, while that of Revelation is not. John also is concerned with what is going on, as exemplified by his letters to the churches. Here he thinks he knows exactly what is going on—and he doesn't much like it! The author of Acts doesn't write letters to churches, so his prose is inevitably different. The closest he comes is Paul's speech to the Ephesian elders, in which he does say a thing or two about that church—and *he* doesn't like it much either!

One could say that the difference lies in different perceptions of the imminence of the eschatological denouement. Yet we don't (and can't) really know how literally the author of Revelation understood his own imagination. The events unfold with breath-taking rapidity in the narrative. How literally is it all to be taken? Most critical scholars see the author as having an awareness of "what is going on," having very strong feelings about that, and using his imagination to put what is going on in a divine perspective. The violent events are John's judgment (he thinks, God's) upon what is going on. Whether he really thinks this is going to happen this year can't be assuredly said, although he has the divine voice say, "Lo, I am coming soon" (3:11; 22:7, 12, 20) and, in the echo of the eucharistic prayer, hopes for this "soon." In the final analysis, what exactly is the difference between the violence of the divine emissaries and the author of Acts' somewhat (at least by comparison) casual mention of a coming day of judgment for all people?

Christianity and Rome at the Beginning of the Second Century

Most scholars, although their reasons vary, tend to date our two documents within, give or take, ten years of each other. Without arguing the issues, I will accept Revelation as composed in the nineties of the first century. While I suspect that Acts was written in the first decade of the second century, even though most scholars place it a bit earlier, there is no need to quibble over a few years. As far as we know, nothing dramatically changed during this general period to demand separate treatment for the two documents. Nor do the possible locations of the authors require different assessments. Revelation is located specifically in the province of Asia; Acts seems to me a writing for the western church at large, including Asia.

What I try to do is to assess the political situation with regard to emerging Christianity at the turn of the century in the Roman provinces. To do this I must begin with the relationship between Judaism and the empire. The evidence seems clear that during the first century C.E. the Jews held what might be called a most-favored-nation status vis-à-vis Rome. This was not due to any particular regard of the Romans toward the Jewish people. Rome had two alternatives with respect to the Jews: either compromise, in order for the Jewish people to maintain their basic interests (which may have seemed bizarre to some Romans), or extermination, an unwise and probably impossible procedure.

Thus the Jews were given certain exemptions or rights not offered to other national groups.[55] They were given the right of assembly, of maintaining their own traditions—which meant living by their own laws, as long as these did not violate Roman sensitivities. They were allowed to ignore pagan religious rites and, to the chagrin of the civic authorities, they were permitted to send gold out of the provinces to pay the temple tax. These exemptions in effect set up a triangle among Rome, the Jews, and the civic governments. Josephus narrates a number of instances in which the civic authorities revoked a privilege the Jews believed was given by Rome; the Jews appealed to the nearest Roman official, and the rights were restored. This no doubt caused a continuous uneasy situation between a Jewish population in a city and the citizens of the city.

Into this situation come the believers in Jesus. At first they are entirely Jewish and live in Jewish populated areas, where rights are assumed because they are Jews. Even in the Diaspora, the earliest communities that believed in Jesus must have been largely Jewish. Paul, however, indicates that there were believing communities who were not Jewish but Gentile. Yet Paul shows not the slightest anxiety over the groups, even to the extent of shipping gold out of the province to take to Jerusalem. Paul obviously assumed the groups were protected by Roman laws with respect to Judaism, and he must have thought of the churches as "the Israel of God" (Galatians 6).

Did the Jewish-Roman War change things politically? Apparently not appreciably in legal ways. Jewish rights were continued (perhaps in some recognition of the basic neutrality the Diaspora communities showed during this period).[56] The main change seems to have been the replacement of the temple tax for a Roman tax, proceeds of which went to support Jupiter Capitolinus in Rome—no doubt a source of much irritation to Jewish sensibilities.

Whether the War raised Jewish anxieties about their safety in the Diaspora cannot be answered but can be guessed. The presence of groups who believed in Jesus, now often largely Gentile, could only have added to the anxiety. What little we know suggests that there was a growing movement by the Jews toward separation from believers in Jesus, now at some time called "Christians." By the time Paul wrote Romans (c. 55–57 C.E.), Jews had ceased to enter believing communities, at least in the Diaspora. And much later, the Jewish council at Jamnia (Javneh), under the leadership of Gamaliel II,[57] inserted a curse on the "Notzrim" and "Minim" into the basic Sabbath liturgy. What the authority of Jamnia was and how widespread the liturgical addition became are disputed issues. For my purposes two things are clear.

The first is that the decision to insert the curse is an indication that some Jews felt it time to draw the line. Get the Notzrim off our back! The second is that there were Roman listeners at the sessions of the Council. What the Romans heard would have been loud and clear. The Jews no longer considered believers in Jesus to be part of them. They did not think such believers merited the rights of protection accorded the Jews by the Romans. Christians were not Jews. I would think such action by the leading Jews would have impressed itself upon the Roman authorities in Syria at least. In chapter 13 of Hebrews, the author seems to be encouraging his hearers and readers to give up the protection of the Jews and to admit they are not Jews. To this one can add the evidence from Pliny's correspondence with Trajan.[58] Pliny writes about an incident around 110 c.e. The implication of his comments, however, leads to the conclusion that as early as 90 c.e. believers, now identified as Christians, had become noticeable as a distinct sect.

What little we know thus suggests that gradually, toward the end of the first century, believers in Jesus became known as Christians. They were increasingly recognized as not being Jews and thus not having the rights of protection as Jews. Soon this new group would attract Roman questions and investigation. Anxieties could have been acute in Christian enclaves, and the sporadic persecution or harassment that began to occur could only have aggravated the situation.[59] It is in this climate that the authors of Acts and Revelation found themselves.

One thing is similar in both of these authors, despite the radical difference in their literary creations: they are both primarily "church persons," not theologians. This is not to say that they do not utilize a theological perspective, but it is to say that in each case their primary concern is not systematically to inform their readers of what the correct theological point of view is. Their concern is to inform the churches about what they see as the correct "political" point of view to take, given the current historical situation. One could even say that they are politicians rather than theologians. Given today's political climate, however, that might be taken as a derogatory judgment. We are too accustomed to think that all our New Testament authors have to be profound theologians—although we do not think all our church leaders today are such—and we may thank God that there are church persons who are primarily concerned about the presence and the future of the church in the midst of a secular world, just as I believe our authors were concerned about the future of their church in an almost too religious world. It was their primary concern, fueled by their anxiety of Roman and civic suspicion of their groups, to suggest to the church a proper stance in response to the general cultural suspicion and harassment and persecution, however sporadic. That each author took a radically different stand does not belie the same starting point.

The Political Perspective of Acts

The author of Acts, writing toward the turn of the century, looks back in his two volumes to the founding of the church, one volume devoted to Jesus, the second heavily emphasizing Paul. Why did he think this enterprise important? Others had written about Jesus. Why did he need to add another volume? For sixty years, the church had had no historian. Why did our author think it important to address that history, especially that of Paul?

There are sufficient clues to suggest that the author felt he needed to defend the political innocence of the church with regard to its origins. After all, Jesus was a "legally" executed insurrectionist. An official Roman governor had set his seal to that. Paul was a known troublemaker, having gotten into disputes with Jewish, civic, and, apparently, Roman officials. By the time of our author, Christianity could no longer claim to be a Jewish sectarian group. Rome had finally become suspicious, and it is likely that local persecutions had begun to occur. In the face of this mounting pressure, a spokesman was needed to argue that Christianity was innocent of any wrongdoing and in fact, while no longer Jewish in make-up, had emerged as the fulfillment of Jewish prophecies and expectations.

Thus the author writes an apology, not to Roman officials, but to the church, to give it a place to stand, both to speak to prospective members and to speak to detractors and attackers. Look, he says, this is our history, our heroes; we have a right to be proud of them. Read my volumes and you will see that we have an innocent past, a past that is the fulfillment of Jewish expectations. Thus we ought to be accorded the privileges the Jews enjoy (he probably thinks: "instead of the Jews," but he is too subtle to say this directly).

The theme of innocence begins in the Gospel, in the scene between Pilate and the Jewish authorities, who are portrayed as pressing for his execution. Pilate emphatically affirms three times that Jesus is innocent, supported by Herod's judgment that Jesus is innocent (Luke 23:4, 14, 15, 22). The blame is placed squarely on the Jewish authorities: "But Jesus he handed over to their [the Jews'] will" (23:25). What Pilate has already said, the centurion repeats at the death scene: "Truly this man was innocent" (23:47). The author makes it clear that Jesus' execution was a miscarriage of justice, and was so acknowledged by the Roman authorities involved.[60]

But it is not just that Jesus is innocent; he is also the fulfillment of the Old Testament prophecies. This is a persistent theme in the Gospel. Perhaps its climactic point occurs in the story of the two disciples on the road to Emmaus. At the end, Jesus tells them: "'Was it not necessary that the Christ should suffer these things and enter into his glory?' And beginning with Moses and all the prophets, he interpreted to them in all the scriptures the things concerning himself" (24:26-27).

In Acts, the trials and encounters with officials tell the story the author wants his readers to absorb. Not surprisingly, the hearings before the Jewish officials turn out badly for the apostles. The Jewish Sanhedrin (except for Gamaliel I) is always hostile to Peter and his cohorts. Before these officials, the apostles stand steadfast in proclaiming the truth about Jesus—with an emphasis upon blaming the Jews for his execution.

Once Paul becomes the hero, however, the story tends to change. Every encounter Paul has with a Roman official turns out in his favor. The proconsul of Crete, Sergius Paulus, comes to believe (13:12). The proconsul of Achaia refuses to take the case when Athenian Jews bring charges against Paul before him. It is not in his jurisdiction, he says, to deal with internal Jewish issues (18:12-17). Indirectly, Paul is exonerated of any wrongdoing in Ephesus. At least the Christian mission is absolved of any guilt for the riot that the author describes so vividly (if a bit unclearly) in chapter 19. After the near riot in the arena, the town clerk denies that the believers (presumably these are those who are said to be to blame) have broken any laws. Rather it is the Ephesian citizenry who might be charged (by the Romans) with *stasis* (a serious charge, running from riot to rebellion). The coup de grâce is applied by the author in the final hearing at Caesarea. Both Felix and Agrippa agree that Paul is "doing nothing to deserve death or imprisonment" (26:31). Agrippa then concludes that Paul could have been set free, had he not already appealed to Caesar. From beginning to end, the Roman verdict on Paul is that he is innocent, just as is Jesus in the Gospel.

Why is the author of Acts so adamant about Paul's innocence? The convincing answer is that Paul was not so considered at the end of the first century. Paul, as well as Jesus, was getting a bad press. And some of that may have been justified. When Paul writes to the Philippians, he is in a Roman prison, accused of a crime serious enough to warrant the death penalty. Although Paul never says where this prison is, many scholars think it may have been Ephesus, a cogent guess. At any rate, here it is Paul who is charged with something like *stasis*, maybe even at Ephesus, where the author of Acts has the town clerk say that it is the Ephesians that might be so charged. Nor do we know what other encounters with Roman officials he might have had, although it is true that his catalogue of sufferings in 2 Corinthians 11:23-27 does not suggest Roman imprisonment. That the author of Acts passes over this imprisonment in silence, though he must have known about it, is instructive of his efforts to clear Paul of guilt.

How Acts portrays Paul's encounters in the cities is different. Here, he acknowledges trouble and persecution (*diōgmos*) against Paul. He consistently blames the Jews for starting it. This is the case in Antioch of Pisidia (13:50); Iconium (14:2, 4-5); Lystra (14:19); Thessalonica (17:5-6; here it is not Paul but Jason and other believers); Beroea (here Jews from Thessalonica, 17:13); and

Corinth (18:12-17). The disturbance at Ephesus I have already mentioned as an at least indirect statement of innocence vis-à-vis Roman law.

The one exception to the above occurs at Philippi, in an unusual episode (Acts 16:19-24). Here there are no Jews involved except Paul and Silas themselves. They as Jews are "disturbing our city. They advocate customs which it is not lawful for us Romans to accept or practice" (vv. 20-21). The tables are turned. Citizens of the city (who also seem to claim Roman citizenship; Philippi was a colony) attack Jews. Here it is the Jews who are arrested, beaten, and thrown in prison. Only at the end is it revealed that both Paul and Silas are themselves Roman citizens. The point of the story (which includes the elaborate scene in jail with the jailer) is not certain—at least not to me. It seems to focus around the issue of citizenship. Paul and Silas are itinerant Jews, by definition certainly not citizens of Philippi. They are treated by the civic court as non-citizens, who have come into the city and disturbed it. The citizens of Philippi may imply that they are also Roman citizens. At the end the itinerant Jews turn out to be Roman citizens themselves. At any rate, this is the one instance in Acts of civic punishment not instigated by Jews, but by citizens against Jews. This story is, however, an example of the triangle among Jews, citizens, and Rome, mentioned above. Jews have their rights taken away from them by civic authorities. The Jews then appeal to Rome (by claiming Roman citizenship).

In the rumor mill at the end of the first century, *who* instigated the trouble in the city was probably long lost to memory. What was told was that Paul was a troublemaker in the cities he missionized. Paul himself acknowledges in his catalogue that (by the time of 2 Corinthians) he had been beaten by rods (a civic punishment) three times (2 Cor 11:25). Considering the number of cities Paul was involved with, this is not a too impressive number; nevertheless it shows Paul *was* considered a troublemaker by some in his own time. Rumor has its basis in some fact.

So Jesus is innocent. Paul is innocent. For what purpose does the author of Acts go to such care to make this a believable story? If this is a document aimed at believers at the turn of the century, the likely answer is that he wants to convince his fellow believers that Christianity is innocent of wrongdoing. He wants to indicate that neither Rome nor the cities ought to have suspicions that would make harassment or persecutions legitimate or desirable. That is, the author of Acts is trying to establish a *modus vivendi* with the political powers in the empire. Rome and the provinces are not evil beasts. They are assumed to be legitimate governments with whom Christians ought to be given a chance to show that they can live as acceptable and responsible participants. The politics of Acts means accepting the Greco-Roman political structures.[61] Its perspective is to live with rather than to live against. In the typology of H. R. Niebuhr, it is

"Christ above culture."[62] Or in the words of Mark: "Whoever is not against us is for us" (Mark 9:40).

The author of Acts is too good a storyteller to say, didactically, that Rome is benign. Instead he implies this throughout in the stories themselves. Using the Q story of the healing of the centurion's slave, already something of a paragon in Q, Luke adds the judgment of the Jewish elders: "He is worthy to have you do this for him, for he loves our nation, and he built for us our synagogue" (Luke 7:8f.).[63] Whether or not the centurion is himself a Roman (we are dealing with auxiliaries, not legions here), he certainly is an official representative of the Roman army. Pilate bends over backward to free Jesus. The centurion at the cross declares Jesus innocent (an accurate judgment, from Luke's standpoint).

In Acts there is the example of Cornelius, named as a centurion of the Italian Cohort, who becomes the first Gentile believer, according to Acts.[64] He also is a pious man, who "gave alms liberally to the people, and prayed constantly to God" (Acts 10:2). The next reference to a Roman official has the proconsul of Cyprus, Sergius Paulus, becoming a believer (Acts 13:12). Then follow all the instances I have listed above. Judging from the stories, Roman officialdom and the Roman army were filled with high-minded and judicially fair people! Clearly Rome is not to be feared but to be missionized. The narratives draw a picture of a benign and fair government, even one in part inclined to accept the faith.

The Political Perspective of Revelation

The action of Revelation is filled with what we can call mythical personae. By that I mean more than human figures. On the good side, this includes God, the angels (only Michael is actually named, Rev 12:7), and the woman in chapter 12. On the evil side there are more. There is, of course, Satan (the dragon). Then there are the two beasts, one from the sea and one from the land, and the whore. We should perhaps include Babylon. That the evil characters have a long history in myth has been underscored by many commentators and need not be repeated here. The question for us is whether they point to realities other than mythical.

That these characters all, in some way or another, stand for the reality of the Roman Empire has been a standard interpretation for many decades, although questions have been raised about the cogency of this reference.[65] One problem with this "historical" interpretation of the mythic is that the details do not seem always to fit what little we know about the imperial period. Even the identification of the number 666 with Nero is uncertain (as any detailed commentary will demonstrate). It is not my intention here to argue these details. The question is whether there is an identification of the evil characters with Rome and what such an identification means for the politics of Revelation. With the majority of commentators, I believe the basic identification of the mythic characters with Rome is assured.[66] What attitude toward Rome is indicated by his treatment? Consider the cast of characters:

The dragon (drakōn). The dragon, who appears in the New Testament only in Revelation, enters the stage for the first time in 12:1-6, as an enemy of the woman (probably a symbol for the church). In the next section (12:7-12), Michael and the good angels fight against the dragon and his bad angels. Here the dragon is identified as the devil and Satan; he is defeated, evicted from heaven and thrown down to earth; and now can use his time (as 12:11 says) to prey on those who are on earth—the believers, using as tools the evil humans on earth, namely, the Roman Empire.[67] When the dragon could not harm the woman, he "went off to make war on the rest of her offspring" (12:17). So far what we have learned is not remarkable. Satan opposes God and thus is an implacable enemy of the church. The question is how he will act out his enmity.

The beast (thērion) from the sea. This character appears for the first time in chapter 13. In a parody of Christian language and ideas, the dragon "enthrones" the beast. "And to it the dragon gave his power and his throne and great authority" (13:2). "And authority was given it over every tribe and people and tongue and nation" (13:7). "The whole earth followed the beast with wonder" (13:2-3). Just as they (presumably the whole world) worshiped the dragon, so they also worshiped (*prosekynēsan*) the beast (13:4, 8). He also persecutes the saints (13:7). The beast is widely understood to be the Roman Empire in general, and perhaps the emperor specifically. Which emperor is less than certain, although most exegetes seem to point to Nero and the Nero *redivivus* rumor. At any rate, the worship of the beast is taken to refer to the emperor cult, which was prominent in Asia Minor.

The beast (thērion) from the land. This beast is also evil and is subordinate to the beast from the sea. Yet it exercises the authority of the beast from the sea and makes all people worship that beast (13:12). The beast from the land also causes an image of the beast from the sea to be erected (13:14) and to force people to worship it (13:15). The identity of this beast is less certain. Presumably the beast stands for the imperial cult, which is involved in devotion to the emperor. Some think of manifestations of this cult in Asia.[68] However the details are to be decided, which must always remain at best educated guesses, the beast from the land is clearly related to Rome and is equally as evil as the beast from the sea.

The great harlot (pornē). In chapter 17 emerges another symbol of evil, the great harlot. The woman is named "Babylon," which prepares the reader for the dirge over Babylon in the next chapter. That the harlot who is Babylon stands for Rome is made clear from the fact that she sits on the beast (from the sea), and the seven heads of the beast turn out to be the seven hills of Rome (17:9). At the end of the description she is identified as "the great city that has dominion over the kings of the earth" (17:18). She is therefore as evil as are the beasts: she is the mother of harlots and abominations, and she is "drunk with the blood of the martyrs of Jesus" (17:6). The dirge over the (now) fallen city is filled with scorn (envy?) about the socioeconomic superiority that everything associated with Rome has enjoyed, including slavery.

While there are other markers of the writer's attitude toward the empire, these are sufficient.[69] Rome is the enemy, and the author has mythologized Rome into Satan. Thus, just as Satan is an implacable enemy of God, so Rome has become the ironclad foe of what is good in the world, which seems to be limited to the "martyrs" in the church. Certainly, not everyone in the church is worthy of being a foe of Satan.[70] The author has constructed an either/or dichotomy of human society, the good guys (however few in number) against the bad guys (who seem to be virtually everyone else), divine forces against Satanic ones. Perhaps the overwhelming odds create the anxiety that makes him attribute such violent actions to the divine powers. At any rate, his view of society is clear. It is church *against* the world. In H. R. Niebuhr's typology, it is "Christ against culture."[71] Or, in the words of Q, "Whoever is not for us is against us."

Theology and Politics

Acts and Revelation are remarkably different in their politics, yet reasonably similar in structure. The conclusion is that the theological structure does not determine their political perspective. Does this mean that theology and politics have nothing to do with each other? Does it mean that one's theological structure, as important as that is in showing one's relationship to the world, is not the only determining factor? I think there is only one solution. The two authors have significantly different views of the reality of God. This difference does not get expressed in the structure, but it can change everything, as it has in our case. In our case, the structure is the mold, but what is poured into that mold may create quite a different statue from some other "material," especially when the implications for life in the world are concerned.

The God of Revelation

The God of Revelation is a God of vengeance. The die is cast; the righteous have been separated from the wicked; what lies ahead is the wreaking of violence and destruction upon the wicked, who have been mythologized into Satanic forces. While I suggested above that the author puts some distance between God

and his Messiah and the pouring out of violence upon humankind, nevertheless God is behind it all. There is only one possible fate for those labeled as evil:
destruction and torment. There is little language in the book about reflection,
repentance, and conversion.[72] In fact, the martyrs complain that God has not
yet acted to avenge their deaths (6:10). Even in the idyllic description of the New
Jerusalem in chapter 21, the wrath of God is not yet finished. After a catalogue
of vices (21:8), the angel (surely speaking for God) determines that their "lot
shall be in the lake that burns with fire and sulfur, which is the second death."
To repeat, the God of Revelation is a God of *vengeance*.

The God of Paul

Paul is not a subject in this chapter. Nevertheless, his view of God is so opposite
that of Revelation that it provides a helpful foil.[73] Acts is, furthermore, difficult
to get at, in part because of its narrative structure. Since I will locate the perspective of Acts somewhere between that of Paul and Revelation, it seems a function
of clarity to set up a typology of opposites as a background.

   Paul's gospel is centered around the God of sheer grace—a God who gives
persons life, not on any achievement but simply because it is God's nature to
love and accept people into fellowship with him. God justifies the doer of deeds
and equally justifies the one who rebels against God. Ultimately both are in the
same place. In Jesus God has acted to grace humankind. Life is sheer gift. Yet
one has to dare to trust that God is such a God. This is what faith is—trust that
God *does* grant life without human striving. Yes, all who have faith are united
with God. Faith is an opening of the gift package. One must trust, hope against
hope, that God is this kind of God. Otherwise one's relationship with God is,
in Paul's view, with a false God. Thus faith is radical trust, and it is this radical
trust that makes what Bultmann called "authentic existence" possible. Faith
restores one to true humanity, to the relationship God intended from creation.
It is symptomatic of this understanding of God that Paul apparently has no
belief in hell—at least he never mentions it. Those who don't come to know
the God of grace will simply die. Thus the God of Paul is a God of *sheer grace*.

The God of Acts

It is extraordinarily difficult to arrive at a sure judgment about the God of Acts.
The author of Acts clearly does not imagine that he is promoting a novel or
different view. He assumes that his readers accept what he at least implies in
his document. If anything, one would expect the major speeches to reveal such

novelty. Even in Paul's speech in Athens, however, the view of God, while perhaps stated in terms that are supposed to be compatible with Greek philosophical religiosity, says nothing really unusual. In fact, the major strangeness about that speech is the insertion of the Jewish apocalyptic notion of the eschatological judgment day.

It is thus fair to judge that the author of Acts assumes that he and his readers share the same view of God. Making this judgment, however, does not get us very far. Which view or views are assumed? And how do we decipher those views, if he assumes them and thus feels no need to explain them didactically or have his characters teach them?

Given the importance Acts puts on the Pharisaic Jewishness of its hero, Paul, as well as the importance to his theology of the fulfillment of the promise of the Hebrew Scriptures, one can safely start with the premise that Acts' view of God is Jewish, stemming from the Hebrew Scriptures. But again this does not get us very far either, since there are a variety of views detailed in those Scriptures, and it was as easy in the first century, as in ours, to construct a coherent view of God that can be claimed to have its roots in the Scriptures. The obvious example here is Paul himself. He thinks his God is the true God of the Scriptures, and he sets this over against another view, which he thinks is a distorted view.[74] Needless to say, his opponents thought it was Paul's view that was distorted.

So how does one proceed? One can look at the major speeches, the dialogue in the narratives, and the direction of the narratives themselves. While one would think that it is in the spoken words of the characters that substance is to be found, this is largely an exercise in futility, since the point of the speeches is hardly a description of who God is. It may be that it is through the direction of the narratives that one can learn more.

The Spoken Word. God is the creator of the world. This need not be emphasized to Jewish hearers. Twice, however, Paul makes the point to Gentile ears. In the speech at Athens, Paul refers to the "God who made the world and everything in it" (Acts 17:24). To the Gentiles at Lystra, Paul points beyond himself to the "living God who made the heaven and the earth and the sea and all that is in them" (14:15).[75] At the beginning of speeches to Jewish audiences Acts prefers to begin with the fathers, as would be appropriate (e.g., 7:2; 13:17). In fact, both Stephen and Paul structure their speeches according to a typical narration of God's relations with Israel. Peter's opening speech implies this narration but begins with words from scripture which justify picking up the story with Jesus' arrival (2:14-22). Thus the structure of the "story" in Acts begins with creation, continues with Israel, and inserts Jesus into the narrative of Israel as the essential part of it. So far, there is nothing remarkable about such a narrative, given the view that Jesus is the fulfillment of the promise to the patriarchs. The story climaxes with Jesus as Lord and Messiah by virtue of the resurrection (2:34-36) and concludes with language about expectation of judgment (e.g., 10:42; 17:31), although the expectation about judgment is spoken to Gentiles. Paul does add the theme of a general resurrection from the dead, when it serves his purpose (23:6; 24:21; 26:6-8), but this claim is not in evidence in the earlier speeches, though it is certainly implied in the notion of final judgment.

There is only one eye-opening statement about God from the speaker's point of view. When Peter realizes what the meaning of his vision is, he exclaims: "Truly I perceive that God shows no partiality [*ouk estin prosōpolēmptēs ho theos*] but every one among any people who fears him and acts righteously is acceptable to him" (10:34). The equivalent Hebrew phrase, which is awkward in Greek, means showing no partiality in judgment. Only here does the phrase occur in Acts.[76] The point is clearly that God works his single will upon both Jew and Greek. In the Hebrew Scriptures, the most similar statement to the Acts passage appears in Deuteronomy 10:17. Again the analogy is with the judge, for God shows no partiality and takes no bribe. Yet the immediately following passage reads: "He executes justice for the fatherless and the widow, and loves the sojourner" (Deut 10:18). The conclusion Moses draws is that the Israelite should "love the sojourner." That is, the non-Israelite should receive the same treatment as does the Israelite, with God as the model. Peter likewise affirms that God equally accepts the Gentile into relationship with him—and thus is to be baptized and receive the same salvation hoped for by Jewish believers in Jesus. Later Peter affirms this in language more familiar to the church: "We believe that we [the Jews] shall be saved through the grace of the Lord Jesus, just as they [the Gentiles] will" (Acts 15:11). One can, of course, find such sentiments in the Hebrew Scriptures (just as Paul does in Jeremiah 1:4). Thus it is not sure how novel the idea is, but in the narrative it is a dramatic breakthrough for Peter and the story. From now on, Gentiles will be equal partners with Jews in the Jesus movement.

Granted that Gentiles now have access to grace, just as do Jews, the question becomes how any person "joins the group." At the end of the first speech, Peter is asked just this question. He responds: "Repent and be baptized . . . in the name of Jesus Christ for the forgiveness of sins . . ." (Acts 2:38). It is interesting to see that the call to repentance is mentioned before baptism. Indeed, this seems to be the author's actual emphasis, for repentance and forgiveness are repeated and insistent motifs throughout the story.[77] If one asks, however, what one is to repent of and what one is forgiven for, the answers are surprisingly vague. After the initial chapters, one might suppose that the Jews should repent for their participation in the execution of Jesus. But the author quickly leaves that scene, and when he insists that Gentiles also have need to repent, then clearly more is at stake. Or is it that Jews and Gentiles repent of different things?

Is it that Jews are to repent of sins committed against Torah requirements? There are two statements, one by Paul, the other by Peter, that might suggest that Jewish sins have something to do with failure in relation to the Torah. The first occurs in Paul's speech in the synagogue at Antioch of Pisidia. "Let this be known to you, brothers, that through this one [Jesus], forgiveness of sins is proclaimed and [or, "even"] from everything that you were not able by the law of Moses to be acquitted, by this one [Jesus] everyone who believes is acquitted" (13:38f.). This strikes me as such a convoluted sentence that it is at least unclear, and perhaps obscure even to the author. The first part of the sentence gives the author's consistent view that forgiveness is available through the resurrected Jesus. The second part brings in Pauline words and, in part, slogans, even if it distorts Paul's teaching as we know it. Does the verse intend to say that the Torah acquitted one from nothing? Or does it intend to say that one could be acquitted for some things by the Torah but not by others? While I think it precarious to be sure one knows what the statement intends to say, I suspect that neither position just stated is likely. I think, rather, that it is saying in presumed Pauline terms what Peter says in 15:7-11. One is not acquitted if one does not follow the Torah, not because one cannot, but because, in the daily course of life, one simply doesn't. It is not the failure of the Torah but the failure of humans.

This second statement, by Peter, occurs in his defense of Paul's view that Gentiles do not need to be circumcised. The issue seems larger than just that of circumcision, however, and circumcision apparently stands for accepting the yoke of the Torah (as Paul himself says in Galatians 5:3). At any rate, the conclusion of the conference is to lay minimal requirements upon the Gentiles, rather than the law itself. This is how Peter's comment is to be understood in 15:10. The yoke of the Torah is something that "neither our fathers nor we have been able to bear" (15:10). That is, it is too hard to be adequately obedient. Then follows the sentence, quoted earlier, that for both Jew and Gentile, salvation is through grace.

Both Paul's and Peter's statements imply, especially when seen together, that Jews were not committed enough to fulfill the law, and thus there is some defect in their relationship with God. This is not, of course, the position of Paul or other Pharisaic intellectuals. That it might represent the views of the peasants in Palestine (if they attended to the law at all) or Hellenistic Jews who sometimes sat loose in the saddle when it came to following requirements, but perhaps also cast a somewhat suspicious eye at the whole system, is uncertain. The statements, however, must represent what the author took to be the position of many Jews, presumably those of the Diaspora. I rather doubt, however, that the author's primary point about the necessity of Jewish repentance has much to do with failure to obey Torah requirements, although that may have been in his mind, since Gentiles are equally exhorted.

Equally unspecific are statements about the necessity of Gentile repentance and concomitant forgiveness. The first reference to Gentiles occurs in Peter's speech to Cornelius. "To him all the prophets bear witness, that every one who believes in him receives forgiveness of sins through his name" (Acts 10:43). That sentence could be directed equally well to Jews. A bit more specific is Paul's admonition to the Athenians: "The times of ignorance God overlooked, but now he commands all people everywhere to repent"—and the warrant for the need to repent is the coming day of judgment (17:30-31). The times of ignorance must refer to the Gentiles before they had knowledge of the truth. And he reminds the elders of Ephesus of his preaching, that it could be summarized as "testifying both to Jews and to Greeks of repentance to God and of faith in our Lord Jesus Christ" (20:21). Here specifically any distinction in the content of repentance with respect to Jews or Greeks is abolished. The same message is addressed to both. But what the content of the sins is and what the nature of repentance might be are never specified.

The contrast with the paraenetic topic, a reminder of what "you Gentiles" used to do, is instructive here. We find this topic primarily in Colossians, Ephesians, and 1 Peter—documents that are roughly similar in date to Acts.[78] Perhaps the most elaborate example is Ephesians 2:1-3. The author addresses "you" (plural), his readers, who are assumed to be Gentiles and describes their past life as "dead through trespasses and sins, walking according to the *aiōn* of this world, according to the chief of the power of the air, that spirit which now works among the sons of disobedience, in which we all formerly lived in the desires of our flesh, doing the will of the flesh and mind, and we were by nature children of wrath as were the rest [of the Gentiles]." One has to admit that even this passage is not very specific about just what were the sins, but at least it indicates that the sins of the Gentiles were caused by a specific allegiance to evil powers and were different from those of the Jews.

The author of Acts doesn't seem to think this way—acknowledging that for the Gentiles the past was a time of "ignorance" (Acts 17:30). Does the author think Jewish sin and Gentile sin are the same in content, or only the same in guilt? A comparison with Paul would be interesting here. Suffice it to say that Paul also makes no real distinction between Jews and Gentiles—unbelievers are even under the same evil power (Gal 4:8-9). Most importantly, both Gentile and Jew are similar in that they both live out of pride and anxiety—both are estranged from the true God. I rather doubt that the author of Acts has a clue as to what Paul thinks. And he gives us no clue about his own meaning either.

We simply have to acknowledge that both unbelieving Jews and Gentiles are equally sinners and equally in need of repentance and forgiveness. The main thing we learn is that such repentance and forgiveness is open to all people—this is what God makes possible through Jesus. It seems to me this is a far cry from the general assault on humankind narrated in Revelation, although that author does refer to the possibility of repentance, however little he anticipates its success.[79] The criteria for sin, repentance, and forgiveness in Acts are simply not stated with any specificity. The author seems to have some general notion of righteousness, which he assumes his readers will acknowledge. That these criteria include faith in Jesus is obvious, but there seems to be, in addition, a general expectation of behavior that is "righteous."[80]

The Narrative. In Acts 3 Peter heals a man born lame (3:1-10). The theme of this healing is clearly important to the author of Acts, since its "memory" is recalled through the rest of the chapter and even in chapter 4 (cf. 3:16; 4:16, 21-22). Peter becomes a noted healer in Jerusalem (5:12-16). He heals Aeneas in Lydda (9:32-35). He raises Dorcas from the dead in Joppa (9:36-42). Peter also performs a miracle of death in the case of Ananias and Sapphira (5:1-11).

Paul also has the gift of healing. He enables a cripple from birth to walk (Acts 14:8-10). He exorcises a slave girl, although Acts reports that Paul healed her for less than divine reasons (he was "annoyed," 16:16-18). In a remarkable summary Acts reports that Paul healed diseases and exorcised, apparently at long distance (19:11f.). He raises Eutychus from the dead (at least the people think so, 20:9-12). After the shipwreck, Paul heals the father of Publius on Malta, as well as other residents of the island (28:8-9). These miracles may not constitute an extensive list, but they do show that Peter and Paul are concerned about the welfare of others, not all of whom are believers. At any rate, the list is at the opposite extreme from the "list" of violence narrated in Revelation.

The overarching theme of the narrative in Acts is mission. The book's narrative is a series of examples of the theme stated in chapter 1: "You shall be my witnesses in Jerusalem and in all Judea and Samaria and to the end of the earth" (1:8). God wishes them to convert the whole world to faith in Jesus, "since there is no other name under heaven given among people by which we must be saved" (4:12). The apostles travel tirelessly, endure hardship, missionize fearlessly, perform miracles of healing. Thus the God of Acts is a God who calls the world to faith, righteousness, and eternal life.[81]

God is a God of mission to and for the world. The God of Revelation is a God of vengeance. It would be theoretically something to hope for if I could show that these different views of God are rooted in a different theological structure. But as I have confessed above, I do not think that is possible. While there are, as suggested, differences in their structures, they are similar enough to suppose similar views about God might emerge. But this is also true of Paul. Paul's

God simply cannot be read out of the structure of the Cosmocrator trajectory, as modified by an eschatological direction.

The differences must lie, to one extent or another, in the author's experiences. Paul's experience can, I think, be delineated (although it is not the subject for this book).[82] Unfortunately, the experiences of our two authors are not accessible from their books. To attempt it would produce a circular argument that I eschew.

THE GOSPEL AND FIRST EPISTLE
OF JOHN AND THE THREE TRAJECTORIES

The Gospel of John

Readers are wont to reserve their superlatives for the Gospel of John. The most profound book in the New Testament! The most confusing! The most anti-Jewish! The most theologically influential! The most spiritual! The most ethically ingrown! Over-adored, over-maligned, the Gospel fascinates with its uniqueness and comprehensive clarity. This clarity makes it easy to love or to hate—perhaps both at the same time.

For one who wants to locate the theology of John within one of the trajectories I have discussed above, the document is no less frustrating. It just does not fit! It certainly does not fit the Cosmocrator trajectory. First, there is no enthronement as a result of the resurrection. Jesus as the incarnate Logos has always been God. No enthronement is needed, and there is no enthronement language. The resurrection is simply a return to where the Logos has always been. Second, there is no language that indicates that the resurrected Jesus exercises lordship over the world. True, the world has not overcome (*katalambanō*) the light (1:5), just as Jesus claims that he has become victorious (*nikaō*) over the world (16:33). Nevertheless, the world is darkness and seems to be left in darkness. There is a radical separation between the believers who are children of light and the rest of humankind who makes up the world; e.g., "I pray for them, not for the world" (17:9). The radical sectarian thrust of the Gospel is hard to deny. There are the insiders and there are all others.

The Cosmocrator acclamations are thus missing from the Gospel. The earthly Jesus is indeed called *kyrios*, most frequently in the vocative, but only once in an acclamation. Thomas confesses at the conclusion of the Gospel that

Jesus is his *kyrios* and *theos* (20:28). This is not Cosmocrator language. Not surprisingly, Cosmocrator language for the rulers of the cosmos is also missing. For that matter, Satan occurs only once (13:27), as a synonym for "devil" (13:2), and the devil, only once (apart from 13:2) in its usual meaning, the infamous 8:44.[1] There seems to be no cause assigned for the creation of the Logos to have fallen into darkness, not even the devil, a missing link noted by all students.

The *Christos* trajectory is certainly present, but it is presented in such an ambiguous way that one could claim either that it remains the dominant and constant trajectory, or that it has essentially been discarded for concepts more amenable to the later reflection of the community. On the positive side, the title, as discussed in chapter 3 above, occurs more times (19) than in any of the other Gospels. Apart from *Logos*, it is the only title to appear in the prologue: "Grace and truth came through Jesus Christ" (1:16).[2] And *Christos* is central in the presumed original ending of the Gospel: The signs narrated in the Gospel have as their intent that the reader "may believe that Jesus is the Christ, the Son of God, and that believing you may have life in his name" (20:31).

On the other hand, the majority of occurrences of *Christos* within the Gospel are in contexts of controversy, controversies that are not resolved in the narrative. The title is there, but the community does not seem to stake its confession on it. It is clear that for some, at least, other views of Jesus are primary. Perhaps the community knows that it has lost the battle with the synagogue. Only once does a traditional two-name designation of Jesus appear (1:16). And it is crucial to note that in the original closing, believing in Jesus as *Christos* is associated with the doing of signs, an indication of a thaumaturgic, popular view, but not the expected political understanding of the *Christos*.

As I said earlier, the abundant use of the title *Christos* in John is primarily associated with controversy with the synagogue. Is Jesus or is he not the Messiah? The dispute may even reflect controversy within the synagogue, where there are sympathizers as well as antagonists toward the Jesus movement.[3] The story of the man born blind in John 9 may help pinpoint the issue of the controversy. J. L. Martyn has cogently pointed out that that story reflects a situation in the life of the Johannine community in which members were separated by the Jewish leaders from membership in the synagogue.[4] In 9:22 this separation is explicitly linked to the *Christos* title: "The Jews had already agreed that if any one should confess him to be Christ, he was to be put out of the synagogue." It may not be accidental that the appearance of the Son of Man title in the story occurs at the end, after the man has been separated from the synagogue, suggesting that this title had nothing to do with his expulsion.

I will dare to speculate on the situation. Within the synagogue, discussion arose about Jesus of Nazareth. This is only what should be expected in any area where Jews who came to admire Jesus were located. The discussion grew heated, with arguments on both sides. Finally the leaders of the synagogue decided to draw the line. To admire and respect Jesus is one thing; to declare him to be Messiah is another. Anyone who made such a confession was to be expelled from the synagogue.[5] Some believers in Jesus were expelled and formed the nucleus of the Johannine community. Some other Jews remained sympathetic to the claims about Jesus but shrank from saying anything that would cause a rupture with the synagogue. No doubt, some of these had notions about Jesus that could be contained in synagogue obedience; some others may have felt the social pressure too great to say what they really believed. In other words, there was probably a wide spectrum of ideas about Jesus. On one end were the synagogue leaders who may have felt matters were getting out of control; on the other was the new Johannine community. In between were most likely Jews who had various attitudes, not all of them hostile, by any means. The frequent reference in the Gospel to Jews sympathetic to Jesus suggests such a spectrum. Of the various arguments for and against Jesus as *Christos* the one most powerful for the Johannine community seems to have been the miracles of Jesus.[6] Thus, as has been widely suggested, there may have been a "Signs Source" that touted and listed the miracles of Jesus.[7] The original end of the Gospel would seem to belong to this set of affirmations, when it enlists the signs of Jesus as "proof" that he was the Messiah. This could well have been an ending affixed to an earlier stage of the community's belief, when the argument about Jesus' messiahship was still central, and to which the later writer has added the final clause: "and that believing you may have life in his name."

Thus we do not need a later "high" Christology to explain the split between synagogue and Jesus movement; the split occurred due to debate about Jesus as Messiah. In fact, the later christological movement may actually have been motivated by the feeling of defeat about Jesus as *Christos*. To continue to claim *only* that Jesus was Messiah was not enough. Something more was needed, a view of Jesus that could not be called into question by "facts" such as those that propelled the argument about Jesus as *Christos*. Hence entered the Son of Man.

In the present Gospel the title "Son of Man" has assumed a prominent, yet surprisingly ambiguous place.[8] The title occurs thirteen times.[9] One can only wonder how the term emerged in Johannine reflection. As we have seen, it clearly is not an offshoot of any *Christos* reflection. Yet the Synoptic traditions show that the *Christos* and Son of Man traditions sat side by side, however incongruously. The simplest suggestion is that the contact (however it may be imagined) between the Johannine communities and other Jesus communities may have provided the impetus for the concurrence of these traditions.[10]

At the same time, the Son of Man logia in John show distinct linguistic peculiarities when compared with Synoptic texts. Of the thirteen occurrences, eight (or nine) relate to the idea of ascent (and descent), a motif not prominent in the Synoptic traditions, where eschatological coming and judgment are the dominant ideas, even after the earthly Jesus has been identified as Son of Man. Even when, as in Mark 14:62, the ascension is implied, it is not mentioned; the emphasis remains on the exalted, coming Son of Man. Clearly, after the Son of Man trajectory entered into Johannine christological reflection, it underwent modification to meet the needs of some other theological reflection.

Very few of the logia would sound familiar to a Synoptic audience. Perhaps the saying most typical would be that in John 5:27: The Father "has given him authority to execute judgment because he is the Son of Man." Even here, given the context, the logion's meaning is ambiguous. For the context speaks of both a typical future judgment as well as a present reality, more like judgment motifs elsewhere in the Gospel. In either case judgment is vested in the Son of Man, a traditional feature of the Synoptic traditions.[11]

All of the other occurrences of "Son of Man" are "deflected"; that is, they have been molded to Johannine language and do not reflect the images typical of Jewish and Synoptic literature. For example, in chapter 6 on the feeding and its meaning, the Son of Man is said to give eternal life (v. 27).[12] While the point is roughly the same as that in Mark 13:27 (the angels gather the elect at the eschaton), the vocabulary has been recast and set within the metaphors of the feeding section, and the eschatological future turned back to the time of the church. Twice more in this chapter the title appears. In the midst of the eucharistic section on eating (6:51b-58), Jesus warns that all who would have life must eat the flesh and drink the blood of the Son of Man. Whether the Eucharist is seen as bestowing eternal life in the present is unclear. The language moves in two directions—one toward the present ("He who eats my flesh and drinks my blood has eternal life"), the other toward the future ("And I will raise him up at the last day"). Probably the meaning is that the partaking of the Eucharist assures one of what will actually happen in the eschatological future. Although in this section it is the Eucharist specifically (not Jesus in general) that bestows eternal life, the saying is functionally similar to verse 27. In both, it seems to me likely that it is the exalted Son of Man who fulfills these promises. Clearly the Eucharist is a post-resurrection event for the community. The third occurrence of the title in chapter 6 is one of the "ascension" sayings, which I will discuss shortly.

While the uses of "Son of Man" in chapter 6, discussed above, hover mysteriously between present and future, earthly and exalted, a clearly present usage seems to occur in 9:35. Jesus asks the man with the recovered sight: "Do you believe in the Son of Man?" Here the title is introduced almost diffidently, as if it were a standard one for the Johannine community. Jesus is Son of Man whenever and wherever. That the title is nevertheless an exalted one is indicated by the man's worship of Jesus (*proskyneō*) when he learns that he is the Son of Man.

But what about the title in the nine ascent/descent contexts? What is going on? The last four occurrences in the Gospel all speak of the glorification of the Son of Man as an imminent event.[13] As all know, glorification in the Gospel of John refers primarily to the revelation of the reality of God as manifest through Jesus. The cross is glorification and revelation because Jesus' death most truly shows that reality of God. Glorification also implies the exaltation, the resurrection to heaven of the Son of Man. Thus the statements about the glorification of the Son of Man refer both to revelation of God and ascent to the transcendent realm. In one sense these statements are similar to the predictions in Mark that the Son of Man must suffer and die. But John suggests two major changes or additions: (1) the death is revelation, and (2) the death is exaltation—it is ascent. Surprisingly, the Synoptic statements never talk about ascent, although it is clearly implied.

In themselves, however, the Johannine references discussed so far could mesh with those of the Synoptics that affirm (or imply) that death and resurrection mark the movement of Jesus to become Son of Man. In the Synoptic traditions Jesus clearly *becomes* the Son of Man by virtue of death and resurrection. There is no preexistence; thus there is no return. Thus also the Johannine statements about Jesus' glorification through death could be taken as implying that Jesus becomes something he was not before. They may, in fact, reflect a stage in the Son of Man Christology before preexistence entered the Gospel theology.

There are two logia, however, that claim explicitly that ascent is a result of descent.[14] Jesus says to Nicodemus (if he is still around by this point in the dialogue): "No one has ascended into heaven but he who descended from heaven, the Son of Man" (3:13). In fact, according to this statement ascent logically implies descent. There can be no affirmation about ascent (glorification, Jesus becoming Son of Man), without the prior confession that all this depends upon descent. In other words, the crucial addition this passage makes is about the preexistence of Jesus. It is this claim that makes the distinction between Johannine and Synoptic Christology. In the following verse, the exaltation of the Jesus on the cross implies ascent (in the double entendre of John), but in this context, ascent depends upon descent.

The second logion that affirms descent seems a harsh insertion into a context that does not require it. In John 6:60, Jesus' disciples respond, negatively it would seem, to a prior statement by Jesus, judging it to be a "hard saying" (*sklēros logos*). The meaning is uncertain. Is the saying hard to understand or hard to accept? Interpreters vary in the nuance they give the phrase, but in the final analysis, from the author's point of view, a saying that is unacceptable is just one that is not properly understood.

For our purposes, it is more important to determine, if possible, which saying of Jesus has been judged to be *sklēros*. Given the present context, the most likely target is the immediately previous comments about eating and drinking Jesus (vv. 53-58). Already, however, I have sided with Rudolf Bultmann, who argued that 6:51b-59 was a later addition by the ecclesial editor. Thus the best judgment about the hard saying is that it is verse 51a: "I am the living bread which came down from heaven; if anyone eats of this bread he will live forever." What the "many" disciples cannot accept is the claim that Jesus has descended from heaven, that is, that he is preexistent.

Jesus then retorts that the complement of the descent is the ascent, now phrased in terms of the Son of Man (it would make little sense to say that bread ascended!). "Then what if you see the Son of Man ascending where he was before?" The ascent implies a descent, that is, preexistence. The claim of preexistence, descent, and ascent causes a rupture in the community (6:66). One wonders whether this hints at a historical break in the Johannine community about the "new" Christology of Jesus as the preexistent Son of Man.

But how did the notion of preexistence enter the reflection of the community? As we have seen, preexistence is not a necessary part of the structure of Son of Man Christology in the early church.[15] The sayings in John about the glorification of the Son of Man do not in themselves force an interpretation of preexistence on the logia. Although the vocabulary is radically different between John and, say, Mark, the basic structure could be seen as congruent. One could speculate, indeed, that the original Son of Man Christology in the Johannine community was similar (structurally) to that of the Synoptics. The earthly Jesus after death becomes Son of Man in heaven, from which he oversees judgment and bestows eternal life on his followers, whether at the eschaton (perhaps an earlier stage) or (later) a continuously present reality.

Judging from the information the Gospel itself gives us, then, the cause for the introduction of preexistence into the Son of Man trajectory was the emergence at some point of Logos speculation. If Messiah Christology was the first stage, and Son of Man the second, then one can see that Logos Christology was the third and final stage. Since the Word is God, then obviously preexistence is structurally a necessary part of the Christology. Furthermore, there is a descent from the transcendent realm to that of the world (1:14). The prologue sets all this out clearly. It does not, interestingly enough, refer to the death and thus does not speak of ascent. Perhaps that is left to come out in the narrative.

Scholars have argued whether or not the prologue was an original part of the Gospel. I doubt that issue will ever be resolved. What seems clear to me, however, and I would consider this a more important issue, is that ideas of divinity run through the *narrative*. Such claims of divinity are not necessary for a *Christos* or Son of Man Christology. For our purposes, what is important is to note that the Logos Christology has significantly modified the Son of Man

Christology by attaching it to the preexistence of Jesus, thus necessitating a descent motif to be added to that of ascent. Once this is done, it would be easy to reinterpret the ascent sayings of the Son of Man (which may originally have had nothing to do with descent) to mean a return to the transcendent realm "where he was before."

Thus we have, I suspect, three stages of historical development in the Johannine tradition. As the community grows, an original *Christos* Christology has added to it an overlay of the Son of Man. And over that overlay comes eventually that of the Logos—the divinity and preexistence of Jesus. Even the first stage caused enmity with the synagogue leaders and led to separation and ostracism. By the time the Son of Man Christology infiltrates the thought of the community, the split with the synagogue is in the past. The fact that the original Gospel concluded with the statement that the purpose of the narrative was to show sufficient signs so that people would believe that Jesus was the *Christos* suggests that there were members of the community who remained theologically at that first level. If my suggestion about the split in the community implied at the end of John 6 has merit, then there were other believers who were offended by the new additions of descent/ascent Christology to Jesus as Son of Man. Perhaps the claims of preexistence seemed unnecessarily grandiose. The prayer by Jesus for unity in the community (17:20-23) begins to sound not like a projected anxiety about the split visible in the Johannine epistles, but like a bad memory of past and present disputes.

Determining where the Logos Christology came from and how long it had simmered in theological reflections before the Gospel itself was completed is a task I shall not set myself. Where it came from is one of those eternal arguments of scholars. That it was not a recent import into the community is suggested to me by the continued presence of notions of Jesus' divinity and, to a lesser extent, of preexistence in the narrative. This must have taken some years of reflection. If the Gospel was written in the mid-nineties, then the community must have been in some turmoil for at least two decades, trying to work to an understanding of the deeds of Jesus and his relationship to God. Whether the Logos theology "won over" the entire community is probably not a fair question. That the author was committed to this theology seems clear. Whether he was writing to a community all of whom agreed with him is less likely. Strands of *Christos* and Son of Man (without notions of preexistence?) seem too important in the Gospel for them to be mere relics of the past. The community may have had quite divergent views, although there seems to have been enough goodwill that a split had not yet occurred by the time of the Gospel's composition. By the time of the epistles, however, the split is a reality.

The Preexistent Logos as the Revelation of the Reality of God

With the appearance of the Logos Christology and its decisive imprint upon the Gospel in its present form, we have arrived at a place from which we can look at the whole, attempting to create a coherence among the various layers still evident in the narrative. As all acknowledge, and as I have tried to show, the Gospel is not a seamless garment. The traditions the author uses are not entirely consistent; almost certainly the community itself had various perspectives, not all of which agreed with one another. It may well be that ancient mentality was more comfortable with a both/and acceptance of inconsistent elements than we can accept today.

Nor is it possible here, any more than in the other documents we have looked at, to give any detailed analysis of the text as a whole. I must content myself with an attempt to understand why the author of John found the Logos Christology compelling. I am not interested in the origin of such thought; I am very much interested in the function this thought served in his portrait of Jesus. I present my suggestions as the solution to a problem of which I think the author was aware, a solution which seemed to the author to validate the truth in Jesus and to show how Jesus could be claimed to be "the way, the truth, and the life" (14:6).[16]

In the religiously pluralistic world of antiquity, there were many competing claims to truth. At a cruder level, one could argue for the efficacy of one god or goddess over another. At a more sophisticated level, one could make the argument that the known world of divinities represented various manifestations of a single power, which might be named as the highest God or Goddess[17] or given an abstract name to indicate that the power lies behind any specific manifestation of a known deity.[18] With so much competition, how did a serious thinker attempt to resolve the vagaries of ancient religious traditions and to protect his own claims that truth resided in his tradition, rather than some other? The Jesus movement had its own problem with Judaism. How did one safeguard the claim that Jesus is the ultimate revelation of Yahweh, especially in the face of emphatic denials by the synagogue?

The author also lives in a "world"[19] in which there is a wall between the transcendent reality, where ultimate truth exists, and the immanent world, where humans exist. Foreign to his world is the constant flitting between heaven and earth of the Olympian deities. Humans cannot breach that wall. Only the revelation of and by the transcendent is salvatory.[20] Unfortunately for the status of religious language, human language, even about the divine, belongs to immanent reality.[21] How then can the status of revelatory words be defended? How does one know that what a presumed revealer says is true? This is particularly problematic in Judaism and most of the early Jesus movements, where the word(s) of God result in actual sentences by God's spokespersons, Moses and the prophets.

The author discovered that the Logos Christology spoke to these issues.[22] In this structure the Logos is divine—thus is not some intermediary between God and the world, as a human or even an angel might be. The Logos *is* God. Thus when the Logos reveals itself, it reveals God. This is the brunt of such statements as "I and the Father are one" (10:30) and "He who has seen me has seen the Father" (14:9). When one is in the presence of the Logos, one is in the presence of God. This brings echoes of the old debate between Rudolf Bultmann and Ernst Käsemann. For Bultmann the offense in the Gospel is that the Logos became *flesh*; thus one had to overcome the offense that the revealer was clothed in ambiguity just like all humans. Käsemann rejoined that Jesus in the Gospel was docetic, was "like a God striding the earth."[23] I think Käsemann is primarily correct; the author wants to use Jesus as a window opening to the actual transcendent reality. Yet Jesus' opponents surely take offense that a mere man should make such outrageous statements (5:18).

Thus the descent/ascent motif is essential to the structure of the Gospel. As the divine Logos, Jesus descends from the transcendent reality into the immanent; from there he ascends "back to where he was before." This is why the more traditional Son of Man trajectory has to have added to it the descent motif. "No one has ascended but he who descended" (cf. 3:13). Ascent is wedded to the glorification through death. But in the present structure, descent is necessary, implying divinity and preexistence. In fact, the effectiveness of the ascent that is the glorification of the Son of Man through death now depends upon descent. Glorification in John is revelation. Glorification of the Son of Man is revelation of the reality of himself. But the glorification of the Son of Man is at the same time the glorification of God (12:23, 27-28). The mutuality of the revelation in the cross depends upon the identity of God and Logos.

Implied in all that has been said above is the Johannine understanding of the salvatory act of the Logos. It is, purely and simply, the revelation of the reality of God. This means it is not verbal disclosure of any sort, nor is it ethically oriented—salvation is not a "do right" program. Salvation means standing and abiding in the presence of God. Seeing is believing ("Come and see!" 1:39; 12:21). But what does it mean to see?

In the great divide between the transcendent and the immanent worlds, words belong to the latter. God cannot be captured in words, slogans, creeds, or even sacred writings. Humans are inevitably forced to use words. The wise person, however, while she knows that words may point to transcendent reality (what other tools do we have but pointers?), also knows that words, however profound, are not the equivalent of transcendent reality. What then is left? If salvation is abiding in the presence of the transcendent reality, what sort of salvation is that? Again Bultmann puts the matter succinctly. He asks: Who is Jesus in the Gospel? Answer: He is the revealer. Question: What does he reveal? Answer: He reveals that he is the revealer.[24]

While the Gospel has a radical understanding of salvation as the presence of God, the general view is not foreign to Jewish apocalyptic. For there salvation in heaven is being in the presence of God forever and ever. In Revelation, for example, the elders on their thrones continually worship God. What is unique to the Gospel is that the presence of God is not relegated to heaven and to the future. It exists now in the presence of the Logos. Jesus says to Philip: "He who has seen me has seen the Father" (14:9). To see Jesus means to be in the presence of God. And to be in the presence of God is to "have eternal life." This is why eternal life is not postponed into the future in Johannine theology. It is a present reality. As long as one abides in that presence, one lives eternally. In fact, one could say that if eternal life does not begin in this life, it never begins.

I still have not answered the question: What kind of "seeing" is the salvatory presence? It is not an intellectual, optic seeing. It is participatory seeing. To "see" is to be transformed into that reality of our seeing. While the later letter we name 1 John knows primarily a future, eschatological salvation, it states clearly the relationship between seeing and being (3:2). "Beloved, we are God's children now; it does not yet appear what we shall be, but we know that when he appears we shall be like him, for we shall see him as he is (*homoioi autō esometha, hoti opsometha auton kathōs estin*). In the future eschatological moment believers will become realities like that of God. That is an incredibly bold statement, colored only by the ambiguity of "like" (*homoioi*).

The Gospel of John uses the language of "abiding in." The author, in the tour de force of chapter 14, gradually leads the reader to understand that the "dwelling," which seems to start out in verse 1 in heaven, is actually the present dwelling of the divine reality in the believer (14:23). The development takes place in several steps. The Father and Jesus indwell one another (14:11). Thus whoever has seen Jesus has seen God. That is but the beginning. The Spirit (a notion to which I shall shortly return) dwells in (with) the believer and is (will be) in them (14:17).[25] In verse 20 the mutual indwelling involves Father, Jesus, and believers. Finally, in verse 23, "we [both Father and Son] will make their home with them," the believers (the word "home" is the same word as in 14:1).

The text clearly speaks of mutual indwelling as the present act of salvation. Just what the author means by "indwelling" is not as certain. Most Christian theology bristles at a literal, "mystical" interpretation. If one takes the language literally, it sounds like divinization. The believer becomes divine! Thus Bultmann, as a neo-Reformation theologian always at odds with mysticism, interpreted the indwelling as "faith." The passages mean that (in a good Lutheran understanding) the believer absolutely trusts that in the ambiguous flesh of Jesus shines the divine reality.[26] Bultmann thought that this was one place where the Gospel, so often indebted to gnostic myth, broke the myth, often called the "saved Savior."[27] I agree that John is not "gnostic" in the way the term is often used. The revealer does not seek out those who already are divine (have a divine spark in them). The revealer brings into the presence of God those who come to the light (3:16-21).

On the other hand, the Gospel seems conflicted over whether those coming choose of themselves to come or whether the coming is God's determination.[28] I suspect the author of John had not thought through the problem any more systematically than most of the other New Testament authors had. On the outside it appears to be choice. What is the inward cause, no one can really say for sure.

On the issue of faith, however, I object to Bultmann. It seems to me there is no way around a basically mystical interpretation. That is, the divine reality inhabits the believer. This is surely another way of verbalizing the transformation that comes through "seeing." Let's put the reality in terms of the transcendent versus the immanent. In the act of salvation, of "seeing," the believer becomes part of the transcendent reality. The whole purpose of the Word becoming flesh is to bring people into that realm, which is the realm of eternal life. It is, in fact, the meeting of revealer and believer that causes divinity. I do not think we should shrink from the idea of "divinization."[29]

At the same time, there is no language in John that hints at the believer becoming an equal part of God. God and Logos take all the initiative. The believer receives divinization as a gift, whether or not the person comes voluntarily to the light. In one sense God is the only Actor. Believers are passive recipients. There is no sense of arrogance or super-human activity on the part of the believer.

A final comment needs to be made about Johannine mysticism. The author never writes about the experiences of the believers. As far as I know, most religious phenomena in the ancient world that have been called "mystical" are primarily ecstatic experiences, as, for example, early Jewish "Merkabah" mysticism. Paul speaks of his ecstatic experience in the heavens (2 Cor 12:1-4). Not so John. The coming to the light reads like an objective event, as if there were no experiential component. The author can speak positively of love, but even that seems more objective than experiential. Thus, based on what the text actually says, I think we have to speak of a non-experiential mysticism, of events in which the believer encounters the transcendent realm and becomes part of it, without having an emotional reality that gives assurance that he or she has encountered the divine. Here, I think, is the place where Bultmann would ask: When one makes a decision, is that decision not an act of faith?

As the author viewed the already vast panorama of his theological vision, at some point he may have realized that he had overlooked one important problem, a problem that is fulsomely addressed in the present Gospel. The Logos becomes flesh and dwells among us. Well and good. As long as that unique flesh is on earth, the light shines and people can encounter the transcendent through it. But it is also the case that Jesus returns to the Father, is crucified and rises, returning back to where he was before. Has the light left for good? Is the world yet once again in darkness?

The author finds his answer in a unique description of the reality and activity of the Holy Spirit, which he calls the Paraclete. In the early church at large, the Spirit was seen as the cause of more than human activity on the part of humans, such as glossolalia (that is, it was something experienced). Paul begins the process of elevating the Spirit closer to the activity of the resurrected Christ (2 Cor 3:12-18). But nothing prior to John prepares one for the breathtaking transformation he makes. The Paraclete descends as Jesus ascends. The Paraclete indwells in the church (the church is the flesh of the Paraclete) and recreates the reality of the Logos. The Paraclete replicates Jesus, so that the world will never again be in darkness.[30] That is, the Paraclete remains as the permanent presence of the transcendent reality. And it abides in the church. The church is called to be the vehicle for the light of the transcendent. Whether the light in fact shines depends upon the obedience of the church to its call. This is why it is important for the author to state that the Paraclete dwells in the believers (14:17).

What lies ahead for the church is not some eagerly awaited eschaton. That, apparently, is not part of the scenario. What lies ahead is the dangerous job of being the light in a world of darkness (16:1-4). Although the world hates them (17:14), and although there is no expectation of miraculous escape from the travail (17:15), they at least have the assurance that God will protect them from falling away. In the midst of danger, the church is called to be faithful. Only in the assurances that living in eternal life in the present and in the call to remain true to the Paraclete lie the confidence and hope of the believing church.

Conclusion

The unique creative work of the author of the Fourth Gospel is awesome. With a sure and sovereign hand he has constructed a vast and, I think it fair to add, profound interpretation of the meaning of Jesus for his communities. With wisdom he has threaded his way through the three trajectories that are the subject of this book, allowing to stand what was not antithetical to his own program, and molding what necessary to fit. The *Christos* trajectory he kept in some prominence. His own structure did not call for it, but for reasons important to him, he made it present in the narrative. I have suggested that one reason is that in the Johannine communities there were some who still held Jesus to be the

Messiah as their primary faith perspective. Also apparently important to others was the belief that Jesus is the Son of Man. Here he had to create modifications to make that older view, which may have had no idea of Jesus' preexistence, fit his own perspective of divinity and preexistence.

We are now at a place where we can ask why the author so ignored the Cosmocrator trajectory. One reason may be that the Johannine community was so rooted in a Jewish perspective that it did not come into significant contact with communities for whom the Cosmocrator trajectory was important. But surely the prime reason, whatever may have been earlier contact, is that the author would have found that trajectory an obstruction to his own perspective—and this for several reasons.

1. The author's radical sectarianism would have found the political tones of the Cosmocrator trajectory conflictive with its own sense of God and the world ("My kingdom is not of this world," 18:36). God's people do not participate in victory over the world as a political event; they are victorious over the world ("I have overcome the world," 16:33) only in the sense that the world is powerless over the faithful.

2. Even where the Cosmocrator trajectory asserts the preexistence of Jesus (as, perhaps, in Phil 2:6; Col 1:15), the resurrection leads to an enthronement by virtue of which Jesus attains a power he did not have before. The Cosmocrator trajectory looks forward to enthronement. The Johannine perspective, with its emphasis upon the Logos as preexistent divinity, has no place for an enthronement. Death/resurrection is Jesus' return "to where he was before." The exalted Jesus needs no further status. Furthermore, the salvatory work of the Johannine Jesus is revelation of the reality of God, not victory over the powers and principalities. Granted, the death/exaltation/resurrection of Jesus has special significance for the Johannine author, since the death is the clearest glorification (i.e., revelation) of God. But that even more pinpoints the difference between John and the Cosmocrator trajectory. Death/resurrection for John remains revelation; for the Cosmocrator trajectory it is enthronement.

3. Since all structures are interwoven motifs, to think about one evokes another. All the trajectories we have looked at involve some claim for new knowledge. The Cosmocrator trajectory "reveals" that the risen Jesus is the ruler over the powers and principalities. In some developments (especially in Colossians and Ephesians) the new knowledge involves the plan of salvation that has been hidden. In the Son of Man trajectory, at the eschaton there will be revelation that is new. But none of these trajectories suggests that the revelation is of the divine reality itself, and none of the trajectories understands the revelation to be non-verbal and transformation into the transcendent reality, as does the Gospel of John.

The conclusion is unavoidable. The theological structure of the Gospel of John at its heart is different from any of the trajectories. It is unique among New Testament documents. Could we call it a new trajectory? Certainly it is *new*. Whether we identify it as a *trajectory* depends upon whether or not succeeding documents emulate sufficiently the theological structure that they can be said to be inheritors of the theological structure.

The answer here is ambivalent. The Johannine epistles are, of course, the most likely candidates for such a legacy. Yet they evince such modifications that it is not clear whether they represent more the inheritance or the movement back to the mainstream church of the second century. One might suppose that the "antichrists" of 1 John might have evoked clearer lines of relationship with the Gospel itself. Yet that offshoot seems to have already moved in a docetic direction, unlike and unnecessary to the structure of the fountainhead. The Valentinian *Gospel of Truth* manifests some remarkable affinities with the thrust of the Gospel, but yet shows many differences. Even after the Gospel of John was accepted into the mainstream church, it did not seem to have been interpreted as its author would have wished. The Gospel thus remains a unique creation, a brilliant star alone in the heavens, not belonging to any constellation.[31] Perhaps a church modeled on its theological structure is yet to emerge.

The First Epistle of John

Majority opinion seems to regard the Johannine Epistles as later documents than the Gospel of John, although emanating from the same "school" or circle.[32] Consonant with this judgment is the widespread view that the author of the epistles (or at least that of 1 John) shows a tendency to move Johannine theology to be more in line with an emerging synthesis of the "great church." Thus some of the radical ideas of the Gospel of John have been modified to be more in line with more traditional positions accepted in this emerging consensus. I have found myself squarely within such a description. To look at 1 John, however, from the perspective of this book, may suggest some possible new perspectives that may better explain the document.[33]

Not surprisingly, just as with the Gospel of John, all Cosmocrator elements and terminology are lacking. There is no enthronement, no acclamations, no powers and principalities to conquer. Yet while not surprising, one might expect some intruding language, if the document is designed to pull the Johannine community back toward the more ordinary views of the emerging consensus, if only in lip service. Key here is that Jesus is never called *kyrios*, nor is God, for that matter.[34]

What *is* surprising is that there is no trace of the Son of Man trajectory. Obviously important, at some stage, to the Johannine community, the author(s) of the epistles are completely silent about it. Why the silence? There are three options. (1) The epistles represent a very early stage of the community before that Christology emerged within it. The problem here would be to find a rationale for the split-up of the community so poignantly described in the epistle. (2) The thought of the epistles represents a late development of Christology, in which the Son of Man trajectory has been completely replaced by what in the Gospel is the dominant Christology of the Logos. Here the difficulty is that there are no explicit statements of divinity or preexistence in 1 John. Scholars have found such views implied in the text, but that may be a result of finding what one already expects to find. (3) The community has rejected the Son of Man trajectory in favor of the earlier *Christos* trajectory. Has the community split from the main Johannine community in protest over the increasingly "high" Christology of the Son of Man, after it has been influenced by the Logos Christology? If so, the split may be alluded to in John 6:66. I think this is the likely position in which to place 1 John, a view I argue for below. This location of the thought of the epistle, however, in no way speaks directly to the issue of its dating.

The *Christos* trajectory is the obvious location for the document. Not only is it the only title, apart from *huios*, occurring in the text, five of its eight appearances reflect the double name, *Iēsous Christos*, which was becoming standard in the later church.[35] In 1:3 a phrase, perhaps functioning as an acclamation in this trajectory, appeals to the Father "and his son Jesus Christ." In 2:1 the *paraklētos* with the Father is "Jesus Christ the righteous." God's command in 3:23 is to believe in the name of his Son, Jesus Christ. The confession that Jesus Christ has come in the flesh is extolled in 4:2. In 5:6 Jesus Christ has come through water and blood. In the grammatically problematic 5:20, it is at least clear that the title is "Jesus Christ." Since in the Gospel of John "Jesus Christ" occurs only twice (1:17; 17:3), the use of the double name must be seen as a significant difference between the two documents. Apparently, this is not a controversial title but the ordinary one within this community. In 4:2 and 5:6 there is controversy, but it is not about the title itself.

On the surface, then, 1 John seems to represent an early christological position in the Johannine spectrum, a stage before the emergence of the Christology of the Son of Man. Since, however, the document is considered late by the majority of scholars, it is necessary to look at other forms of expression that to some have seemed to indicate acceptance of some, at least, of the later strata of that community.

The use of the title *huios*, is, if anything, even more prominent than that of *Christos*, since it occurs twenty-two times referring to Jesus. The main question for us is whether the author uses *huios* as a synonym for *Christos* or whether it carries other meanings as well. I think it can be argued that to identify the precise meaning of *huios* in christological texts is the most daunting task facing anyone trying to locate an author's thought. From a Jewish perspective, its origin seems clearly located in the notion that the Messiah is God's Son, as stated explicitly in Psalm 2, a text appealed to by early Christian writers. How Hellenistic thought moved the title more in the direction of a God and Son, perhaps with preexistence implied, has never been easy to answer. Paul uses *huios* frequently, sometimes with the verb "send." Whether Paul implies a preexistence in such vocabulary is uncertain.

In John the linguistic data leads to no sure results. Three times, *huios* is linked with the double name, Jesus Christ (1:3; 3:23; 5:20), indicating that the author understands *huios* to be at least a synonym for "Messiah." The explicit phrase "Son of God" occurs six times (3:8; 4:15; 5:5, 10, 13, 20). In five other instances, the nearest antecedent for *huios* is *theos* (1:7; 3:23; 4:9, 10; 5:9, 10). In four occurrences, *huios* is specifically linked with *patēr* (2:22, 23 [twice], 24; 4:14).

The evidence suggests that the author most readily associates *huios* with *theos*. Four of the five occurrences of *huios* and *theos* are found in a section where the author is hotly contesting some opposing point of view. This is the section of the infamous antichrists—former members of the community now turned into bitter enemies by the author (2:18-25). He says that the liar is the one who denies that Jesus is the Christ. The antichrist is "he who denies the Father and the Son. No one who denies the Son has the Father. He who confesses the Son has the Father also. . . . If what you heard from the beginning abides in you, then you will abide in the Son and in the Father" (2:22-24). It is strange that this conjunction of Father and Son occurs in such a concentrated area. One suspects that *patēr* is a term for God that the "antichrists" use when speaking about the relationship of God and Jesus. The alternative is that the "antichrists" deny any significance to Jesus and use the term *patēr* for God. Before I try to make sense out of this puzzlement, let me add the final occurrence of Father and Son in the document, a passage that also may be implicitly a controversy. In 4:14 the author writes that "we" are sure that "the Father has sent his Son as [the] *sōtēr* of the world." This is the only occurrence of *sōtēr* in the document. Likewise there is only one occurrence in the Gospel—and the phrase is almost identical. The Samaritans confess that Jesus is "the Savior of the world" (John 4:42). Why would the author of 1 John use the term *sōtēr*, especially since he clearly has a view of the world basically as negative as that of the Gospel of John? Of the many uses of *kosmos* in 1 John, only one other tends to the positive side. Jesus is the expiation for our sins and also "for the sins of the whole world" (*peri holou tou kosmou*, 2:2).[36] Thus there are two unusual features of this sentence. One is the association of Father with Son; the other, the positive intent for the world. This might well count toward seeing the phrase as capturing the vocabulary of the opponents. But the solemn beginning of the sentence, with the emphasis upon witnessing, suggests that the author wants to claim the vocabulary as his own. Is the purpose to wrest that vocabulary away from its possession by his opponents? Or is there here some vague echo of Samaritan theology?

But let us return to the cluster of Father/Son passages in 3:22-24. On the surface, it would seem the case that the "antichrists" claim to have the Father but do not allow significance to the Son. The author, on the other hand, claims that unless one confesses the Son, claims to the Father are useless. Claiming the Father without the Son does not save. To confess the Son would seem, in the context of 3:22, to lay claim to the notion that Jesus is Messiah. There are two apparent claims in other passages. In 4:2, it is necessary to claim that Jesus Christ has come "in the flesh." In 4:15 and 5:5 it is added that one must confess that Jesus is the Son of God. Are these independent assertions or, in some way, do they all mean the same thing?

I take it that the usual view, based on the premise that 1 John is a later Johannine production, is that 1 John represents the mainstream Johannine perspective, although pulled back toward the "great church," while the opponents represent the radical, gnosticizing segment, that would eventuate in second-century gnostic Christianity. In this case it is usually assumed that 2:22 really means what 4:2 says, so that the christological issue is about docetism. But how then do 4:15 and 5:5 fit into this picture? There are so many possible meanings to "Son of God" that it would seem unlikely that gnosticizing opponents could not have fit a title such as Son of God into their framework, especially since it is so prominent in the Gospel of John.

I suggest as an alternative that, from the author's perspective, all three of these criteria fit the tenets of the opponents. The author thinks the opponents (a) do not believe that Jesus is the Messiah (although they obviously have a positive view of Jesus); (b) do not believe that Jesus in his appearance on earth was truly human; (c) do not believe Jesus is the Son of God as he understood it. The question is, what situation would such claims fit as well as the author's perhaps mistaken ideas about what the opponents actually claimed?

I want to turn to the sixth chapter in the Gospel of John. In the monologue of Jesus as the living bread, one can see a Christology influenced by the Logos idea. Clear statements of descent appear. Jesus is the living bread (v. 35). More, he has come down from heaven (v. 38). The "Jews" correctly hear him as saying: "I am the bread that has come down from heaven" (v. 41). Jesus then confirms their suspicions when he says in verse 51: "I am the living bread that came down from heaven." This descent is entwined with the Son of Man Christology (obviously influenced by the Logos descent ideas, thus a late development of the Son of Man trajectory in John). Jesus says that the heavenly bread is to be given by the Son of Man (v. 27). By implication, the descending Son of Man and the descending living bread are the same.

Then in verse 60, many of his disciples bristle at what they consider a "hard saying." I have already argued that this hard saying is the one about Jesus as the descending living bread.[37] Jesus then retorts that, by implication, they will find it even harder to accept the idea that Jesus as the Son of Man will ascend where he was before (v. 62). This prepares for the rejection of "many of his disciples" who no longer follow him (v. 66). What are we to make of this startling rejection? Is it a supposed event in the life of Jesus? Or is it not, more likely, a reflection of a split within the community that had already taken place before the Gospel of John was composed?[38] Contemporary interpreters have become alert to the possibility of "palimpsest" readings of the Johannine texts.[39] That is, what is on the surface an event in the life of Jesus is also an event in the life of the community.

Read in this way, the story chronicles a split in the community over the descent/ascent Christology of the Son of Man. And, as I suggested above, this is clearly here the later interpretation of the Son of Man, influenced by the Logos Christology, in which the Son of Man descends and ascends.[40] The dissenters (seen from the standpoint of the Gospel) clearly believe in Jesus—but in what way? The rather obvious conclusion is that they believe in the earlier Christology that had once been the dominant (only?) point of view of Jesus as *Christos*. What they may have thought of a Son of Man Christology, uninfluenced by Logos Christology, cannot be stated.

I propose that the dissenters left the Johannine community and maintained their own, earlier belief in Jesus as *Christos*. I also think it worth considering that these dissenters are represented in the community that lies behind 1 John. This community clearly has the *Christos* Christology as its centerpiece. All Son of Man ideas have been rejected, perhaps because they all seemed too "contaminated" by the Logos influence. And perhaps we have read too literally the claim by the author that "they" went out from the community of 1 John. It is notorious that sectarians always claim the original truth; thus any dissenters from that truth have been the ones who left the truth. Of course, from the perspective of the Gospel of John, the disciples who could not accept the descent/ascent Christology were the ones who left.

Granted that there are no Son of Man sayings in 1 John, are there passages that nevertheless indicate preexistence? Raymond Brown has listed five texts that he thinks indicate that the community of 1 John had no problem with the Logos Christology, despite the fact that it is never mentioned directly. These texts are 1:2; 3:8; 4:9, 16; 5:6, 20.[41] I will discuss these in roughly reverse order.

First John 5:6, 20 both use the language of the Savior figure "coming." "This is he who comes (*elthōn*) through water and blood. . . ." "We know that the Son of God has come" (*ēkei*). As Brown himself acknowledges, the language of God's agent "coming" is at best ambivalent.[42] The question is where the agent comes from. In almost all instances in biblical language the assumption is that he comes from some earthly location. One would have to have specific indication to think otherwise. Brown can only appeal to the Gospel of John, where it is obvious that in the final christological move, Jesus comes from heaven (e.g., 6:51). But if the issue is whether that view is found in 1 John, it is inappropriate to appeal to the Gospel. Thus these two passages in 1 John remain ambiguous; the assumption should be, I think, that they do not imply preexistence, if there is no explicit evidence in either these passages or elsewhere in 1 John to make one think otherwise.

The second two passages Brown appeals to are 4:9, 14. Here the language is that of God sending the Son. Again Brown acknowledges that the sending language (here *apostellō*) in itself is ambiguous and is used of prophets as well as other emissaries.[43] For him, however, the association of "sending" with *kosmos* implies a sending to the world from outside the world—hence descent/preexistence. But it seems more likely in the passages of interest in 1 John, that *kosmos* is more a theological concept than a geographical destination. In 1 John 4:14 the text reads *ho patēr apestalken ton huion sotēra tou kosmou*. The purpose of the sending, not the location, is the theme. That is, the world defines the scope of operation, not the geographical object of the sending. In the same way, the Samaritans confess in John 4:42 that Jesus is the Savior of the world, without any knowledge of his preexistence.[44] The passage in 4:49, also using the perfect tense, says that God has sent his Son *eis ton kosmon* for the purpose of salvation. Again, *kosmos* is the (potential) place of salvation. I do not think this passage implies preexistence.

When introducing his list, Brown says: "It is not surprising to find him [the author of 1 John] too speaking in the uniquely Johannine language of preexistence."[45] He then appeals to the use of *phaneroō*. But it is interesting to see how few occurrences of the verb in the Gospel of John could be taken to refer to preexistence. The verb appears nine times in the Gospel.[46] Most of these clearly have nothing to do with preexistence, referring to Jesus' supernatural revelation in historical reality (e.g., 2:11 and 7:4). Some do not even have a relation to Jesus in any form (3:21; 9:3). There is certainly no question that the author of the Gospel of John pushes a notion of preexistence; the question is whether he uses the verb *phaneroō* to do it, and I think the answer is clearly no. One may take two occurrences as test cases. In 17:6, Jesus speaks to God: "I have manifested [*ephanerōsa*] your name to those who you gave me out of the world." In Johannine Christology, obviously the reason Jesus can manifest the name of God is that he is the Logos. The verb in this passage, however, refers specifically to Jesus' historical work in calling the church into existence. In 1:31, John the Baptist confesses that he came baptizing, so that Jesus might be manifest (*phanerōthē*) to Israel. Clearly the manifestation has something to do with the historical act of John baptizing.[47]

Phaneroō is also a popular word in 1 John, occurring eight times, in a much shorter document than the Gospel.[48] Again, as in the Gospel, the majority of these instances clearly have nothing to do with preexistence (e.g., 2:19, 28; 3:2). Brown appeals to two locations, 1:2 and 3:8. The first instance occurs in the "prologue" or preface to the document, and here the verb appears twice, both in the aorist passive, "was manifest" (*ephanerōthē*). The preface contains grammatical and syntactical problems, but the first two verses can be translated:

> That which was from the beginning, which we have heard, which we have seen with our eyes, which we have looked upon and touched with our hands, concerning the word of life—the life was made manifest, and we saw it, and testify to it, and proclaim to you the eternal life which was with the Father and was made manifest to us. . . . (RSV)

Most commentators seem to read this prologue out of the ideas of the prologue in the Gospel of John. There are, however, significant differences. In the Gospel the prologue is clearly about the transcendent reality and its impingement upon the earthly. It is cosmic in its perspective. The words of 1 John, however, suggest a beginning point in some beginning which "we" have experienced (seen, touched, heard). Who the "we" are, of course, is one of the issues. It certainly refers to historical persons who are doing the witnessing. Painter names them the "foundational witnesses" who have communicated the "foundational message."[49] Brown, after carefully assessing the possibilities, concludes that "'what was from the beginning' means the person, words, and deeds of Jesus as this complexus reflects his self-revelation . . . to his disciples after his baptism."[50] Thus, while the prologue to the Gospel is cosmic, that of 1 John is "historical," in the sense that the beginning point is not the transcendent realm with the preexistent Logos, but the earth with the salvific work of Jesus.[51] If this is the case, the Gospel cannot be allowed to be the principle of interpretation of 1 John, as so often happens.[52] What is then manifest is the salvific revelation of a historical phenomenon, which, from the author's perspective, is certainly revelatory of God and of God's salvific intent. Thus "the life" and "eternal life" was made manifest to believers. The manifestation carries no necessary connotation as a manifestation of the preexistent.

The other occurrence of *phaneroō* to which Brown appeals is 3:8b. "For this purpose the Son of God appeared (was manifest) to destroy the works of the devil." Again there is no convincing reason (other than reading 1 John out of the Gospel) to take *phaneroō* to necessitate a manifestation from some preexistent state. The word here can most simply be translated "appeared." We should ask, however, what the author means by destroying (or "loosing" believers from) the works of the devil. It seems clear that "the works" of the devil in this context refers to people who sin. To loose them from the devil is to release them from sin. How does the author think Jesus did that? He does not say. The emphasis in the document upon the death of Jesus as an expiation for sin (e.g., 2:2) would be the most likely avenue. If so, 3:8b refers, indirectly, to the salvatory death of Jesus in his historical existence. It seems to me that there is no need to read pre-existence out of a salvatory death, any more than one reads it into passages such as Matthew 26:28 or Romans 3:24-25.

Brown's appeal to these passages do not convince that 1 John asserts the preexistence of Jesus, if one reads the document independently of the Gospel, as I think one must. Thus the Christology of 1 John does not refer to preexistence, the Logos, descent/ascent, or Son of Man beliefs. Its single focus is on Jesus as the *Christos*, who is God's Son. If this is the case, then the Christology of 1 John represents an early stage in the beliefs of the Johannine community, a stage prior to the development of "high" Christology as represented by the Gospel itself.

Two further features of 1 John call for mention. The first is the heavy emphasis upon sin. As all commentators note, the ideas expressed by the author seem confused. On the one hand, the presence of sin in believers is assumed, as in 1:8-10 and 5:16-17. On the other hand, believers do not have the burden of sin, as in 3:6, 9. It is not my intent here to try to resolve the apparent contradictions but simply to mention that sin is an issue here that does not surface in the Gospel of John.

The second feature is related to the above, and that is the role of Jesus as expiation for sin (2:1-2; 2:12; 3:5, 16; 4:10). This is again hardly the focus of the Gospel, where apart from the Baptist's statement in 1:29 the death of Jesus serves as the revelation of the reality of God (chap. 12), not the eradication of sin and guilt. The question again is whether the different emphasis represents a later development of the Johannine community in 1 John or whether it reflects an earlier Christology of the community before the Logos Christology took over. While no sure tests exist to prove one or the other, it is certainly possible that both the emphasis on sin and expiation are the earlier of the two views. Is it accidental that both the Baptist's and Samaritan language is reflected in 1 John, while that of the Johannine dominant emphasis upon the Logos Christology is not?

I suggest that the indications coincide to strengthen the judgment that 1 John represents an earlier view of the Johannine community. It is pointed to in by the statement in John 6:66 that there was a split in the community, before the Gospel was composed, between some, at least, of those who held earlier views of Jesus as the *Christos* who atoned for sin and those who believed in the Logos Christology.

This, if correct, would not say anything decisive about the dating of 1 John. The split would have taken place at the latest stage of christological development, thus perhaps not long before the Gospel was published. First John could have been written after the Gospel, perhaps in response to it. Ultimately the issue of the date is of little significance for my purpose. The conclusion I would draw, however, is that 1 John cannot be used as evidence that there was a trajectory of Johannine Logos Christology. The Gospel stands unique, even though developments are visible in the Gospel itself. What happened to either community is lost to us. Certainly, later gnostic appropriations of Johannine Christology buy in on the Gospel and not 1 John.

Notes

Notes to the Foreword

1. See the comments in a tribute to Robin Scroggs by his long-time colleague at Chicago Theological Seminary, Graydon Snyder, in *Putting Body and Soul Together: Essays in Honor of Robin Scroggs,* ed. Virginia Wiles, Alexandra Brown, and Graydon Snyder (Valley Forge: Trinity Press International, 1997), xix.

Notes to Introduction

1. This attempt was directly due to the Enlightenment, which emphasized the priority of science and historical fact as the key criteria for "truth."

2. The famous names here are Hermann Samuel Reimarus, David Friedrich Strauss, Joseph Ernest Renan, and Adolf Harnack.

3. "In his *Vorlesungen über die neutestamentliche Theologie* Ferdinand Christian Baur goes directly from his presentation of the teachings of Jesus, which are 'not theology at all but religion' (1864), to Paul as the first Christian theologian and to Paul's 'doctrinal conception.'" So W. Schmithals, *The Theology of the First Christians* (Louisville: Westminster John Knox 1997), 81.

4. Harnack's theme, emphasized in his famous lectures, *Das Wesen des Christentums,* delivered at the University of Berlin in 1889–90; English trans.: *What Is Christianity?* (New York: Harper, 1901).

5. W. Bousset, *Kyrios Christos* (Nashville: Abingdon, 1970).

6. Harnack, *What Is Christianity?* 4.

7. *Theology of the New Testament* (New York: Scribner's, 1954), 1:3. The German was published in 1948.

8. Albert Schweitzer, *The Quest of the Historical Jesus: A Critical Study of Its Progress from Reimarus to Wrede* (New York, 1956). Schweitzer's German original, *Von Reimarus zu Wrede,* was published in 1906.

9. In today's scholarship there are two diametrically opposing trends that influence any recovery of the factual Jesus. On the one hand, we have had decades of research into the theological bases of each of the canonical Gospels. In this case who Jesus actually was, what he taught, and what was his self-understanding recede (and in most cases disappear) behind the faith of the believing writers as they draw a portrait of Jesus who is Lord of the

church. In this case, the Gospels must be interpreted in the same way as Paul, who also portrays the Lord of the church, albeit in a different genre.

At the other extreme are the many scholars of the same recent decades who have struggled to recapture the earliest records about Jesus in Q and elsewhere. Perhaps the best known is John Dominic Crossan, e.g., *The Historical Jesus* (San Francisco: Harper SanFrancisco, 1991). Some of these scholars are quite ready and confident to say who Jesus actually was (in this case leaning on what they consider to be the first "edition" of Q). Cf., e.g., Burton Mack, *The Lost Gospel: The Book of Q and Christian Origins* (San Francisco: HarperSanFrancisco, 1993). The Jesus who emerges is a Hellenistic wisdom teacher, who says little directly about theological truths and who certainly does not belong within the Jewish religious circles we know anything about. He need not even have been Jewish. At any rate, this Jesus is of even less worth to Christian theology than was Albert Schweitzer's apocalyptic madman. Even if this was the true, factual Jesus, he is not the same Jesus as proclaimed in Christian theology. If the dogma of the Enlightenment still holds ("Only the historical saves"), then perhaps Christianity is indeed called into question. Fortunately, the historic Christian church has, apart from the two most recent centuries, not been enslaved to Enlightenment dogma.

10. Cf. the interesting comments of W. Schmithals in *The Theology of the First Christians* (Louisville: Westminster John Knox, 1997), chaps. 1 and 2.

11. According to Graydon F. Snyder, *Ante Pacem: Archaeological Evidence of Church Life before Constantine* (Macon, Ga.: Mercer University Press, 1985), the earliest archaeological remains that can be demonstrated to be Christian occur not before c. 180, a date beyond the purviews of most early Christian theologies.

12. Antoinette Wire argued in an interesting way for a women's movement in the Corinthian church, which runs theologically counter to Paul's understanding (*The Corinthian Women Prophets* [Minneapolis: Fortress Press, 1990]). I think Wire is most convincing when the women are seen as leaders in the community rather than a "popular" strand that included most or all of the female members in the community.

13. I use the term "Christian" with some desperation. It is generally agreed that the term is a late-first-century coinage. At the time of which I am speaking there was no such thing as "Christianity"—believers in Jesus were mostly Jews who perhaps stood somewhat apart from the other Jewish communities because of their claims about Jesus.

14. Confidence in Gospel form criticism began to erode in the late 1950s, when scholars began to sense that the final authors of the Gospel played a larger role in composition than had previously been thought. Form criticism led to redaction criticism, which led to composition criticism. In the last-named perspective some scholars denied any claim that material in the Gospels was prior to the authorial composition, at least that any earlier strand was recoverable. Jesus, as well as the early communities, disappeared. In my judgment this is too sweeping a view, and I still think one can speak of the historical Jesus and communities who believed in him. The matter is, alas, very complicated.

15. As the early work of Gerd Theissen suggested, e.g., *Sociology of Early Palestinian Christianity* (Philadelphia: Fortress Press, 1978). One could also consult my early publications, collected in *The Text and the Times* (Minneapolis: Fortress Press, 1993), 20–45, 46–68.

16. For a summary cf. R. H. Fuller, *The Foundations of Christian Theology* (New York: Scriber, 1965). For a more up-to-date and detailed treatment, cf. J. Habermann, *Präexistenzaussagen im Neuen Testament* (Frankfurt: Peter Lang, 1990).

17. Theodore W. Jennings Jr., *Beyond Theism: a Grammar of God-Language* (Oxford: Oxford University Press, 1985).

18. Hovering about this whole discussion is the enterprise of sociology of knowledge, a popular tool in today's biblical guild but one that I have avoided here for the sake of brevity. This perspective believes that a society's ideational creations are products of the social matrix. The going phrase is that systems of thought are "social constructions of reality." The "Bible" of this perspective in the biblical guild is by Peter Berger and Thomas Luckmann, *The Social Construction of Reality* (Garden City, N.Y.: Doubleday, 1966). If thought is a social construction, it does not necessarily have the referent it claims to have. Religion, for example, claims to speak about God but it "really" is a vehicle for legitimizing the societal (political) status quo. In Berger's words, religion is a "sacred canopy." Cf. *The Sacred Canopy* (Garden City, N.Y.: Doubleday, 1969). This sounds easy, and one thinks it can be demonstrated (as indeed it can in many instances). Questions have been raised, however, about how such a correlation can in general be proved. By the very nature of the magnitude of the data to be controlled, any sure correlation can hardly be convincing.

19. For this purpose I have, gratefully, borrowed a term from the classic and insightful book by James M. Robinson and Helmut Koester, *Trajectories through Early Christianity* (Philadelphia: Fortress Press, 1971).

20. I have tried my hand at distilling such profundity in two of my books: *Paul for a New Day* (Philadelphia: Fortress Press, 1977), and *Christology in Paul and John: The Reality and Revelation of God* (Philadelphia: Fortress Press, 1988).

Notes to Chapter 1

1. Pliny, *Epp. ad Trajan* 10.96.7, trans. H. Bettenson, *Documents of the Christian Church* (London: Oxford University Press, 1963), 4.

2. Paul does mention the place of hymns (*psalmoi*) in worship but does not specify the subject matter (1 Cor 14:26).

3. I need to concede the obvious. The term "Cosmocrator" is never used in the New Testament to refer to the resurrected Jesus. Although an honored term in Greek culture to refer to presumed world rulers, both divine and human, the word occurs only once in the New Testament, and that in reference to the divine enemies of the Christian faith, i.e., the evil world rulers (Eph 6:12). The term was probably avoided by early believers because of negative associations with competing cults. The word is so apt, however, for what the early believers thought about the resurrected Jesus that I dare to use it as a key word in my structure.

4. Obviously there is dispute about details in all of the materials. Whether there is preexistence implied or stated (e.g., Phil 2:6-11) is important for the meaning of the materials but does not diminish the importance of the theme of enthronement. What counts as additions by an author are debated points. The debated lines in general, however, clarify rather

than obscure the theme of enthronement and, as added interpretations, specify the direction an author wishes to take the theme. They do not call the theme itself into question.

5. Cf. the discussion by J. Habermann, *Präexistenzaussagen im Neuen Testament* (Frankfurt: Peter Lang, 1990), 99–110, 135–38.

6. Here I can agree with Leander Keck that titles often obstruct attempts to find meaning, rather than help (cf. Keck, "Toward the Renewal of New Testament Christology," *NTS* 32 [1986]: 368–70).

7. My translation, as are the next several New Testament quotations.

8. Cf. R. H. Fuller, *The Foundations of New Testament Christology* (New York: Scribner's, 1965), 165–66, 187–88.

9. Again a convenient summary of the discussion is found in Habermann, *Präexistenzaussagen*, 230–39).

10. R. Bultmann, "Bekenntnis- und Liedfragmente im ersten Petrusbrief," *ConNT* 11 (1947): 1–14.

11. Evidence is divided between the readings *epathen* and *apethanen*. The former fits better the letter's content; the latter, the more usual formulaic tendency. The meaning is essentially the same, since the suffering of Jesus included his death.

12. The phrase is *peri hamartiōn*. While the phrase can refer to a sin offering in the LXX, the following phrase, which expresses the intent of the suffering, does not especially lead in that direction. The suffering/death enables the resurrected Jesus to present believers to God, presumably in a favorable light such that God will accept them (cf. Rom 5:2). The meaning is close to the idea of the resurrected Jesus interceding to God on behalf of believers (cf. Hebrews and Rom 8:34). At any rate, it is an activity of the resurrected, not the dying Jesus.

13. These materials are surely sufficient for the structural pattern to be clearly seen. Other materials could be added but they contain nothing new. The clear liturgical formula in 1 Tim 3:16 points to exaltation of the resurrected Christ but does not explicitly mention enthronement. A pre-authorial statement is sometimes seen in Heb 1:2-4 (or parts thereof). Climactic here is the enthronement (sitting at the right hand, bestowal of the most excellent name). I believe it also likely that in Hebrews 1–2 is contained a catena of Old Testament citations that were originally used to support the faith of resurrection/enthronement. This catena, in so far as the author of Hebrews shows it to us, climaxed with the reference to the subjection of *ta panta* to the exalted Christ (Ps 8:7 LXX). Thus Christ as Cosmocrator was the motif of this catena. As I argue below, however, the author of Hebrews has eliminated the political thrust of the Cosmocrator Christology. For the author, the Cosmocrator becomes the High Priest.

One could also appeal to the final story in Matt 28:16-20. Here, in words reminiscent of Dan 7:14, the resurrected Christ claims to be the possessor of complete authority over the cosmos. This pericope, however, almost surely belongs to the Son of Man trajectory; cf. below.

14. The appropriate analogy, I think, is the election (e.g., in the United States) of a president whose avowed policies fit closely with one's own (say in distinction to the previous officeholder) and one can thus rejoice that the future may hold positive and meaningful events. One hardly expects perfection.

15. Despite talk about "pagan eschatology," e.g., Dieter Georgi, *Theocracy in Paul's Praxis and Theology* (Minneapolis: Fortress Press, 1991), 7, I do not think evidence for such an orientation is at all strong. My own judgment is that the Jewish notion of a future perfection of the world under the rulership of Yahweh (perhaps meaning the end of the corporeal order) would be completely strange to Gentiles. This would be reason enough to explain its absence in the liturgical materials. One might cite 1 Cor 4:8-13 as an example of a "realized" eschatology among Gentiles. But here the stated contrast is between the satiated existence of the Corinthians and the constrained and humiliating life of the "we" (apostle or apostles). The metaphor of kingship is parallel to those of wealth and food. Nothing requires that Jewish notions of eschatology be in the background.

16. Habermann argues forcefully that faith in the preexistence and thus the agency by the preexistent in creation itself stems from a prior faith in the exaltation/enthronement (*Präexistenzaussagen*, 421–22). Agency of creation thus secures the belief in the restoration of the cosmos to its rightful owner, its creator.

17. There is no space to pursue here the intriguing ideas of some sociologists of knowledge. The general premise is that expressed ideas are inseparably related to social experiences of a community. The question then becomes, Which is prior, the social experience or the expressed ideas? This issue runs head-on into the question whether experience or language is prior. That is, does the liturgy of enthronement *produce* the sense of liberation, or is it the other way around? Does a social experience of liberation in the early Christian communities lead to the Cosmocrator Christology? Or is it a mutually fructifying dialogue, so that questions of origin become chicken and egg? For an overview, cf. Peter L. Berger and Thomas Luckmann, *The Social Construction of Reality* (Garden City, N.Y.: Doubleday Anchor, 1966); Peter L. Berger, *The Sacred Canopy* (Garden City, N.Y.: Doubleday, 1967).

18. Such is the famous, and I think correct, view of Ernst Käsemann with regard to the hymn in Phil 2:6-11. Cf. E. Käsemann, "Kritische Analyse von Phil. 2,5-11," in *Exegetische Versuche und Besinnungen* (Göttingen: Vandenhoeck & Ruprecht, 1960), 1:51–95, esp. 73–74. The same understanding fits the materials in Colossians and 1 Peter.

19. We have, perhaps, been too influenced in our reading by someone like a Paul, who clearly does not accept such a replacement. He may have added, as correction, "To the glory of God the Father" to the hymn in Philippians. And his eschatological vision in 1 Corinthians 15, while affirming Christ as Cosmocrator, nevertheless ends with Yahweh alone on center stage (vv. 27-28). We should not interpret the materials from a Pauline perspective.

20. So L. Rost, "Zur Deutung des Menschensohnes in Daniel 7," in *Studien zum Alten Testament* (Stuttgart: Kohlhammer, 1974), 74.

21. C. Colpe, *TDNT*, 8:419. While it is disputed whether this is appointment or usurpation, many scholars agree that there is a transfer of power and authority. Cf. J. A. Emerton, "The Origin of the Son of Man Imagery," *JTS* 9 (1958): 225–42; J. Day, *God's Conflict with the Dragon and the Sea: Echoes of a Canaanite Myth in the Old Testament* (Cambridge: Cambridge University Press, 1985), 164–65; J. Collins, *The Apocalyptic Vision of the Book of Daniel* (Chico, Calif.: Scholars, 1977), 101; A. Lacocque, *The Book of Daniel* (Richmond: John Knox, 1979), 132–33; idem, *Daniel in His Time* (Columbia: University of South Carolina Press, 1988), 147, 152.

22. Cf. Emerton, "Origin," 229; Day, *Conflict*, 161–65; Colpe, *TDNT* 8:415–19; Collins, *Vision*, 96–101; Lacocque, *Book of Daniel*, 129.

23. Cf. J. Day, *Conflict*, 164–77; Lacocque, *Book of Daniel*, 133; idem, *Daniel in His Time*, 71.

24. Although many scholars take that structure back originally to the myths of El and Baal, there must have been an intermediary stage between Ugarit and Daniel, which is now inaccessible to us.

25. Cf. Emerton, *JTS* 9 (1958): 233; Lacocque, *Daniel in His Time*, 152.

26. Cf. Douglas R. A. Hare, who attempts to deny titular status to any of the New Testament usages; Hare, *The Son of Man Tradition* (Minneapolis: Fortress Press, 1990).

27. Emerton, *JTS* 9 (1958): 238.

28. Cf. Emerton, *JTS* 9 (1958): 229–39; Collins, *Vision*, 96–101; Day, *Conflict*, 161–65; Lacocque, *Book of Daniel*, 129, 135; M. Pope, *El in the Ugaritic Texts* (Leiden: Brill, 1955), 27–29.

29. So T. Mann, *Divine Presence and Guidance in Israelite Traditions: The Typology of Exaltation* (Baltimore: Johns Hopkins University Press, 1977), 50; M. Pope, *El in the Ugaritic Texts*, 27–30; A. S. Kapelrud, *Baal in the Ras Shamra Texts* (Copenhagen: G. E. C. Gad, 1952), 86–93; J. Gray expresses the matter more cautiously, *The Legacy of Canaan* (Leiden: Brill, 1965), 159–67.

30. Cf. J. J. M. Roberts, "The Davidic Origin of the Zion Tradition," *JBL* (1973): 329–44. Idem, "The Religio-political Setting of Psalm 47," *BASOR* 221 (1976): 129–32. He is supported by O. Eissfeldt, "Jahwes Königsprädizierung als Verklärung national-politischer Ansprüche Israels," in *Kleine Schriften* 5 (Tübingen: Mohr-Siebeck, 1973); Emerton, "Origin of Son of Man Imagery," 240–42, and Mann, *Divine Presence*, 224.

31. The term is from W. Hallo and J. van Dijk, *The Exaltation of Inanna* (New Haven: Yale University Press, 1968), 68.

32. Roberts, "Religio-political Setting," 132.

33. Mann, *Divine Presence*, 49.

34. Hallo and van Dijk, *Exaltation*, 9. Their argument is supported by Mann, *Divine Presence*, 30–33.

35. Hallo and van Dijk, *Exaltation*, 65.

36. Ibid., 68. Were space permitting, a number of other examples of replacement themes could be discussed. *Greek*: The replacement of Kronos and the Titans by Zeus, according to an older view, represented a change of religious systems due to successive movements of different people into Greek territories. While there may be something important to hear in that theory, much depends upon the myths narrated by Hesiod.

Hatti: Since 1935, in an article by E. O. Forrer, Hesiod is seen as dependent upon myths from Hatti, so that the replacement motif in Hesiod is merely a literary creation and not related to any social setting ("Eine Geschichte der Götterkönigtums aus dem Hatti-Reiche," in *Melanges Franz Cumont* [Brussels: Secretariat de l'Institut de philologie et d'histoire orientales et slaves, 1936] 2:687–713. For our purposes a loss is also gain, for Forrer believes that the replacement theme in the Hatti myths do reflect successive movements of people. "In the ancient Orient, world history as the struggle of people for dominance in the Near East becomes the history of the fight of the Gods for dominance in the sphere of heaven and earth" (p. 689). Forrer's views are accepted by F. Dornseiff, "Altorientalisches zu Hesiods Theogonie," in his *Antike und alter Orient* (Leipzig: Kobler & Amelang, 1956), 55–56.

Germanic: Especially interesting, but unfortunately highly speculative, is the view that in ancient Teutonic cults, different gods were espoused by different classes of people. Here the primary statement is by O. Höfler, "Der Sakralcharakter des germanischen Königtums," in *La Regalit, Sacra* (Leiden: Brill, 1959), 665–701. Höfler argues that the propertied and established class focused on the god Tiwaz, while the unpropertied, unmarried and young warriors honored Wotan. In war situations the cult of Wotan might gain ascendance over the otherwise dominant Tiwaz, since the warriors became in that situation the dominant group. The sociologist Werner Stark portrays this situation as a struggle between an establishment and an outcast group, thus providing a socioeconomic setting *within* a people (*Sociology of Religion*, vol. 2: *Sectarian Religion* [New York: Fordham University Press, 1967], 42–43).

37. It needs to be emphasized that hope alters experience. It seems obvious that "hopelessness" is an experience of despair. The change from despair to hope is indicative of a decisive change of experience.

Notes to Chapter 2

1. I despair about finding an adequate term to describe the believing communities embedded in Jewish culture in the areas we label Judea and Galilee. We have become comfortable with the phrase "Hellenistic Christianity" to describe communities outside of these areas. Obviously, this is such a general term that it is almost meaningless, although as a useful term scholars (including myself in this book) continue to use it. The term most frequently used to describe the other reality is "Palestinian churches." And this term is used to contrast "Hellenistic." But this is a geographical term as a correlate to a cultural term. Furthermore, "Palestinian" often is broadened to include areas in the Roman province of Syria outside of Judea and Galilee. (What does "Palestinian" include anyway?) I have adopted the term "Aramaic" as a cultural correlate to "Hellenistic," but this is itself admittedly awkward. At least it correlates better with "Hellenistic," although in each instance one should not take the linguistic indications literally. Who knows what other languages people spoke? What we need is a term to speak of a Jewish *culture* as widely diverse as that of Jewish peasantry in Judea and Galilee and the Pharisees, priests, and others who claimed authority and wisdom. And such a term would have to be able to differentiate between this Jewish culture and the possibly different Jewish culture in the Diaspora. For the moment, "Aramaic" seems as good as I can do.

2. Cf. Arthur Drews, *The Christ Myth* (London: Unwin, 1910), and Burton Mack, *A Myth of Innocence: Mark and Christian Origins* (Philadelphia: Fortress Press, 1988).

3. The use of the term "title" is obviously a divisive issue in scholarship. See below.

4. "Son of Man" occurs 80 times in the Gospels: Matthew 31; Mark 14; Luke 24; John 11. *Christos* occurs 53 times: Matthew 15; Mark 7; Luke 12; John 19. In the Synop-

tic Gospels, Son of Man is used twice as frequently as *Christos*. In John it is the reverse; as I show below, the *Christos* title plays a highly specific role in that Gospel.

5. It has been said that the only sure place where this can be demonstrated is Rom 9:5. So W. Kramer, *Christ, Lord, Son of God* (Naperville, Ill.: Allenson, 1966), 210.

6. Should one capitalize either or both of the nouns? It will be my custom to capitalize both "Son" and "Man" as a title, except when I clearly indicate that it simply refers to a human form or being.

7. For a helpful summary of perspectives, see the article "Son of Man," by G. Nickelsburg in the *Anchor Bible Dictionary* (New York: Doubleday, 1992), 6:137–50.

8. See ibid.

9. Cf., e.g., chaps. 46; 47; 48; 51; 62. In a remarkable conclusion to the section, Enoch *becomes* the Son of Man. There has been debate about the possible dating of the "Parables" of *1 Enoch*. Based on the fact that there are no extant fragments from this section at Qumran, among many fragments of other sections, J. T. Milik concluded that the Parables were late and post–first century; cf. Milik, "Problèmes de literature Hènochique à la lumière des fragments araméens de Qumran," *HTR* 64 (1971): 33, 78. If they were this late, they could hardly be used for purposes of comparison with New Testament texts. Milik's conclusion, however, is rejected by several scholars, e.g., E. Isaac, in his translation of *1 Enoch* in *The Old Testament Pseudepigrapha*, ed. J. Charlesworth (Garden City, N.Y.: Doubleday), 1:7, and G. Nickelsburg, *1 Enoch* (Minneapolis: Fortress Press, 2001), 7.

10. One could reflect on Matt 8:30 and the Q sayings in Luke 7:33-34. It can be argued that the term is used here as simply an oblique reference to the earthly Jesus.

11. E.g., Matthew changes the "Son of Man" in Mark 8:31 to a personal pronoun in Matt 16:21.

12. R. Bultmann, *Theology of the New Testament* (New York: Scribner's, 1951), 1:30.

13. Because the priority of Mark is predominant in scholarly circles, Q continues to be a useful hypothesis. It depends not only on the priority of Mark but also on the independence of Matthew and Luke. If one rejects these two judgments, however, then Q disappears. Arguments about the priority of Mark continue. Moreover, many composition critics doubt that traditions prior to the final composition of the texts can be detected. Other scholars, however, have confidently isolated various strands of Q, finding at least three successive versions. Caution is called for.

14. There is a possible covert allusion to Jesus' death when Q asserts that persecution and death are the typical (inevitable?) fate of the prophet (e.g., Luke 11:47, 49; 13:34). But (a) Jesus is nowhere called a prophet in Q (although he was seen as such in other quarters) and (b) John the Baptist is acclaimed as more than a prophet (Luke 7:26). Would Q accord John more status than Jesus?

15. The quotations of Q are from the NRSV.

16. To be sure, it is possible that it is the *preaching* of the earthly Jesus that is compared with that of Jonah. I think it unlikely, however, that the "sign" is that of the eschatological appearance of the Son of Man. Matthew's version, however, clearly is molded to refer to the death of Jesus and must therefore be secondary.

17. So J. Fitzmyer, *The Gospel according to Luke I–IX* (Garden City, N.Y.: Doubleday, 1981), 635.

18. G. Nickelsburg, *1 Enoch* (Minneapolis: Fortress Press, 2001), 63–64.

19. Ibid., 63.

20. Ibid., 64.

21. There are two kinds of objects removed. The second are "evildoers." The first translates a plural neuter noun, *skandala*. In the New Testament the verb is frequently used to indicate someone causing another to fall away from faith (e.g., Matt 5:29-30; 18:5). This would fit the context, even if wrenching the neuter into the masculine plural does violence to the grammar.

22. Trans. E. Isaac, in *The Old Testament Pseudepigrapha*, 1:44.

23. The meaning of this sentence is uncertain but does not concern me here.

24. Just what *pistis* means as the object of the Son of Man's coming is not clear. It does not fit any vocabulary I have looked at that mentions the Son of Man. Perhaps "trust" or even "trust in the Son of Man" conveys the intention. In any case, it cannot be taken in a Pauline sense.

25. A partial parallel in Luke 22:28-30 raises the possibility of a Q saying. The first part of the material, however, has few similarities, and it seems best to consider them separate logia, with, in part, similar content. The main thing they have in common is the disciples judging the twelve tribes: "That you may eat and drink at my table in my kingdom, and sit on thrones judging the twelve tribes of Israel" (Luke 22:30).

26. In Matthew Jesus twice identifies John with Elijah, once (11:14) in a passage seemingly Q, although Luke does not make the identification, and once in 17:9-12, following Matt 9:9-13, a passage that Luke omits. Yet in the poem about John in Luke 1:14-17, John is expressly identified with Elijah. How early are these traditions?

27. But an early tradition explains Jesus' power by saying that John has been raised "in" Jesus (Mark 6:14-16).

28. My present position—which is somewhat different from that of a few decades ago—makes the most sense if Jesus did, in fact, proclaim the coming Son of Man. Whether Jesus learned this perspective in his days as an apprentice in the Baptist circle is an enticing possibility, but one I do not think can be demonstrated.

29. As I will show, however, the *Christos* as miracle worker is a strong motif in the Gospels.

30. It is granted that there could be sublimations of the military enterprise. In *Psalms of Solomon* 17, the king Messiah is to rule over the nations but is to act benignly with his people, Israel. In *4 Ezra* 13, God's son continues to have traits of military conquest, even though he is peaceful at times.

31. Cf. my essay "The Earliest Christian Communities as Sectarian Movement," in *The Text and the Times* (Minneapolis: Fortress Press, 1993), 20–45.

32. Cf. also Luke 24:7, 20, 26, 46 for other formulations of the death/resurrection formulas. Variations occur here, with the exception of "on the third day," which is always chosen over "after three days."

33. The stories of appearances to the disciples in the Gospels are late and cannot reflect accounts as early as 1 Corinthians.

34. In the excursus at the end of this chapter I argue that Mark 8:27-29 was not originally a resurrection narrative.

35. It is true that in Luke 24:6-7 the two men call the resurrected Jesus the Son of Man, but that is clearly a spinoff from the Markan passion predictions.

36. E.g., J. Fitzmyer, *The Acts of the Apostles* (New York: Doubleday, 1998), 390.

37. The Greek here is *ton Christon Iēsoun*; the consensus is to insert a comma after *Christon*.

38. "The Earliest Hellenistic Christianity," in *Religions in Antiquity: Essays in Memory of Erwin Ramsdell Goodenough*, ed. J. Neusner (Leiden: Brill, 1968), 176–206.

39. Even relative dating is difficult. One could suggest that the tradition would have to be later than the list in 1 Cor 15, both since Paul does not mention Stephen and also because the assumption is that stories are later than lists. It is surprising that the appearance to Stephen is not in the list in 1 Cor 15, since the list seems to stem from Jerusalem. But there are several reasons why the appearance is not on the list. (1) Paul does not explicitly say that the list is inclusive. (2) The creation of a tradition about an appearance to Stephen may have developed in the Stephanic group after it fled from Jerusalem and so might not have even been known to the Jerusalem church. (3) Since the list seems to have a political function, even if the Jerusalem church knew of a tradition of an appearance to Stephen, it might not have been considered politically important, since Stephen's group, having to flee, was out of the political loop in Jerusalem.

40. For example, Raymond Brown, *The Gospel according to John* (Garden City, N.Y.: Doubleday, 1966), 1:xlvii; C. H. Dodd, *Historical Tradition in the Fourth Gospel* (Cambridge: Cambridge University Press, 1963), 423–24; Barnabas Lindars, *The Gospel of John* (London: Oliphants, 1972), 26–27; Robert Kysar, *John* (Minneapolis: Augsburg, 1986), 2; and Craig S. Keener, *The Gospel of John* (Peabody, Mass.: Hendrickson, 2003), 40–42. Keener has an excellent bibliography on this issue.

41. I have not discussed the two other occurrences in the New Testament of a Son of Man Christology identified with Jesus—Heb 2:5-9 and Rev 1:12-20. The passage in Revelation, I think, is clearly late in comparison with the texts I am discussing above. The passage in Hebrews is more problematic. I consider the reference to Psalm 8 to be the end of a pre-authorial catena, which is the backbone of 1:5—2:9, which includes authorial comments because the author uses the catena for purposes not germane to the catena itself. The catena itself celebrates the exaltation of the risen Jesus and is part of the Cosmocrator tradition. Since the dating of Hebrews is uncertain, and since the passage belongs to the Cosmocrator tradition, it seems wise to table discussion of this passage. It is interesting as the only Cosmocrator tradition to refer to Son of Man.

42. E.g., Werner Kelber, *The Kingdom in Mark* (Philadelphia: Fortress Press, 1974), 67–71; J. Donahue and D. Harrington, *The Gospel of Mark* (Collegeville, Minn.: Liturgical, 2002), 264–66.

43. Nowhere else does Mark duplicate an ailment that Jesus cures.

44. Rudolf Bultmann, *The History of the Synoptic Tradition* (Oxford: Blackwell, 1963), 257–65; see also his *Theology of the New Testament* (New York: Scribner's, 1954), 1:26.

45. See the list in J. Meier, *The Vision of Matthew* (New York: Paulist, 1979), 107, n. 104.

46. Most scholars now do not even discuss the possibility that the passage is a post-resurrection appearance story, although they also tend to give a positive evaluation of the

story (e.g., it is for Mark positive that Jesus is seen to be *Christos*). Cf. R. Gundry, *Mark* (Grand Rapids: Eerdmans, 1993); L. Williamson Jr., *Mark* (Atlanta: John Knox, 1983); R. T. France, *The Gospel of Mark* (Grand Rapids: Eerdmans, 2002); J. Donahue and D. Harrington, *Mark*; E. Laverdiere, *The Beginnings of the Gospel* (Collegeville, Minn.: Liturgical, 1999).

47. The Gospels say nothing about the Baptist's miracles, but then the Gospels suppress much material about John.

48. Bultmann explicitly says this about 8:27; cf. *Synoptic Tradition*, 257.

49. D. Harrington, *The Gospel of Matthew* (Collegeville, Minn.: Liturgical, 1997), 250, says that it is still a live option, but he does not build it into his exegesis.

50. Ulrich Luz, *Matthew 8–20* (Minneapolis: Fortress Press, 2001), 356 (v. 17 is Matthean; vv. 18-19 partly pre-Matthean and partly compositional); W. D. Davies and Dale Allison, *The Gospel according to Saint Matthew* (Edinburgh: T&T Clark, 1991), 2:604–15. Davies and Allison even entertain the possibility that it is a historical memory about Jesus.

Notes to Chapter 3

1. This is disputed by M. de Jonge, "Christ," *Anchor Bible Dictionary* (New York: Doubleday, 1992), 1:914–21.

2. The reading varies in the manuscripts. A majority, including most of the early witnesses, read some form of "Jesus Christ, Son of God." A few omit "Son of God," and there are other minor variations. I accept the longer reading but note that "Son" is anarthrous, just as the last occurrence of "Son of God" in the Gospel—the centurion's acclamation (Mark 15:39). Is the lack of an article at 1:1 significant? The title is an acclamation, but is notable for not including *kyrios* as part of it. In fact, I do not think *kyrios* appears anywhere in the Gospel as a title for the exalted Jesus.

3. This will be true whether the confession was originally a post-resurrection appearance story or whether it originally was located in the earthly ministry.

4. Cf. the persuasive arguments of John Donahue, *Are You the Christ? The Trial Narrative in the Gospel of Mark* (Missoula, Mont.: Society of Biblical Literature, 1973).

5. In 8:27-29 Peter confesses Jesus to be *Christos*. In v. 30 Jesus commands silence and in the next verse teaches about the Son of Man. Peter's following argument with Jesus is often seen as a conflict between the two notions of Messiah and Son of Man. If so, the preference for the Son of Man title is clear.

6. The form does not fit a traditional pronouncement story. Here Jesus provokes the issue, and there is no rejoinder except the positive response of the bystanders. For some this casts doubt on the saying as a pre-Markan tradition. Since Mark shows no particular interest in discussion about the title, I think it likely to be a traditional unit.

7. Yet shortly before in the narrative Mark inserts a healing story in which the blind beggar, Bartimaeus, twice cries out "Jesus, son of David" in the narrative. Nothing in the story suggests that this vocative is wrong, even if the crowd tries to silence him. A very unusual address—is this an implicit messianic vocative? Without further

evidence, it is difficult to say. I will discuss below possible linkage between miracles and Messiah.

8. It is true that Matthew changes Mark 13:6 to imply that Jesus admits he is Messiah (Matt 24:5).

9. After the saying in question, Mark adds the vivid scene of the enthronement of the Son of Man. Controversy about Messiahs on earth is puny compared with the cosmic event to come. That this context is due to Mark's tradition is usually assumed.

10. Cf. Matt 23:10, which may be compositional.

11. I think it likely that the pericope is traditional and its location fixed in pre-Markan chronology.

12. The words in Mark are those in the LXX, although the syntax is different.

13. Since the Mosaic motif is not a Markan interest, it seems likely to me that it belongs to the tradition. In this context one must mention the strange saying in 13:32, which also assumes an intimate relation between Father and Son—and yet ignorance on the Son's part. Here only the Father knows the hour, while neither the Son nor the angels in heaven do. Unusual here is the absolute Father and Son. Structurally similar is the saying in Matt 11:27, to which I shall return.

14. The scholarly term for such miracle workers has become "the divine man," and I will use this term in the discussion. As a term applied to Jesus, it carries no disparagement. The phrase became popular due to the enormous collection of Ludwig Bieler, *Theios Aner: Das Bild des "Göttlichen Menschen" in Spätantike und Frühchristentum* (Vienna, 1935; reprint, Darmstadt: Wissenschaftliche Buchgesellschaft, 1967). Cf. M. Smith, "Prolegomena to a Discussion of Aretalogies, Divine Men, the Gospels, and Jesus," *JBL* 90 (1971): 174–99.

15. Some manuscripts read *Christos* at 16:21. The title is likely an addition to the original text.

16. This seems like a strange "title," but cf. John 11:27, where Martha confesses, "I have believed that you are the *Christos*, the son of God, who is coming (*ho erchomenos*) into the world."

17. Cf. R. Scroggs, "The Earliest Christian Communities as Sectarian Movement," in *The Text and the Times* (Minneapolis: Fortress Press, 1993), 39–42.

18. This saying bears some family resemblance to Mark 9:41, where the missionaries are "of *Christos*." That is, in both instances the community specifically acknowledges its leader to be *Christos*. Apart from these two instances, as far as I know, the claims about Jesus as *Christos* are made independently of any relationship to the community.

19. Matt 3:17; 8:29; 17:5; 24:36; 26:63; 27:40; 27:54.

20. To note that Matthew (or Luke) has added to the Markan prototype leads one at first thought to assume that the addition is by the final author. Careful reflection, however, indicates that another option is possible: the added element may have been in the final author's oral tradition of the Markan pericope. In this case, the added element is traditional and not compositional. How to decide between the two alternatives is obviously a difficult matter. The only criterion we have is the consonance of the added element with the final author's point of view. In the case of Matthew's addition to the sea miracle, it seems to me more likely to be traditional than compositional.

21. 9:27; 12:23; 15:22; 20:30, 31; 21:9, 15.

22. Again, if Q has no inclination to describe Jesus as Messiah, and if Luke presumably has the more original wording of Q, then Matthew's reading in 12:23 is probably compositional.

23. Matthew's compositional work is significant at 21:9. Mark's text reads: "Hosanna! Blessed is he who comes in the name of the Lord! Blessed is the kingdom of our father David that is coming! Hosanna in the highest!" (11:9-10; punctuation from the RSV). Mark models his refrain upon the pilgrim Psalm 118:25 but adds the mention of David. Mark has all the crowd ascribe David as *their* father. Matthew changes this to the singular "son of David" and then adds the phrase from Mark (and Ps. 118:25) "Blessed is he who comes in the name of the Lord." Now "he" means Jesus as son of David, not a generic pilgrim.

24. The classic study here is that of Krister Stendahl, "Quis et Unde," *BZNW* 26 (1960): 94–105.

25. In the Gospel of John that Jesus be born in Bethlehem is listed as a criterion for messiahship, with the counter that Jesus comes from Nazareth. The Johannine narrative does not dispute either judgment.

26. Luke 9:20; 20:41; 22:67; 23:35.

27. The only other occurrence of *sōtēr* in the Gospel is also in the birth narratives (1:47) but is there used of God. It appears only twice in Acts (5:31; 13:23). *Sōtēr* as a title for Jesus is usually seen as a later addition to the christological repertory. Paul does, however, use the title once in an acclamation not dissimilar to Luke 2:11: "We await a Savior, Lord Jesus Christ" (Phil 3:20). The Lukan birth narratives have in places strong political overtones. It is possible that the use in 2:11 implies deliverance from some perceived oppression. Since Luke himself does not portray the Christian movement as revolutionary in character, the birth narratives surely must have arisen independently of authorial concern. It is true, however, that the disciples ask the resurrected Jesus in Acts 1:6, "Lord, will you at this time restore the kingdom to Israel?" This seems very much like a reprise of the angel's announcement in 1:32-33. But how is Jesus' replay to be interpreted? " It is not for you to know times or seasons which the Father has fixed by his own authority" (v. 7). As a rejection of an earthly kingdom? As a postponement?

28. It is perhaps possible that Luke has in mind Mark 3:7-12, which he hints at in 6:18.

29. This is one of those curious Lukan similarities with the Gospel of John, in which the Baptist also denies emphatically that he is the Messiah (1:20). Luke also knows that even in Ephesus the baptism of John is practiced (Acts 19:1-3). Does he know or suspect that communities continued to exist which honored John after his death with titles such as Messiah? Many scholars, following Bultmann, think that the Gospel of John implies such communities.

30. It is remarkable that charges do not appear elsewhere in the Gospel tradition. Here they are political and I have always thought they had an authentic ring to them: that is, while current judgment is that the charge is a Lukan creation, I suspect Luke finds this in his tradition. The charge that he is "perverting" the nation is closely related to the Rabbinic charge that Jesus "led the people astray" (*b. Sanhedrin* 43a).

31. I say "apparently" because I think Luke is following a tradition of the last supper which is different from Mark, and it is possible that 22:15 comes from that tradition.

32. E.g., Ferdinand Hahn, *The Titles of Jesus in Christology: Their History in Early Christianity* (London: Lutterworth, 1963).

33. In Acts 2:36 Peter says: "God has made him both Lord and Christ, this Jesus whom you crucified." The context is the resurrection; thus the resurrection/exaltation is the beginning time of Jesus' messiahship. One can argue whether this statement is Lukan or pre-Lukan tradition. The point is that Luke accepts the statement.

34. In 1:27 Joseph is said to be of the house of David.

35. See 1:27.

36. I do think there are some early traditions reflected in the Gospel, but in general these are not relevant for my discussion. More difficult is to come to terms with the different layers in the Gospel that seem to reflect perspectives of the community itself at different times. Does a layer that does not seem consonant with the final author's view (if we can be sure what that is!) present in the Gospel because of antiquarian interest? Or does it mean that the community is not monolithic, and the layers represent different and *present* points of view within the community? Unless there is evidence to the contrary, I think the latter is the better operative principle. Thus the argument with the Jews about Jesus' messiahship discloses a *reality* within the Johannine community at the time of the final author.

37. The final confession, however, of the Samaritans in Jesus is that he is *sōtēr* (4:42).

38. Here the title is merged with that of the Son of Man, since for the author of John the departure, i.e., exaltation is tied with the latter title.

39. Since this phrase occurs on the mouth of Peter at a crucial moment in the narration of John, it would seem appropriate that the acclamation would be couched in the most exalted terms available to the author. Instead he writes what is on the surface an enigmatic confession. The Greek uses an adjective, *ho hagios,* to which one must supply a noun. What is the noun meant to be supplied: Messiah, Son? Rarely do we find this phrase elsewhere in the New Testament as an acclamation of Jesus. The man with the unclean spirit in Mark exclaims to Jesus: "I know who you are, the holy [one?] of God" (Mark 1:24). The angel announces to Mary that the child to be born "will be called holy, Son of God" (Luke 1:35). Is there an equation here between "holy" and "Son of God"? Twice in Acts Jesus is named with the adjective *hagios:* 3:14; 4:27. In the latter the noun is supplied—"child" or "servant," to which is added that God had anointed him. Is this a messianic anointing? The least to be said is that *ho hagios* reverberates with a sense of awe, which puts it close to identity with an acclamation—whether to *Christos* or to Son of God cannot be said with precision.

40. A variant reading of 1:18 also uses this terminology, but textual scholars today prefer the reading of *theos* (God) to that of *huios* (son).

41. The title son of David does not occur in the Gospel of John. Once, in controversy about the criteria for messiahship, Jesus from Galilee is contrasted with the Messiah, who is to be born in Bethlehem as a descendant of David. The Gospel writer apparently has no answer to that put-down.

42. J. A. T. Robinson argued that this was "the most primitive christology of all" in his article "The Most Primitive Christology of All?" *JTS* 7 (1956): 177–89.

43. Not even in the later endings of Mark and John is there reference to *Christos*.

44. Cf. John 11:27 where Martha acclaims Jesus as *Christos*, Son of God, who is coming into the world—a phrase quite similar to that in Q. It is well known that the *Christos* title does not appear in Q—although the reason for this is not. The connection of the two sayings cited above with Messiah notions seems apparent. Could it be that Q has suppressed the *Christos* title?

45. Of course, the Son of Man also comes. But that is not a coming to earth, nor is there ever any hint that the Son of Man is to perform miracles. In the Matthean context, the "coming" is clearly an earthly appearance.

46. In an early compositional approach to the Gospel of Mark, T. J. Weeden argued that in Mark's perspective, the confession of Peter was a pivotal point in the Gospel. Weeden interpreted the confession that Jesus is Messiah to be based on all that had gone before in the Gospel—which seems to emphasize the powerful miracles of Jesus. Peter is thus proclaiming Jesus to be Messiah on the basis of his miracles. Jesus proceeds to interpret himself in terms of the suffering Son of Man and excoriates Peter for having the wrong idea of messiahship. If there is probity in this interpretation, then the author of Mark must have known that for some people miracle and Messiah could be linked. T. J. Weeden, *Mark: Traditions in Conflict* (Philadelphia: Fortress Press, 1971).

47. Cf. Luke 1:32-35, where the angel announces to Mary that Jesus will be Messiah (vv. 32-33) and Son of God (v. 35). Here the two terms must be synonymous.

48. Believing in Jesus because he does miracles is, of course, an ambiguous value in the Gospel of John. What seems apparent is that *some* people who "believe in" Jesus because of his miracles believe in him as the Messiah.

49. This linkage was held to be almost axiomatic by Morton Smith in his *Jesus the Magician* (San Francisco: HarperSanFrancisco, 1978), e.g., 13, 14. Unfortunately, Smith asserted the relationship but did not try to explain why such a linkage was possible or believable.

50. A passage based on 2 Samuel 7, a late postexilic (?) encomium on the throne of David and his descendants. Cf., e.g., R. Brown, *The Birth of the Messiah* (Garden City, N.Y.: Doubleday, 1979), 310–11.

51. If this perspective is correct, then Wayne Meeks's well-known and generally accepted argument needs some revision. Cf. W. Meeks, "The Man from Heaven in Johannine Sectarianism," *JBL* 91 (1972): 44–72. There Meeks proposed that increasing hostility between the Johannine community and the synagogue led the Johannine community to a higher and higher Christology. This only intensified the hostility because the increasingly high Christology made increasingly less sense to the synagogue. It may be that the community in fact presented its case to the synagogue in terms of a concept known to the synagogue, namely, *Christos*, but kept the "high" Christology to themselves (just because they did not want to antagonize more than they had to?).

Notes to Chapter 4

1. This change is not due to the passing of time. That even the final authors of the Gospels (cf. also Acts) are aware of the titular significance of *Christos* means that the completely divergent perspectives are temporally parallel, not consecutive. That is, it is too simple to say that an early Palestinian view was replaced by a later Greek view.

2. According to W. Kramer, Rom 9:5 is the only place where one can be reasonably sure that Paul uses *Christos* as a title. Cf. the carefully argued book of W. Kramer, *Christ, Lord, Son of God* (Naperville, Ill.: Allenson, 1966), 210.

3. Suetonius, as late as the early second century, does this (*Vita Claudii* 25.4). *Chrēstos*, meaning "kind" (as in helpful, gentle), was a name given to slaves.

4. In philosophical logic, if "A" means everything, it means nothing.

5. To get a cross-section of the Hellenistic church I have analyzed the following documents: 1 Thessalonians, Philippians, Galatians, Romans, Acts, Colossians, 1 Timothy, 1 Peter, and Hebrews. I will mostly limit my comments to these writings, which I use as trench studies.

6. Cf. the argument of Kramer below.

7. In the documents analyzed (cf. n. 5 above), *Christos Iēsous kyrios* occurs three times, *Iēsous Christos kyrios* three times, *kyrios Iēsous* six times, and *kyrios Christos* three. *Iēsous* alone occurs infrequently, except in Acts and Hebrews.

8. I follow Kramer here. Cf. below.

9. Again, the appeal to the name of Jesus in Phil 2:10 is startling. Clearly here the "naming" refers to the post-enthroned Lord. The oddity is that "Jesus" refers to this Lord, not his earthly past. Cf. also the uses of *Iēsous* in Hebrews, noted below.

10. In the Gospels, "Jesus" is usually without addition. When a need is felt for an addition, it is "Jesus of Nazareth," e.g., Mark 1:24; 10:47; Matt 26:71; Luke 24:19.

11. Cf. the discussion below about the use of *Kyrios Iēsous* in the church.

12. E.g., the phrase repeated for two hours by the Ephesians, "Great is Artemis of the Ephesians," according to Acts 19:34.

13. For example, it appears five times in 1 Thessalonians, once in the salutation (1:1), once in the thanksgiving (1:3), twice in the benediction (5:23, 28), and only once in the body (5:9).

14. Cf. n. 7 above.

15. It is true that *Kyrios Iēsous* appears five times, compared with none in Philippians, Galatians, and Romans. Cf. the discussion of this usage in the section on Acts below.

16. As mentioned above, Kramer acknowledges that Rom 9:5 indicates Paul knows *Christos* is a title.

17. Kramer, *Christ*, 203–14.

18. "Allerdings ist er (Paul) sich noch deutlich bewusst, dass das Wort 'Christus' kein Eigenname ist, wie die gelegentliche Voranstellung des Christustitels vor 'Jesus' beweist." *Die Christologie des neuen Testaments*, 2nd ed. (Tübingen: Mohr, 1958), 135.

19. In our trench-study documents, the order *Christos Iēsous* appears twice as frequently as the other.

20. Cf. Kramer, *Christ*, 203–6.

21. Ibid., 206–11.

22. 1 Cor 1:13; 10:4; 11:3; 12:12; Rom 9:5; 15:3, 7. Cf. Kramer, *Christ*, 209–12.

23. Ibid., 213.

24. The problem here is that we are operating in a time frame of less than twenty years. If Jesus was crucified in the early 30s and Paul is writing 1 Thessalonians in the late 40s, there is only a fifteen-year span, give or take, for such a transfer of meaning to have taken place, and for its significance to have been lost.

25. Probably *Christos* occurs 24 times. In some key manuscripts it also occurs in 20:21, but this is so uncertain a reading as to exclude it from our survey.

26. Cf. H. Cadbury, "The Titles of Jesus in Acts," in *The Beginnings of Christianity*, ed. F. J. Foakes Jackson and K. Lake (reprint, Grand Rapids: Eerdmans, 1979), 5:354–75; cf. esp. 357–59.

27. Acts 11:17; 15:26; and 28:31.

28. In 10:48 it is the baptismal formula (there are textual issues here, but it seems to me the appearance of *Christos* is reasonably certain), and in 16:18 it is the exorcistic, healing formula.

29. The question is not what Peter might have meant, but what the author of Acts intends.

30. Some manuscripts omit *Christos*.

31. Acts 2:31, 36, 38; 3:18, 20; 4:10; 26:23 (I assume that Agrippa is considered a Jew).

32. In the Greek the apostles preach *ton Christon Iēsoun*. This is one of several places where the Greek, strictly speaking, is ambiguous. One could translate "preaching Christ Jesus." All the commentators seem agreed, however, that a comma should be placed between *Christos* and *Iēsous*, indicating that the terms are in apposition, meaning "preaching the Christ to be Jesus," or the reverse. Other similar passages are 3:20; 17:3; 18:5, 28.

33. I have already noted the uncertainty of 20:21, where some witnesses read the full acclamatory title, "Our Lord Jesus Christ." If the shorter reading is to be preferred, this is the only occurrence of *Kyrios Iēsous* in Acts with the possessive "our."

34. 1:21; 4:33; 9:17; 15:11; 20:24; 20:35; 21:13.

35. 8:15: The Samaritans have been baptized in the name of the Lord Jesus. Since the implication of v. 12 may be that the Samaritans were baptized in the name of "Jesus Christ," the distinction between "Lord Jesus" and "Jesus Christ" may not be significantly different in this passage. 11:20: At Antioch some preach to the Greeks the Lord Jesus. 16:31: The jailer at Philippi is admonished to "believe in the Lord Jesus." 19:5: Some disciples, knowing John's baptism, are now baptized "in the name of the Lord Jesus."

36. The full acclamation is used only in 1:3. *Kyrios Christos* occurs only once (3:24, in the context of slavery—perhaps indicating that the slave's master is Christ). *Christos Iēsous* appears three times (1:1, 4; 4:12). Perhaps the most interesting use is in 2:6, where the author writes of the church having received *ton Christon Iēsoun ton kyrion*. If anywhere in Colossians, this usage may hint at a titular meaning for *Christos*.

37. The other three appear in the apparent name "Jesus Christ."

38. "Jesus" appears with "Son of God" in 4:14 and with *kyrios* in 13:20.

39. It is striking that the full acclamation, *kyrios Iēsous Christos,* does not appear in the document. Is this because the function of the resurrected figure is focused on priestly activity, while the acclamation, at least originally, emerged out of a royal setting?

40. 1 Tim 1:2, 12; 6:3, 14.

41. In 5:11 young widows enrolled in the order of widows (if this is what it is) may "grow wanton against Christ" and desire to marry. What this might mean is unclear. Most interpreters take enrollment in the order to be equal to a spiritual marriage with Christ; hence to desire to marry an actual persons is taken to be an act of unfaithfulness toward Christ. Why the word *Christos* appears solo, against the clear preference of the author, need not be debated here.

42. *Iēsous* does not appear in the epistle independently of *Christos.*

43. Most scholars take seriously its claim to be a circular letter to churches in several provinces in this territory, despite the difficulty of imagining how the problems of such a scenario could be overcome.

44. There are two passages with textual variants. (1) 3:15. The majority of early witnesses read "*kyrion de ton Christon* sanctify in your hearts." The use of the article with *Christos* and not with *kyrios* suggests one should translate "sanctify Christ as Lord." That is, one should not take *kyrios Christos* here as a double-word title. Hence, the passage is evidence for the solo use of *Christos.* Other witnesses read *theos* instead of *Christos,* but this is probably a later reading aligning 1 Peter with Isa 8:13, a text probably in the background of 3:15. (2) 5:14. Several witnesses, mostly later, add *Iēsous* to *Christos* at the benediction. If this later reading is correct, 5:14 is the only place in the letter in which "Christ Jesus" occurs. Probably the shorter reading is correct, although it is surprising that a benediction does not have a fuller title than *Christos* alone.

45. The topic in the later chapters is some sort of persecution and the use of Jesus as a model for a requisite Christian response. If tradition determines the heavy appearance of *Christos* solo in these chapters, there may not be a content connection. One could, of course, argue that the concurrence of name and tradition means that the connection between *Christos* and suffering had already been made in the earlier tradition.

46. It is true that certain names have a way of pointing to a particular facet of a person, in private familial context, or even in public societal situations. One uses nicknames in ways one would not use the "real" name of a person. This does not make the various appellations titular.

47. Or could it have retained its Hebrew sound as transliterated into Greek? *Ben adam* = something like *benadam.* So it would be *Jesus benadam.* Why not?

48. Poor Trypho has little chance to argue his side and appears mostly as a willing tool in the onslaught that Justin mounts. Justin is adamant and haughty; Trypho is mostly deferential and concessive (although his companions occasionally cannot hide their amusement). Clearly the text portrays a very "Christian" view of the matter. To what extent the *Dialogue* has historical roots, and even the theological "location" of such a debate, is much disputed. Cf. the helpful discussion on what the author calls a genre of "anti-Jewish polemical literature" in M. Simon, *Verus Israel* (Oxford: Oxford University

Press, 1986), 135–78. Simon argues that it does, in fact, reflect a basic accuracy with regard to the issues and the texts debated. It is important to note that Justin's *Dialogue* is what Simon calls the "prototype" of the dialogic literature (p. 140) and is thus the earliest of that form. It also seems to be the earliest of all of the texts Simon discusses. Thus one must exercise some caution. Was Justin repeating traditional motifs, or did he create a new form, to be emulated by later theologians?

49. The Greek text I use is *Corpus Apologetarum Christianorum* 1/2, ed. Johann Carl Theodore Otto (Wiesbaden: Dr. Martin Sändig Otto, 1969; reprint of the 1876 edition). The translation I have consulted (though I make my own translations) is that of Thomas B. Falls, *Saint Justin Martyr* (Washington, D.C.: Catholic University of America Press, 1977). One needs to read this translation with the Greek in hand. At times the author glosses the Greek with his interpretation—perhaps correctly, but nevertheless such a procedure is sometimes disconcerting when one is trying to get an exact reading on the titles and words Justin uses.

50. Justin frequently uses the phrases "his [God's] *Christos*" and "*Christos* of God." It has been argued that this is a peculiarly Lukan phrase, but Justin uses it without any apparent reference to the Lukan texts.

51. The translation glosses with the title "Messiah," which does not appear in Justin's text. I think it dangerous to assume that the titles are equivalent. Trypho may be making an important distinction in this passage.

52. The translation reads "Jesus Christ"; the Greek is a simple *houtos*. I concede that "your Jesus" is also a gloss, but it avoids a false suggestion of a title.

53. It is interesting that Trypho ridicules Justin's defense of the virgin birth ("You Christians should be ashamed"), by claiming that it is a repeat of the birth of Perseus by the virgin Danae (chap. 67).

Notes to Chapter 5

1. As far as I can reconstruct the teaching of the actual Jesus, they would have heard him correctly. I do think that the parables, especially, present a view of a God who sympathizes with the hardship of the outcasts and who embraces them into a loving relationship.

2. One is struck by the frequent occurrence in this section of *Christos* solo (both with and without the article). The only other title is "Son." It is tempting to enlist this as evidence of a messianic argument with Jews, but the possibility I am suggesting does not depend on any titular significance in and of itself.

3. It may well be that the issue of the Messiah "having" to suffer was yet another item in the synagogue debate.

4. It remains likely that in the debates between Jews and Christians it is the latter who introduced the *Christos* title. The Jews may have, for obvious reasons, preferred the term Notzrim, that is,"Nazoreans." In a version of the *birkath ha-minim* discovered by Schechter, the text reads: "May the Notzrim and the heretics perish in an instant." Cf. the discussion in W. D. Davies, *The Setting of the Sermon on the Mount* (Cambridge: Cambridge University Press, 1977), 275–76. In other early rabbinic texts, such as *b. Sanhedrin*

43a and *Aboda Zarah* 16b–17a, Jesus is called Jeshu or Jeshu the Nazarene. We might glean from this that in such debates it was the Christian side that forced the title *Christos* on the discussion.

5. The ecstatic experiences, at least in some of the early communities, may be expressive of this sense of liberation.

Notes to Chapter 6

1. Antoinette Wire, *The Corinthian Women Prophets* (Minneapolis: Fortress Press, 1990).

2. There are no acclamations, no exalted terms such as *kyrios*.

3. Several scholars consider these "predictions" to be Markan creations. Their unusual wording, however, causes me to question their origin. It still seems conceivable to me that they are pre-authorial. It is granted, however, that there is no earlier hint anywhere else of the identification of Jesus and the Son of Man. We must remain content that it is only in authorial Mark that this idea surfaces. The issue is immensely complicated.

4. The idea of ransom is unique to Mark's Gospel and does not seem to fit his thought. This is another reason to wonder whether the dying of Jesus as the Son of Man is purely a Markan creation.

5. The reverberation of Deut 18:15 in Mark 9:7 might suggest that in this story Jesus is portrayed as the "new Moses."

6. The instances are 8:29; 9:41; 12:35; 13:21; 14:61; 15:32.

7. That this was an issue in the Gospels is clear. The birth narratives both argue that the Messiah is son of David; cf. also the question raised in John 7:40-45.

8. The problem here is that the miracle stories do not explicitly use the term *Christos* but rather related terms, such as "Son of God" or "Holy One of God."

9. Part of the genius of Mark is how he structures his story units in order to communicate the meaning of a narrative. For example, the over-ruling of the food taboos in chap. 7 leads directly to the healing of a Gentile, which leads directly to the second feeding story. In chap. 8, which takes place in Gentile territory and thus must indicate the calling of Gentiles into the community of faith, Jesus' refusal to give a sign (8:11-13) means, in the context, that Jesus refuses to give proof for the entry of the Gentiles.

10. This assumes that none of these were in Q, that it, that Luke reports all there was in Q and doesn't omit any. If he omits, it cannot be said with surety that none of these fifteen sayings are Q.

11. Matthew: *edothē moi pasa exousia en ouranō kai epi gēs.* Daniel: *kai edothē autō exousia.*

12. Matthew turns the Markan story about David and the *Christos* (22:41-46) into a debate, but does not alter the implications of the story itself in any way. Quite a conflict with the birth narrative!

13. Matthew has inserted the title twice in the earlier narrative of the hearing before Pilate (27:17, 21). It is hard to say whether these are supposed to represent Pilate's own

judgment. Probably not. Nevertheless, it is a much less brutal use than that accorded the high priest's entourage at the end of the night trial (26:68).

14. As listed in a previous chapter, four of these are the full acclamatory title; the rest are distributed, sometimes uncertainly, among various joinings with *Iēsous*.

15. Some prefer the translation "righteous"; cf. R. Karris, *Luke: Artist and Theologian* (New York: Paulist, 1983), 109–11.

Notes to Chapter 7

1. Of the making of books on Paul's theology there is no end, and it would be fruitless to try to list even the major newer works. Fortunately for our purposes, I do not need to enter the lists of a battlefield strewn with so many warriors. Yet it is amazing how, true to a Pauline interest, resurrection keeps occurring in this battlefield. I have made my own very modest contributions in *Paul for a New Day* (Philadelphia: Fortress Press, 1976), *Christology in Paul and John* (Philadelphia: Fortress Press, 1988), and in various articles scattered in the literature, some of which are republished in *The Text and the Times* (Minneapolis: Fortress Press, 1993).

2. Paul adds, of course, that because Christ is raised so also will believers be raised, but this does not alter his agreement with the enthronement structure.

3. I realize that this statement is debatable and has been fiercely argued by scholars. For my purposes the issue is not crucial. J. Habermann even argues that preexistence is a retro-movement from the primary affirmation of exaltation. Thus even in affirmations of preexistence exaltation is mirrored. Cf. *Präexistenzaussagen im Neuen Testament* (Frankfurt: Peter Lang, 1990), 421–22.

4. The obvious exception is 1 Pet 3:18a: "Christ suffered once for sins . . . that he might present us to God." "Suffered" rather than "died" is the preferred reading. "That he might lead us to God" is an unclear metaphor but is not specifically sacrificial. The early formula about resurrection appearances in 1 Cor 15:3-7 also refers to the significance of the death of Jesus, but the function of that formula is not to extol Christ as Cosmocrator but to show the chain of authority appearances are claimed to have. That either passage presents the death of Jesus as sacrificial is uncertain. The association of Jesus' death with cosmic reconciliation in Col 1:20 is an addition by the author of the document to an earlier text.

5. Cf. Rudolf Bultmann, *Theology of the New Testament* (New York: Scribner's, 1954), 1:295–96.

6. I say "orthodox," because it may be that the Cosmocrator Christology of the Hellenistic churches *could* have headed in directions that might have been sympathetic to the later Marcionite movement.

7. It seems to me that there are certain hints, usually ignored or reinterpreted, that not all believers thought that they would live after death. After all, this would have been a novel and probably incredible view for a Greek or a Roman. Cf. 1 Cor 15:12 and 1 Thess 3:13-14. It has become accepted in many scholarly circles that the Corinthians did, in fact, believe in continued life for the believer; they just did not believe in *resurrection* from

the dead. According to this view, Paul misunderstood the Corinthians. But I see no reason to question that Paul knew the situation better than we.

8. It seems striking to me that no explicit reference to freedom from fate occurs in the New Testament—with the possible exception of Rev 1:16, if the seven stars that the Son of Man holds in his hand (i.e., controls?) are the planets, which were widely understood to determine one's fate. In fact the vocabulary about fate is completely lacking in the New Testament.

9. Long ago Ernst Käsemann made popular the term "enthusiasm," for him a derogatory word referring to what he considered an emphasis on present salvation without reliance on the cross and what that meant. He applied the term both to the liturgical material as well as to the Corinthian church. The interested reader may look at two particular chapters in *Jesus Means Freedom* (Philadelphia: Fortress Press, 1970). In "The Gospel of Freedom" (pp. 42–58), he dealt with some of the liturgical pieces (among other texts), and in "For and Against a Theology of Resurrection" (pp. 59–84) he strongly argued against the enthusiasm he saw in the Corinthian church. The liturgies exhibited enthusiasm because (1) they proclaimed that God's reign had already begun; (2) they did not connect Christ's reign with Judaism; and (3) they proclaimed freedom as a watchword (p. 49). For the Corinthians, the heavenly world had already invaded the earthly in the individual believer at baptism. All gifts are present; hence they extolled the gifts of the spirit (pp. 62–63). Power is present, but sadly missing is the theology of the cross.

Although I myself was persuaded by his arguments for a while, today they seem to me questionable. His claims about the liturgies' excess of freedom goes far beyond any evidence, and his reading of 1 and 2 Corinthians seems increasingly problematic to me. The problem Paul had with the use of the spiritual gifts of the Corinthians was that it was a misuse, the use of the gifts to vaunt themselves in the eyes of other believers. It was conceit that falsified the gospel, not the presence of the gifts.

10. E.g., 1 Cor 1:18; 2 Cor 2:15.

11. Rom 8:18-23 presents problems to all interpreters. If the general Pauline context were different, one could read the Romans passage as expecting a restored creation. One has to choose between this reading and the passage of 1 Cor 15 quoted above. The odds seem to favor 1 Cor 15.

12. Obviously many sectarian groups have in fact anticipated the eschaton as a soon-to-be-realized event.

13. Cf. Bultmann, *Theology*, 1:246–49. Is death the "last" enemy because it is the temporal or the ultimate "last"? Probably both.

14. This judgment can stand, even if 2:6-11 and 3:8-21 do not belong to the same letter.

15. Whether the contrast is conscious and intentional between the hymn and Paul's own yearnings depends in part on the debated issue of the integrity of Philippians. If the partition theories are correct, then the hymn and the material in chap. 3 are from different letters and, thus, different times. For a convenient summary of the issues cf. Ralph P. Martin, *Philippians* (Grand Rapids: Eerdmans, 1985), 14–21. Whether from the same letter or not, the vivid contrast remains.

16. I am not sure that "everything to everyone" is a happy translation of the

formulaic Greek, but then any translation is precarious. I take it that it is a pleonastic expression that points to the final supremacy of God.

17. This has become a dominant view since Krister Stendahl, *Paul among Jews and Gentiles* (Philadelphia: Fortress Press, 1976), 7–23.

18. It would have been impossible to link the act of creation to the preexistent Jesus without making him an agent of the God of Israel, e.g., Col 1:15-20 and John 1:1-4. I suspect that the motif of creation by Christ as agent functioned to guard precisely against the separation of redemption from creation (although function does not necessarily provide a theory of origin). Paul himself probably knew and accepted the claim that Christ was preexistent (everything depends upon how one reads Phil 2:6-11; 1 Cor 8:6; and 2 Cor 8:9). I do not see anything in Paul's thinking that would have made acceptance of the idea improper. It has to be said, however, that it did not become an important element in his theology.

19. Robin Scroggs, *The Last Adam* (Philadelphia: Fortress Press, 1966), 54–58, 75–112.

20. Cf. my *Christology in Paul and John*, 23–32.

Notes to Chapter 8

1. See also 4:8-10 and 5:14.
2. 1:2, 3, 17; 3:11; 5:20; 6:23, 24.
3. The name "Jesus" appears independently of titles only once in the two documents, and that in a strange expression in Eph 4:21.
4. Cf. the careful analysis of A. Lincoln, *Ephesians* (Dallas: Word, 1990).
5. It is true that Phil 2:6 implies some speculation about Jesus and God prior to, or at the time of, the incarnation.
6. I trust the reader will always take my choice of words as less than literal. It is a constant temptation to use the word "substantial" in speaking of the identity of the *plērōma* of God and of the resurrected Jesus, as well as the inter-relatedness of the resurrected Jesus and the cosmos. Nor am I entirely sure the word would be misapplied. Since, however, the term is so identified with fourth-century theology, I avoid it in these discussions.
7. I take it that this unique use (in the New Testament) of *theotēs* occurs because the author senses that there is something impersonal about the relationship.
8. Cf. the use of *sōma* in 2:17, which has to mean "substance, reality."
9. Note the joining of Pss 8 and 110, something the catena in Hebrews does as well. Paul uses Ps 8 christologically in 1 Cor 15:25-27.
10. There remains an intriguing echo with the Jewish notion of the measurement of the gigantic figure of God, but that would surely be an extraneous element in this complex.
11. The author uses the term in 1:10 in relation to time. I will return to that passage.
12. The word *epouraniois* may seem unusual, but it probably simply denotes the totality of the heavenly reality. The resurrected believers, but also the powers and

principalities, inhabit it (cf. 3:10 and 6:12). He also uses the more usual word, *ouranos*, several times.

13. Cf. my "Paul: Sophos and Pneumatikos (1 Cor 2:6-16)," *New Testament Studies* 14 (1967): 33–55.

14. Cf. also 1 Cor 13:2 and 14:2. Paul's use in 1 Cor 2:1 is textually disputed. The appearance in Rom 16:25 is also post-Pauline, although it bears resemblance to usages in Colossians and Ephesians.

15. If "for the church" is not an insertion in Eph 1:22, then Eph 1:10 contradicts the fragment. Eph 1:10 clearly has a cosmic goal, contrary to the limitation of the fragment referencing the church.

16. This is the first mention of *pneuma* in connection with *mystērion*.

17. Lincoln, *Ephesians*, 187.

18. The issue is the nature of the "decree" that has been held against humans (or just Gentiles?—the issue does not seem to concern Torah, despite the previous reference to circumcision) and the extent to which the powers have been responsible for the decree. Or is this an idea of the position that the author of Colossians is opposing?

19. I admit that translating *en* by "behind" seems far-fetched, but it is the only way I can continue the metaphor.

20. In 1:10 the unusual word is *anakephalaioō*, which is a rhetorical term referring to an orator summing up his arguments in a speech. But what does it mean to sum up all things in Christ? The probable description is voiced by A. Lincoln: "The summing up of all things in Christ means the unifying of the cosmos or its direction toward a common goal" (*Ephesians*, 33).

Notes to Chapter 9

1. The use of Hebrews by *1 Clement* is accepted by most scholars. When this latter document was written is, however, not certain, but a date in the late first century is probable. Does this mean the location of Hebrews (either as place of composition or destination) was in Rome, or simply that a copy reached Rome in time for the author of *1 Clement* to use it? The latter supposition requires even an earlier date, to allow the manuscript time to travel.

2. The author has taken Psalm 8, a hymn that refers to the status of the human being, to refer to Jesus as Son of Man.

3. The difficult phrase is *chōris hamartias*, literally, "without sin." The context forces one to translate it as a contrast to "for salvation," thus indicating not Jesus' sinless state (which would have seemed obvious to the reader), but as the object of his coming.

4. The meaning of "sin" for the author of Hebrews is ambiguous. Cf. below.

5. Harold Attridge, *The Epistle to the Hebrews* (Philadelphia: Fortress Press, 1989), 210, argues that the phrase probably means "completely."

6. Heb 2:2-3 presents a major problem in interpretation, a passage I shall inspect below. Many scholars think the teaching and miraculous activity of Jesus are there referred to. Even if this is the case, it would be the only text in Hebrews that mentions such activity.

7. The phrase is *chōris hamartias*, curiously the same phrase used in 9:28 to indicate that the eschatological Jesus does not come as judge. Paul, apparently, also assumes that Jesus was sinless (2 Cor 5:21).

8. Cf. the excursus in Attridge, *Hebrews*, 83–87.

9. Attridge, *Hebrews*, 86–87.

10. There are a few ethical exhortations in 13:1-9 and 12:12-17. Elsewhere references to failings of the addressees seem to be communal, like failing to meet regularly (10:24f.).

11. That the Torah was given through angels was by this time traditional in Hellenistic Judaism. Our author sees the Torah as a legitimate legal document (at least for its own time).

12. Heb 7:21; 8:2, 8, 9, 10, 11; 10:16, 30; 12:5, 6; 13:6.

13. The term *sōtēria* is certainly not a Gospel term. It does not occur at all in Mark or Matthew; only once in the Gospel of John (4:22), and four times in Luke. Of these four, three are in the infancy narratives, and the other in the story of Zacchaeus (19:9). It is interesting that in the late addition to Mark 16:8 there is a statement that is a closer parallel to Heb 2:3 than any other in the New Testament: "After this Jesus himself from east to west sent out through them the sacred and immortal proclamation of eternal salvation." The phrase *aiōniou sōtērias* may actually be taken from Heb 5:9. And this points to the fact that *sōtēria* is a preferred word of the author of Hebrews. It occurs seven times, more than in any other New Testament document. In all but one occurrence (in 11:7 Noah saves his family by building the boat), the word *is* the final, ultimate eschatological event—which apparently is tantamount to eternal life for believers. Even in our passage *sōtēria* is an event, even though "declared"—in advance of the event itself.

14. Attridge, *Hebrews*, 67.

15. The author is not afraid to add a bit of pathos, by narrating the loud cries and supplications of Jesus (5:7).

16. Again, if 2:3f. refers to the earthly Jesus, that may be one reference to his miraculous activity.

17. This is as close to a masochistic Jesus as we find in the New Testament. Fortunately, Nietzsche did not notice this.

18. Is this one reason the community is gathering together less frequently? Cf. 10:25.

Notes to Chapter 10

1. The word "true" is crucial, since for the author "true" believers are only those who are willing to sacrifice everything in standing against the adversaries.

2. Persecution under Domitian, which used to be the bedrock event for determining the date of Revelation, is now doubted. Nevertheless, a date in the mid-nineties seems to be accepted by even those who most doubt the historicity of Domitian's persecution. Most scholars also date Acts toward the end of the first century. I suspect it may be even a

bit later, but quibbling over such issues of dating does not call into question the contemporaneity of the writing of the two documents.

3. I agree with current judgment that the readership of the book is largely that of believers. That it is also apologetic is true, since its aim is to provide its readership with what the author thinks is the proper perspective of the relationship between government and church.

4. I speak above of Hellenistic civic and Roman structures. The third structure, that of Jewish authorities in Jerusalem, is treated differently. The author rejoices in showing opposition between these authorities and the nascent church, an opposition that supports his religiopolitical theories. By the time Acts is written, such opposition in Jerusalem is long gone.

5. I have already discussed the Gospel of Luke and made some comparisons with Acts. In this chapter I assume what has already been said and focus on what is said in Acts.

6. Cf. 2:22 and 10:38 as exceptions.

7. Most of the theology of Acts has to be gleaned from the speeches, which in their completed form now are largely taken to be creations of the author of Acts. Bits of tradition are certainly incorporated in the speeches.

8. The Greek is ambiguous. The end result, however, seems to be that "justification" comes through faith, not Torah obligations. I discuss the passage in more detail below.

9. Paul claims that this was his message to Jew and Gentile (20:20-21).

10. This is a remarkable shorthand; why not at least kingdom of God? What does "kingdom" mean" Does it have here its usual, presumed eschatological orientation, or does it lack this? The lack of other eschatological pointers in the speech means that the word could be taken in more than one way. Some think it might refer to the church. Cf. 28:23, where in the final scene with the Jewish audience in Rome, the author writes that Paul proclaimed the kingdom of God—but the context is so vague it is not clear just what the author intends.

11. *Boulē* in the New Testament is a predominantly Lukan word. Presumably Paul is claiming here that he not only knows the full intentions of God, he preached them!

12. There is not a single word about Jesus in the speech. Paul presents his case purely on Jewish grounds.

13. This must be an echo of a baptismal formula.

14. It may be purposeful that the three speeches to the Gentiles explicitly include the theme of future judgment. That judgment is based on some criterion of righteousness and will happen to all people is the view of the author. There is little notion of grace in his thought. He seems to want to impress the Gentiles that this is what lies in store for them.

15. I discuss in this section only those references to Jesus' resurrection that seem to suggest how the notion functions in the mind of the author. There are a number of references that mention, even extol the resurrection, without, in my judgment, helping us to understand the author's intents. The noun *anastasis* is the regular word chosen. For the verb, the author alternates almost equally between *egeirō* and *anistēmi*.

16. Cf. *hyperypsōsen* in Phil 2:9. The statement about "at the right" probably echoes Ps 110:1. Even if it doesn't, being at the right has by now become a traditional part of the acclamatory language. In the narrative about Thessalonica, the charge is made by a hostile

crowd that the believers are claiming that Jesus is "another" king (obviously in opposition to the emperor).

17. Acts 20:21 is uncertain. Important witnesses add *Christos*.

18. The word usually means leader, ruler, or founder, none of which fits well here. From the way the author has Paul speak about the resurrection in Jerusalem (23:6), it seems clear Acts does not think the resurrection becomes real only because Jesus has been raised. Nor is the resurrection of the believer tied closely with that of Jesus, as Paul himself does. Is the author of Acts making simply a rhetorical play, that "they" killed one who not only lives but is the first exemplar of the resurrection?

19. One could wonder whether an efficacious act "in the name of Jesus" is an act that appropriated the power of the resurrected Jesus. While this is assumed, it is a follower who is doing the appropriating and not an act of power originating from Jesus himself.

20. Which we know in its Aramaic form from 1 Cor 16:22.

21. The only other juxtaposition of the verb *stauroō* and *kyrios* in the New Testament is 1 Cor 2:8, "crucified the Lord of glory."

22. Rev 11:15; 12:10.

23. It is true, however, that Luke uses essentially the same phrase in Luke 2:26 and Acts 3:18; Ps 2:2 is quoted in Acts 4:26. This expression is not unique to the author of Luke-Acts. It is present also in Revelation. Psalm 2:1-2 is quoted in Acts 4:26. Although Psalm 2 does not seem to be directly cited in Revelation, there are possible allusions, and it is hard to think Psalm 2 has not influenced both Luke-Acts and Revelation. The priority of God in Revelation makes it seem natural to think in terms of "his Messiah."

24. A strange use of the plural "thrones" occurs in Rev 20:4: "And I saw thrones, and they sat upon them, and judgment was given to them, and [that is?] the souls of those who had been beheaded because of the witness of Jesus. . . ." Who is it sitting on the thrones? Most exegetes seem to think they are the saints who have been beheaded.

25. The combination of serpent, devil, and Satan recurs in 20:2. For Satan, cf. 2:13 (twice); 2:24; 3:9; 20:7. For devil cf. 2:10; 12:12; 20:10.

26. Paul, for instance, does not explicitly affirm that God is creator.

27. E.g., Ernst Lohmeyer on 16:15: "Only Christ can be the speaker"; *Die Offenbarung des Johannes* (Tübingen: Mohr, 1953), 136. But to say this he has to argue that the passage has been misplaced.

28. E.g., Mal 4:5; Zech 14:1. Surely that means that God "comes" in judgment (cf. Mal 3:5).

29. In the same way, Paul in 1 Cor 15:28 shows God alone on stage at the denouement.

30. Jewish apocalyptic may indeed state or imply violence at the final judgment itself. I still think a helpful perspective is that of A. Y. Collins, *Crisis and Catharsis: The Power of the Apocalypse* (Philadelphia: Westminster, 1984).

31. This is one of the reasons, no doubt, for those who see essentially a Jewish apocalypse throughout much of the book.

32. The word *pistis* occurs only a few times in Revelation. The phrase *pistis Iēsou* is so notorious from discussions about Paul that there is danger of reading too much into this occurrence in Revelation. "Faith of Jesus" is parallel with "keeping the commandments of

God." Thus the faith is something one "keeps." Thus it can hardly mean the "faithfulness by Jesus," nor Paul's sense of trust in the grace of God through Christ. The simplest suggestion is that it means something like keeping the belief in Jesus. What this is to mean, however, is not clarified elsewhere in the treatise.

33. Rev 1:2; 1:9; 12:17; 17:6; 19:10 (twice); 20:4. In 1:2 the word *martyria* is joined to the double name "Jesus Christ."

34. A particular problem involves the strange statement in 19:10: *Hē gar martyria Iēsou estin to pneuma tēs prophēteias*. Again the subjective or the objective genitive is possible. If the former, then the phrase would mean something like "the testimony by Jesus is the spirit that inspires the prophets." If the latter, "The true test of whether one has the spirit is whether one testifies to the testimony by Jesus."

35. Of the nine occurrences of *martyria* in Revelation, six are connected explicitly with the name "Jesus." One (12:9) is used in connection with the title *arnion*.

36. Strictly speaking, the word is a diminutive, but seems to have lost this force by the time of Revelation. Certainly John's Lamb is not "little lamb." This is indicated, if in no other way, by the fact that the word is used once for an evil creature who opposes God (Rev 13:11).

37. Even other words for an animal, though they might well be appropriate as a metaphor for Jesus, are rare. The term *amnos* occurs only three times in relation to Jesus (John 1:29, 26, and 1 Pet 1:19). Paul refers to Jesus once as the paschal sacrifice (1 Cor 5:7).

38. The word occurs only four times in the LXX: Ps 114:4, 6; Jer 11:19; 50:45. The only possible point of contact would be Jer 11:19. The Lamb of Revelation, however, is not a simple lamb led to the slaughter. He is a victorious figure.

39. Including once where the Lamb is a warrior (17:14).

40. One could perhaps translate into terms of honor/shame: "worthy" would then refer to a person who was in a position of honor to do or act in such a manner.

41. Cf. Gen 49:9-10 and Isa 11:1-3.

42. The author likes to describe objects as having horns. I will not go into the Freudian possibilities here.

43. As usual the metaphor of ransom is tantalizingly vague. Those liberated are people from everywhere; the ransom price is the death of Jesus. But to whom is the ransom paid? *Agōrazō* is perhaps used in a related way in 14:3, 4.

44. There are textual variants with regard to the ending of *basileuō*, but I accept the Aland reading.

45. The Lamb has no throne of his own. This phrase is one of the many in Revelation in which the Lamb almost seems like an add-on.

46. One is tempted to compare the similar acclamation scene in Dan 7:14, but the words are mostly different. Only *timē* occurs in both.

47. Rev 22:1, 3 may suggest that the Lamb shares the throne with God.

48. Despite the fact that John writes to the seven churches, *ekklēsia* does not seem to be his preferred one of speaking of the believers. Between chapter 3 and the final words (22:15), he does not use the word at all.

49. This is similar to the role of the Son of Man in *1 Enoch* 37–71.

50. There are certain similarities with the function of the shepherd sayings in the Gospel of John 10.

51. The metaphor is strained. Obviously those invited to the marriage feast are not guests—they are the bride!

52. The actions correspond to the seals. The fifth seal has no violence; the sixth has violence but not instigator (since there are only four living creatures).

53. Scholars disagree as to whether these armies are divine or human. For our purposes it makes no difference.

54. While *orgē*, lit. "wrath," can be understood as a synonym for judgment, the addition of *thymos*, "anger, fury," intensifies the idea, so that it seems to signify God's active anger. In 6:16, there is reference to the *orgē* of the Lamb, and in the following verse, assuming the slightly preferred reading, to "their" *orgē*, i.e., both that of God and the Lamb.

55. Rome certainly saw the Jews as a race, a "people," not a religion.

56. E.g., the Jewish community at Alexandria handed over some refugees from Masada to the Romans.

57. Gamaliel II was an acerbic and restrictive thinker, according to the Talmud. That is, he was in favor of a narrower definition of who was a Jew than some others may have been. When this addition to the liturgy is to be dated is uncertain. It is usually assumed that Gamaliel II took over authority from Johanan ben Zakkai around 90 c.e., and often the curse is dated near the beginning of his rule, although there is no evidence for this, nor do we know how long his rule lasted. He was even deposed by his fellow rabbis, but apparently he inveigled his way back into power.

58. Text in Henry Bettenson, ed., *Documents of the Christian Church*, 2nd ed. (London: Oxford University Press, 1963), 3–6.

59. Although Domitian may not have instigated a persecution of Christians near the end of his reign (d. 96 c.e.), even the suspicion of it (e.g., *1 Clement* 1) suggests a high anxiety level. Questions have also been raised about the sort of persecution that is reflected in 1 Peter. There are those who prefer to call it harassment; it seems to me that evidence suggests a more explicit legal persecution. Again the dating of 1 Peter is uncertain, although it is surely sometime in the last decade of the first century. We know it was addressed to the provinces in Asia Minor, including the province of Asia, the location of John of Revelation.

60. The tendency to remove blame from the Romans and place it on the Jews is not original with Luke. It had already begun in Mark and was carried almost to an extreme in Matthew.

61. Since by his time the Jewish political structure was a thing of the past, he doesn't have to worry about what Christian attitudes ought to be toward that political reality. Presumably, judging from the early chapters in Acts, he would oppose such structures as opposing the legitimate spread of the truth. The academy at Jamnia (Javneh), whether he knew about it or not, does not count as a government with any legal jurisdiction.

62. H. R. Niebuhr, *Christ and Culture* (New York: Harper, 1951), chap. 4.

63. On a centurion's salary?

64. There is dispute about the accuracy of the presence of this Cohort as early as the

account in Acts requires. But this is how Acts puts the matter. Presumably Cornelius was thus a Roman citizen.

65. Cf., e.g., Leonard L. Thompson, *The Book of Revelation: Apocalypse and Empire* (Oxford: Oxford University Press, 1990).

66. The details the author gives in his descriptions indicate that he wanted to relate the myths to some specific situations which would have been known to the readers, if not us. This gives confidence to conclude that the mythic characters do represent sociopolitical and religious situations in the history of his day.

67. It is interesting that the name "Rome," never appears in the book. One also assumes that Rome is evil before Satan enters into relationship.

68. G. B. Caird, *A Commentary on the Revelation of St. John the Divine* (London: A. & C. Black, 1984), e.g., believes the beast stands for the Asiatic council, one of whose self-imposed duties was to oversee the functions of the imperial cult in the cities of Asia.

69. One should at least add the comment in the letter to Pergamum, which is said to be the place of "Satan's throne" (2:13). This is presumably a reference either to the Roman provincial government, located there, or to the large temple of the imperial cult, prominent there. In either case, Satan is identified with the empire.

70. Indeed, the Nicolaitans (2:6, 15), "Balaam" (2:14), and "Jezebel" (2:10) seem to belong to the side of evil.

71. Niebuhr, *Christ and Culture*, chap. 2.

72. It is true that in the description of the fourth bowl (16:9; cf. also v. 16), people curse God "who had power over these plagues" and did not repent of their works. The context suggests, however, that the purpose of the plague is torture, not repentance. There seems to be no sorrow over the failure of people to repent; that was expected.

73. There are as many views of Paul as there are interpreters. Paul is a hot, controversial person, and there is enough uncertainty in his letters to enable diverging views to emerge—and to be defended or attacked with passion. As the following paragraph makes obvious, I still (many today oppose this view) view Paul out of the Augustinian/Lutheran/Bultmannian perspective. For me the classic work remains that of R. Bultmann, *Theology of the New Testament* (New York: Scribner's, 1951), vol. 1, part 2. My own views can be found in *Paul for a New Day* (Philadelphia: Fortress Press, 1977), and *Christology in Paul and John* (Philadelphia: Fortress Press, 1988).

74. Cf. his major revisionist statement in Romans.

75. The word "create" (*ktizō*) is not prominent in the New Testament. Acts uses instead "make" (*poieō*). This could be a concession to Greek preferences for forming order out of preexisting matter.

76. But cf. Rom 2:11; Gal 2:6.

77. Cf. Acts 3:19; 5:31; 8:22; 11:18; 12:24; 17:30; 19:4; 20:21; 26:20.

78. E.g., Col 1:21; 2:13; 3:7; Eph 2:1-2; 2:11, 13, 19; 4:17; 1 Pet 1:14, 18; 2:10; 4:3. There may be hints of the idea in Paul, but very light hints, if they are even that (cf. 1 Thess 1:9; Gal 4:8; 1 Cor 6:11; perhaps also Tit 3:3).

79. Several times in the letters to the churches the author of Revelation exhorts them to repent. In the description of violence he refers to all those who did not repent

(9:20-21; 16:9-11). These judgments are put in negative terms—a different tone from that in Acts.

80. In Revelation the only criterion in addition to martyrdom seems to be sexual chastity (Rev 14:4).

81. As I have said, the theme of eternal life is strangely muted in the narrative until Paul's appeal to the Pharisaic belief at the end of the document—but it is surely implied in the notion of eschatological judgment.

82. I try to get at his experience in my books *Paul for a New Day* and *Christology in Paul and John.*

Notes to Chapter 11

1. The use in 6:70 does not seem to indicate the supreme evil ruler, but one of the subordinates.

2. It seems now generally accepted that the original reading in v. 18 is *theos*, not *huios*.

3. Cf. 3:2; 6:15; 7:12-13, 27, 31, 40-41; 8:31; 10:21; 12:42; 19:38.

4. Cf. J. Louis Martyn, *History and Theology in the Fourth Gospel*, 3rd ed. (Louisville: Westminster John Knox, 2003). One does not have to think, as does Martyn, that the agent of separation was the famous curse on the Christians inserted at some point in the synagogue liturgy. Synagogues were independent congregations and leaders could make their own rules. That synagogues here and there acted against Jesus communities is not surprising.

5. How the expulsion mechanism worked cannot be known. Since synagogues could make their own rules, it is not necessary, I think, to try to align such mechanism with any set of rules known from later Rabbinic literature.

6. This assumes that the Messiah in popular mentality was to be a miracle worker. The evidence in the Gospels seems compelling, although this view of the Messiah is a far cry from that usually assumed by scholars, based on more "political" texts. Cf. chap. 3 above.

7. So Rudolf Bultmann, *Theology of the New Testament* (New York: Scribner's, 1955), 2:3. And Robert Fortna thought to discover a primitive Gospel oriented around the signs; cf. *The Gospel of Signs* (Cambridge: Cambridge University Press, 1970).

8. Scholars have remained perplexed by the differences between the Synoptic sketch of the Son of Man and that of John. Most of the commentaries deal, at least in passing, with the issue; cf., e.g., R. Schnackenburg, *The Gospel according to St. John* (New York: Crossroad, 1990), 1:529–42. There are monographs on the topic. Cf., e.g., S. Schultz, *Untersuchungen zur Menschensohn-Christologie in Johannesevangelium* (Göttingen: Vandenhoeck & Ruprecht, 1957); F. Moloney, *The Johannine Son of Man* (Rome: Libreria Ateneo Salesiano, 1976); and R. Rhea, *The Johannine Son of Man* (Zurich: Theologischer Verlag, 1990).

9. John 1:51; 3:13, 14; 5:27; 6:27, 53, 62; 8:28; 9:35; 12:23, 34 (twice); 13:31.

10. I am still intrigued by the possibility that the Son of Man may have entered into the Jesus movement from the followers of John the Baptist. Since the Johannine communities seem to have had a relationship with those of John's followers (both positive and negative) it is possible that discussions between the two groups were the avenue of entrance.

11. The solution of priority of present versus future judgments in John 5 remains unclear. In v. 24, the presence of life and judgment is stated clearly. Verses 25-29, on the other hand, suggest a traditional future judgment, and it is in this section that the Son of Man saying appears. Bultmann argued that the present sayings were prior, the future ones being due to the ecclesial redactor; cf. R. Bultmann, *The Gospel of John* (Philadelphia: Westminster, 1971), 260–61. I think it is also possible that the future direction is original (indicating the movement of the Johannine theology from the traditional Son of Man notion) and make more sense of the Son of Man saying. So also R. Kysar, *John, the Maverick Gospel*, rev. ed. (Louisville: Westminster John Knox, 1993), 104–5.

12. The majority of the earliest and best texts read the gift as future: "will give to you." Even so, this is not an eschatological future. So C. K. Barrett: "It refers to the time after the glorification of Jesus (7:39) when his gifts would be fully available"; *The Gospel according to St. John*, 2nd ed. (Philadelphia: Westminster, 1978), 287. Also Bultmann: the passage is "clearly about the activity of the Exalted Lord (it makes no difference whether one reads *dōsei* . . . or the timeless *didōsin* . . . ," *John*, 225, n. 1. The author is looking forward to the time of the church.

13. John 12:23, 34 (twice); 13:31. The two uses in 12:34, although they are spoken by the crowd, clearly are set up by Jesus' word in 12:23 and thus take their meaning from that earlier statement.

14. The saying in 1:51 should probably not be listed with the two to be discussed here. Here it is the angels who ascend and descend upon the Son of Man. Clearly this means that the Son of Man is the revelatory agent of the reality of God. It probably implies that Jesus ascends and descends, but to read this in may push the metaphor. I omit 1:51 from discussion here.

15. The situation is ironic. By definition, in traditional Son of Man conceptions the figure is preexistent, but not human. Jesus (and Enoch) *become* Son of Man, but are not themselves preexistent.

16. The interested reader will find a lengthier statement in my *Christology in Paul and John: The Reality and Revelation of God* (Philadelphia: Fortress Press, 1988), 56–59.

17. E.g., the aretalogy of Isis in Apuleius, *The Golden Ass*, Loeb Library (Cambridge, Mass.: Harvard University Press).

18. As in the Valentinian *Abyss* or the *En Sof* of the later Kabbala.

19. I mean by "world" what the sociologists call a "socially constructed" world.

20. No natural revelation here!

21. This unbridgeable gulf can be taken as a straight ontological judgment, or it can be taken in the more existential perspective of Bultmann. For him, the issue is not a theoretical ontological divide; the gap has its origin in the world of humans turning to darkness rather than light. It is human decision to live one's life independently of obedience to God that causes human minds to be unable to hear the divine word. For practical

purposes, the result is the same; the "world" is unable to know the divine. And I think Bultmann tilts toward the ontological distinction when he says, for example, that "every new statement about God is first and foremost a statement about the self." That is, we "read" God out of our new self-understanding; e.g., Bultmann, *Jesus Christ and Mythology* (New York: Scribner's, 1958), 72–77. Bultmann also shows that in John Jesus has no teaching about God or himself. He reveals only that he is the revealer. For selected passages where Bultmann explains his judgments, cf. *Theology* 2:59–69 (p. 66 for the statement that Jesus reveals only that he is the revealer), 19–21; *John*, 79–83.

22. I am aware that the originator of the Logos Christology in the community may not be the author of the Gospel, but a seer who lies behind the author's creation. I use the term "author" as a convenience.

23. For Bultmann, cf. his comments on 1:14 in *John*; for Käsemann, cf. his *The Testament of Jesus* (Philadelphia: Fortress Press, 1968), chap. 4.

24. Bultmann, *Theology*, 2:66; cf. the entire section, pp. 59–69.

25. Whether the last verb is present or future is uncertain. Given the context of chapter 14, where all is present reality (in distinction from 1 John) one expects the present, a reading that has good attestation (B, D*, and others). The future has better attestation. The context suggests to me that the present has to be accepted as original. So Barrett, *John*, 2nd ed., 463. Bultmann opts for the future, but concludes that the present *menei* and the future *estai* "mean the same" (*John*, 617, n. 6). That is, the Spirit dwells now, not in some eschatological future, in the believer.

26. Bultmann, *Theology*, 2:67–69, 75.

27. Ibid., 2:76. The phrase "saved Savior" (or "redeemed Redeemer") is not much in usage today, being subjected to some skepticism. It is used to show that the Savior figure comes to call back to the spiritual world those people in whom a spark of that reality abides. One can find a story about a saved savior in the so-called Hymn of the Pearl, a section of the *Acts of Thomas*. Cf. the discussion in H. Jonas, *The Gnostic Religion*, 2nd ed. (Boston: Beacon, 1963), 112–29.

28. A sense of God's determination of those who are saved is especially strong in chap. 17; cf. vv. 2, 6, 9, 24.

29. If I understand the matter, the Orthodox church, influenced by Greek notions, has always been sympathetic to the belief that the salvatory act of Jesus was to come to earth to enable believers to live forever, to transform flesh into the reality worthy of life in heaven. The arguments of the Council of Chalcedon were about such issues, with the Eastern bishops favoring a text that would, for them, safeguard Jesus' act of divinizing human flesh.

30. The Paraclete is described in 14:16-17, 25-26; 15:26; 16:7-15.

31. There is an old saw that says no one understood Paul until Marcion—and Marcion misunderstood him. It may not be too audacious to add that no one really understood the Gospel of John until Bultmann.

32. Cf., e.g., R. Brown, *The Epistles of John* (Garden City, N.Y.: Doubleday, 1982); J. H. Houlden, *A Commentary on the Johannine Epistles* (New York: Harper, 1973).

33. I will not consider 2 and 3 John here, since there is no christological insight in either of those documents.

34. The kind of intrusion one might expect is well exampled by the variant reading

in 2 John 3, where a scribe as early as the fourth century (Sinaiticus) added *kyrios* to "Jesus Christ." The variant can hardly be authentic, but it does show what sort of reflexes one would expect from believers familiar with *kyrios*-type acclamations.

35. *Christos* occurs in 1:3; 2:1, 22; 3:23; 4:2; 5:1, 6, 20.

36. In some senses this echoes John 3:17. Here God (not the "Father") sent the Son into the world not to condemn the world but so that the world might be saved through him. Characteristically, the Gospel of John and 1 John differ about the criteria of salvation. For the Gospel it is "believing in"; for 1 John it is forgiveness of sins.

37. I argued that, in agreement with Bultmann, vv. 51b–59 are a later addition by an ecclesiastical editor.

38. Commentators do not seem to have considered this is a possibility. The only suggestion I have found that goes in this direction is that of Francis J. Moloney, who says of v. 66: "The Johannine community and its divisions are behind this presentation of the disciples who have heard and witnessed so much, but no longer go about with Jesus"; Moloney, *Signs and Shadows: Reading John 5–12* (Minneapolis: Fortress Press, 1996), 62.

39. So admirably urged by J. L. Martyn in his *History and Theology in the Fourth Gospel*.

40. One is tempted to go further. The narrator, after the story of the feeding, reports that the awe of the people, based on the sign that Jesus did, leads them to acclaim him the prophet. More, they want to make him *basileus* (Messiah?). But after the "hard sayings" about the descent and ascent, even many of the disciples reject him. Those who are willing to acclaim him Messiah think some in the community have gone too far with the descent/ascent Christology.

41. Brown, *Epistles*, 75.

42. Ibid., 76, n. 169.

43. Ibid., 76, n. 168.

44. Whether the perfect tense of *apostellō* is relevant here is disputed. If taken seriously, it would further indicate that the verse deals with the salvific intent of God, not a once for all geographical movement. Brown disputes any significance of the tense (*Epistles*, 517); more recent scholars still think the tense may be significant, e.g., S. Smalley, *1, 2, 3 John* (Waco, Tex.: Word, 1984), 241, and J. Painter, *1, 2, and 3 John* (Collegeville, Minn.: Liturgical, 2002), 266.

45. *Epistles*, 76.

46. 1:31; 2:11; 3:21; 7:4; 9:3; 17:6; 21:1 (twice), 14. The adjective *phaneros* does not occur; the adverb *phanerōs*, once, in 7:10.

47. One has to be careful in expressing this, since the text nowhere states that John baptized Jesus.

48. 1:2 (twice); 2:19, 28; 3:2, 5, 8; 4:9.

49. Painter, *1, 2, and 3 John*, e.g., 127–28, 130–31, 135.

50. Brown, *Epistles*, 158.

51. I am not convinced that the reference couldn't be to the proclamation of the "foundational witnesses" (so Painter), but I certainly agree that the prologue to 1 John does not begin in the pre-historical, transcendent realm.

52. Brown also reads 1 John out of the Gospel of John. He thinks that the prologue

to 1 John does not correct that of the Gospel; the author interprets it in such a way as to oppose the docetists who are his enemies. "He [the author of 1 John] would say that the Gospel of John is correct: In the beginning before creation there was a divine Word who ultimately became flesh. But he would add that the only way this can be known is from another beginning when the Son began to reveal himself to disciples who could hear him, see him with their own eyes, and touch him with their own hands" (*Epistles*, 131). My problem with this view is that I do not see the evidence that would indicate in any conclusive way that the author of 1 John thought the author of the Gospel was "correct."

INDEX

acclamation: as context for understanding titles in John, 61, 62, 70

Acts
  as Christian apology, 164
  Christology of, 151–52
  and *Christos* trajectory, 57–60, 92, 93
  comparison with Revelation, 160–61
  political perspective of, 164–67
  resurrection of Jesus in, 149–51
  theological structure, 147–52
the all (*ta panta*), reconciliation of, 13
Ancient of Days/ancient of days, 18, 19, 27, 84
antichrists: in 1 John, 192, 193
Aramaic community, 24, 36, 38, 64
Aramaic Jesus movement, 30
Aramaic trajectory. *See* Son of Man trajectory
ascent/descent: and Son of Man trajectory, 179, 180, 181, 182, 185, 194
author: as adversary of community, 99

Babylon: in Revelation, 168, 169
Bar Cochba: as Messiah, 37, 66
beast from the land: in Revelation, 168
beast from the sea: in Revelation, 168
belief, popular, 3–5, 7, 8, 95, 96
  and *Christos* trajectory, 91–94
  and Cosmocrator trajectory, 94–95
  and form criticism, 5
  and heresy, 4
  and Son of Man trajectory, 90, 91
  and three trajectories (Cosmocrator, Son of Man, *Christos*), 89–96

believers
  relation to Lamb in Revelation, 157
  suffering of, 138, 144
Bethlehem: as birthplace of the Messiah, 53, 56, 59, 61, 86, 88
blood: of the Lamb, 157, 158
breakthrough language, 6, 7

chrēstos, 68
Christ
  crucified, 83, 84, 87
  as head of church, 121, 122
  as head of cosmic reality, 121
  as head of the powers, 128, 129
  false, 103
  as *mystērion*, 126
  preexistence of, 84, 86, 87
  as proper name in Hellenistic church, 26, 27, 48, 49, 63, 72, 78, 108
  rule over powers and principalities, 112
  as warrior figure, 115, 157, 159
  See also Christos; Christos Iēsous; Christos trajectory
Christianity
  political situation at beginning of second century, 161–63
  popular: and form criticism, 5
  See also Christians; church
Christians
  and Jewish privileges in Roman Empire, 162
  separation from Jews in first century, 162, 163